Philip Hewitt / Alexander P. Saccaro

Maxi Training

Englisch

Grammatik 5. – 8. Schuljahr

Ernst Klett Verlag
Stuttgart Düsseldorf Leipzig

9 783129 298596

Bibliographische Information Der Deutschen Bibliothek
Die Deutsche Bibliothek verzeichnet diese Publikation in der Deutschen Nationalbibliographie; detaillierte bibliographische Daten sind im Internet über http://dnb.ddb.de abrufbar

Auflage 4. 3. 2. 1. | 2008 2007 2006 2005
Die letzten Zahlen bezeichnen jeweils die Auflage und das Jahr des Druckes.

Internetadresse: http://www.klett.de
Zeichnungen: Andreas Florian, Lübeck
Satz: Meyle + Müller, Pforzheim, Klaus Bauer, Bondorf
Umschlagfoto: image 100
Druck: Medien Druck Unterland GmbH, Flein
Printed in Germany
ISBN 3-12-929859-2

Alexander P. Saccaro

Englisch

Grammatik

5./6. Schuljahr

Inhalt

Vorwort

Liebe Schülerin, lieber Schüler,

dieses Buch macht dich **fit in englischer Grammatik.** Es bietet dir einfache Erklärungen, vielfältige Übungen und Tests, um deine Leistungen in diesem Fach zu verbessern. Vor dir liegt das gebündelte Wissen zur englischen Grammatik vom 5. bis zum 8. Schuljahr – greif zu! Zunächst werden die **wichtigsten Themen** der Schuljahre 5 und 6 bearbeitet; dann folgen die Schuljahre 7 und 8.

Mit diesem Buch kannst du den aktuellen Unterrichtsstoff mitlernen oder Inhalte aus vorangegangenen Schuljahren nachschlagen und festigen. Nimm es einfach immer wieder zur Hand und bearbeite einen Abschnitt daraus. Die folgenden Zeichen helfen dir bei der Orientierung:

Lies zunächst die **Regeln** und **Tipps**.

In zahlreichen **Übungen** kannst du die Regeln und Tipps dann anwenden.

Zusammenfassungen bieten dir einen Überblick über dein Wissen.

Mithilfe der **Tests** am Ende eines Kapitels kannst du kontrollieren, ob du alles verstanden und behalten hast.

Bei vielen Aufgaben hast du die Möglichkeit, deine Lösungen sofort ins Buch einzutragen. Für die anderen lege dir ein **Trainingsheft** an. Die richtigen Lösungen aller Aufgaben findest du am Ende eines Buchteils. Ob du nun Stoff wiederholen oder dich auf eine Klassanarbeit vorbereiten möchtest – dieser Band wird dich Schritt für Schritt zum Ziel führen und bringt dir maximalen Durchblick, maximalen Erfolg und maximale Sicherheit.

Und jetzt kann's losgehen!

1 Substantive

Weißt du noch, was Substantive bzw. Nomen *(nouns)* sind? Grob gesagt, sind es Wörter, mit denen wir Personen, Tiere, Sachen, Gegenstände und abstrakte Begriffe wie Eigenschaften und Gefühle bezeichnen. Viele dieser Substantive können im Plural gebraucht werden. Dazu musst du allerdings wissen, wie man den Plural der Substantive im Englischen bildet.

1. Die regelmäßige Bildung des Plurals

Im Allgemeinen bildet man den Plural im Englischen, indem man an die Singularform ein **-s** anhängt:

Singular	**Plural**
a farm	some farm**s**
a hen	some hen**s**
a sponge	some sponge**s**

Nach den Lauten [s], [ʃ], [tʃ] und [dʒ] steht ein **-es**, wenn kein **-e** im Singular vorhanden ist:

Singular	**Plural**
a bu**s**	some bus**es**
a box	some box**es**
a bush	some bush**es**
a match	some match**es**
a sandwich	some sandwich**es**

Achtung:

Auslautendes **-y** wird nach Konsonant zu **-ies**:	a bab**y**	some bab**ies**
Auslautendes **-fe** wird meist zu **-ves**:	a kni**fe**	some kni**ves**

2. Unregelmäßige Pluralformen

a m**a**n	two m**e**n	a f**oo**t	two f**ee**t
a wom**a**n	three wom**e**n	a g**oo**se	ten g**ee**se
a child	five child**ren**	a m**ouse**	three m**ice**

1.

Mr Mason's farm

Mr Mason ist Toms Großvater. Er hat einen Hof in der Nähe von York. Schau dir das folgende Bild an.

a) Was für Leute und welche Tiere kannst du sehen?

b) Mache dir eine Liste mit allen Substantiven. Setze die Substantive, die in der Einzahl sind, in die Mehrzahl und umgekehrt.

Beispiel: a farmhouse — some farmhouses

a wife — ______________

2.

Animals, animals ...

Wie lautet die Einzahl der folgenden Tiere, die es auf einem Bauernhof auch noch gibt?

cats	bulls	cows	dogs
horses	ponies	mice	geese

3.
On Mr Mason's farm

Was kannst du für die Bilder einsetzen?

There are a lot of  men,  women and  children on Mr Mason's farm today. They all have got  presents for Mr Mason because it is his birthday. Look at those two  boys over there; the big boy is Tom and the small boy is Timmy. They have got presents, too. Tom's present is a book about farms and farm animals. Timmy has got something in his  hand, too. But it is not  a present, it is only his old  teddy. Poor teddy! One  foot is missing and one  arm, too, and it is half-blind because one  eiy is gone. But Timmy has got a present for his grandad, too. It is a wonderful picture of three big  mice. They are in the kitchen and they are eating grandpa's birthday  cake.

Merke

Bei allen Pluralformen müssen auch die Begleiter **this** und **that** in den Plural gesetzt werden:

this book — **these** books
that girl — **those** girls

4.

Timmy's picture book

Timmy hat auch ein Buch. Er zeigt es seinem Großvater. Kannst du dir vorstellen, was Timmy seinem Großvater sagt?

1. This is a boy and these are boys, too.
2. That is a car and those are cars, too.
3. This is a street and ... there are street, too
4. That is a house ... and there are houses, too
5. This is a brush ... and there are three brushes, too.
6. That is a baby ... and there are two ~~baby~~ babies, too.
7. This is a foot ... and there are two feets, too.

5.

Clothes

Lies den folgenden Text und unterstreiche die Substantive im Plural.

Mr Mason is Tom's grandad. He is a farmer, but today he is not wearing his old trousers, his old shirt and his old shoes. He has got his best clothes on because it is his birthday. Mrs Mason is wearing her best clothes, too. She is not wearing her old jeans, but a nice blouse, a new skirt and some nice tights.

Merke

clothes, jeans, trousers und tights (Strumpfhose) werden im Englischen immer im Plural gebraucht. Der unbestimmte Artikel **a/an** ist vor diesen Substantiven nicht möglich.

Auch **police** und **people** werden im Englischen immer im Plural gebraucht. **Homework** steht dagegen im Englischen immer im Singular:

"Help! Where **are** the **police**? Some **people give** us too much **homework**!"

6.

Kate's clothes

Dieses Mädchen heißt Kate und ist Toms Schwester. Sieh mal, was sie anhat: Obwohl ihr Großvater Geburtstag hat, trägt sie nur alte Sachen.
Kannst du die folgenden Sätze vervollständigen?

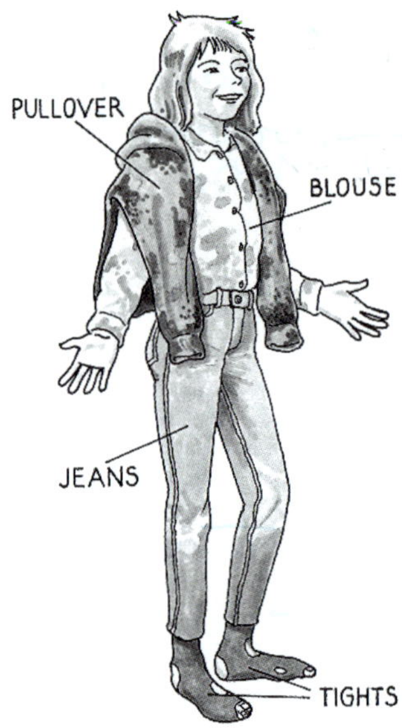

Look at her old pullover.

It's dirty.

Look at her old tights.

There __are__ holes in __tights__.

Look at her old jeans.

__There are__ too small.

Look at her old blouse.

__This__ not clean.

Her clothes __are__ really awful!

7.

Your clothes

a) Was hast du gerade an?

b) Welche Kleidung magst du am liebsten?

Test

1.
In Timmys Bilderbuch gibt es viele Bilder, zum Beispiel:

hens, geese, ducks, rabbits, boys, girls, children, teddies, men, women, houses, brushes, apples and sandwiches

Stelle eine Liste dieser Substantive auf. Wie lautet ihre Einzahl?

singular	*plural*
a horse	some horses

2.
Großmutter mag nicht, was Kate anhat; deshalb fragt sie, weshalb Kate ihre alten Sachen trägt. Setze *it, they, them, this, these* in die folgenden Sätze ein.

Grandma: Kate, why must you wear __these__ old things? What about __this__ old pullover, for example?

Kate: Sorry, Grandma, but my new one is in the gym. I left __it__ there.

Grandma: And what about your jeans? __They__ are too small, and __thes__ are dirty, too.

Kate: Mum put my new ones in the washing machine. __They__ aren't dry yet.

Grandma: What about a skirt then?

Kate: I don't like skirts. We must always wear __it__ at school.

3.
Herr Mason hat viele Geschenke zu seinem Geburtstag bekommen.
Vervollständige die folgenden Sätze.

There are Tom's and Timmy's presents. But there are other __presents__, too. Here is Mum's present. It's a photo album. There are many __photos__ *(photo)* in it. There are many __peoples__ *(people)* on them. There is Grandma's present. It's in __that__ these two big __boxes__ *(that/box)* over there. What's in them? Nobody knows. And there is Kate's present, too. It's only a small present because she had too much __somework__ *(homework)*.

2 Das Personalpronomen

Pronomen stehen immer für (lat. *pro*) ein Substantiv (Nomen). Daher können sie sowohl Subjekt als auch Objekt eines Satzes sein.

1. Das Personalpronomen als Subjekt

Where is **Kate?**	**She** is here.
Where is **Tom?**	**He** is at school.
Where is **your book?**	**It** isn't here.

Ist das Personalpronomen **Subjekt** eines Satzes, so lauten seine Formen:

Singular					**Plural**		
I	**you**	**he**	**she**	**it**	**we**	**you**	**they**
(ich)	(du/Sie)	(er)	(sie)	(es)	(wir)	(ihr/Sie)	(sie)

It steht immer für Sachen; **they** kann für Personen, Tiere und Sachen stehen. Alle anderen Personalpronomen stehen für Personen.

2. Das Personalpronomen als Objekt

Ist das Personalpronomen **Objekt** eines Satzes, lauten seine Formen:

		me	(mir/mich)	**Singular**
		you	(dir/dich/Ihnen)	
Tom	can see	**him**	(ihm/ihn)	
Kate	can help	**her**	(ihr/sie)	
		it	(es)	
		us	(uns)	**Plural**
		you	(euch/Ihnen)	
		them	(ihnen/sie)	

Im Englischen macht man bei den Pronomen keinen Unterschied zwischen dem indirekten und direkten Objekt; die Formen sind gleich. Wie bei den Subjektpronomen steht **it** für eine Sache; **them** kann für Personen, Tiere und Sachen stehen.

Die Objektform des Personalpronomens steht im Englischen auch nach Präpositionen:

Wait **for me**!	Look **at her**!
Look **at him**!	Wait **for them!**

1.

Where are they?

Beantworte die folgenden Fragen. Verwende Personalpronomen in deinen Antworten.

1.	Where is Mr Mason?	(on the farm)
2.	Where's Mrs Mason?	(in the house)
3.	Where's Tom ?	(at school)
4.	Where's Tom's bike?	(at school, too)
5.	Where's Timmy?	(on his potty)
6.	Where are his toys?	(on the floor)
7.	Where are his clothes?	(on his bed)
8.	Where's Kate?	(not at home)
9.	Where is her girlfriend?	(with her)
10.	Where are Kate and Jenny?	(in the park)

2.

Looking for persons and things

Beantworte die folgenden Fragen; verwende dabei Personalpronomen.

1. Where are my clothes?
2. Where is my book?
3. Where are you, Kate?
4. Where is Mike?
5. Where are Tom and Jenny?
6. Where are my photos?
7. Where are my keys?
8. Where is my money?
9. Where is Dad?
10. Where is your potty, Timmy?
11. Where is my teddy?
12. Where are my trousers?

I can't find …
I can't see …
I can't hear …

3.

Looking for Timmy's toy cars

Kate ist in Timmys Zimmer. Sie sucht seine Spielzeugautos, kann sie aber nicht finden. Kannst du die Sätze vervollständigen?

Kate: Timmy, where are your toy cars? Help ________ to look for ________. Are ________ under your bed?

Timmy: No, ________ aren't. ________ aren't there.

Kate: Where are ________ then? Let ________ guess. Are ________ in your bed?

Timmy: No, ________ aren't in my bed. ________ in my teddy's bed.

Kate: In your teddy's bed? Where is ________?

Timmy: ________ 's here.

Kate: But why are ________ in your teddy's bed, Timmy?

Timmy: It's my teddy who wants to play with ________, not me.

Test

1.

Lehrer stellen viele Fragen. Stelle du sie einmal und gib die richtige Antwort darauf. Verwende Personalpronomen.

		in the classroom
	Tom and Mike?	here
	your homework?	on the bus
	your English book?	on the desk
Where is	your book?	at home
Where are	Christine?	not here
	the register?	in my schoolbag
	they from?	ill
	you from?	York
	Kate?	at school

2.

Was musst du tun, wenn …? Beantworte die folgenden Fragen; verwende in deiner Antwort die Verben:

to read / try / wash / brush / play with / talk to / talk about / forget / look after

Beispiel: When I've got a dog, I must look after it.

What must you do when you've got …

a dog?
a lot of homework?
dirty clothes?
a silly neighbour?
a baby?
a friend?
a new computer game?
problems?
a good book?

3 Bestimmter und unbestimmter Artikel

Der bestimmte Artikel

Wie du weißt, gibt es im Englischen nur eine Form des bestimmten Artikels *(definite article)*. Seine Aussprache richtet sich nach dem folgenden Wort. Vor einem Vokal wird *the* [ðɪː], vor einem Konsonant und dem Halbvokal [j] (wie z.B. in *unit, uniform, yellow*), wird er [ðə] ausgesprochen:

[ðɪː]	[ðə]
the **o**ther girl	the boy
the **E**nglish car	the car
the **o**ld uniform	the uniform

Wann benutze ich den bestimmten Artikel?

1. Der bestimmte Artikel steht immer, wenn es sich um bestimmte Personen oder Sachen handelt:

   The colours of Tom's school uniform are blue and grey. **The** girls must wear a grey skirt and **the** boys must wear grey trousers. **The** boys and **the** girls can wear a school blazer, too.

2. Der bestimmte Artikel steht nicht, wenn die Personen oder Sachen nicht näher bestimmt sind. Er steht daher nie bei **most** (people, girls, boys ...) und **most of them**:

   Not all boys and girls in Britain like **school uniforms. Most of them** could do without a school uniform.

3. Er steht auch nicht bei Eigennamen und bei Verkehrsmitteln, wenn man sagen will, wie man irgendwo hinkommt:

   Tom goes to school **by bike.** Some children go there **by bus.**

Beachte:
Im Unterschied zum Deutschen steht der bestimmte Artikel nicht bei Straßennamen: They live **in Park Road**.

Bei Wörtern wie **bed** und **school** steht kein Artikel, wenn man ausdrücken will, was man dort tut. Ist dagegen das Möbelstück oder das Gebäude gemeint, so steht der bestimmte Artikel:

Let's go **to bed**.	Let's look **under the bed**.
Gehen wir ins Bett (= schlafen).	Schauen wir unter dem Bett nach.
He goes **to school**.	His mother is going **to the school**.
Er geht zur Schule (= in den Unterricht).	Seine Mutter geht in die Schule (= zum Gebäude).

1.

What's right?

Musst du die folgenden Wörter mit [ðə] oder [ðiː] sprechen? Schreibe zwei Listen.

Beispiel: [ðə] box, [ðiː] empty box

___ old women	___ young girls	___ American cars
___ English children	___ silly answers	___ difficult questions
___ examples	___ bad ideas	___ school uniforms
___ yellow apples	___ afternoons	___ empty pages
___ wrong numbers	___ easy units	___ terrible teachers

2.

Jenny

Wo muss der bestimmte Artikel stehen, wo nicht?

Jenny isn't x Tom's sister, she is x Tom's friend. She lives in the Apple Street. The Apple Street is a small street in the north of ___ York. In winter she goes to x school by ___ bus, in summer she goes to ___ school by ___ bike. ___ Tom is in her class. She doesn't like all the girls and boys in her class, but she likes ___ Tom very much. She thinks he is the nicest boy in her class. But Jenny doesn't only like ___ Tom, she also likes the maths. The maths is ___ subject she likes best. Before the tests, she always helps ___ Tom.

3.

How you can get there

Heute haben die Schüler Erdkunde. Sie reden in der Stunde darüber, wie sie zu anderen Städten oder Ländern reisen können. Achtung! Tom und die anderen leben nicht in Deutschland, sondern in York.

Beispiel: What about London? How can you get there?
I can get there by train.

Germany

New York

Scotland

Ireland

Denmark

France

The Isle of Wight

Wales

California

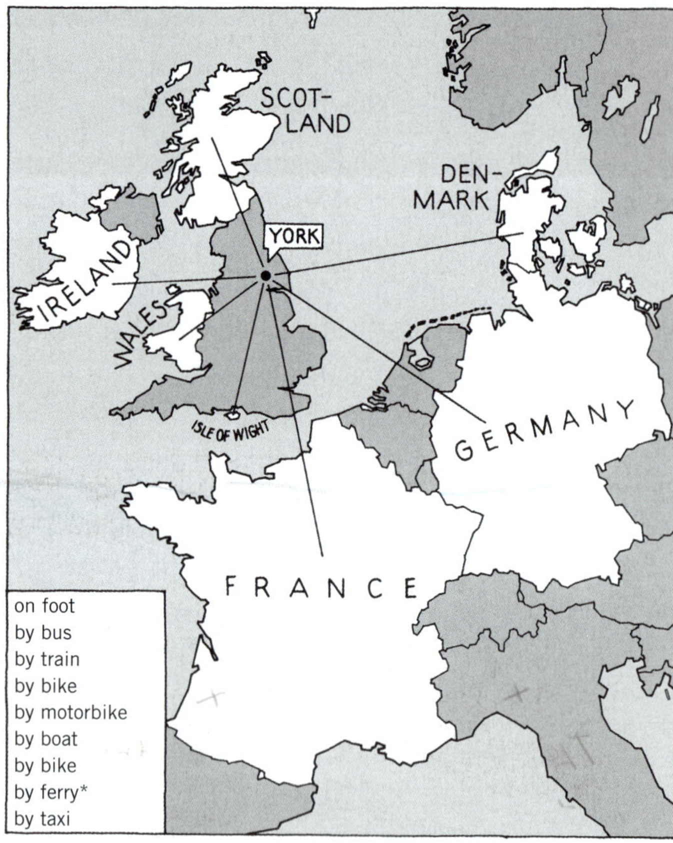

*ferry – Fähre

4.

Definite article or not?

Setze den bestimmten Artikel da ein, wo er stehen muss.

1. ____ boys like ____ girls.
2. ____ Tom likes ____ Jenny.
3. Do you like ____ boys in your class?
4. Do you usually like ____ girls more than ____ boys?
5. What about ____ girls in your class? Are they nice?
6. Which of ____ boys/girls do you like best?
7. Who is ____ nicest boy/girl in your class?
8. What's ____ name of ____ girl/boy you like best?
9. Which boy/girl do ____ most of you like best?
10. Are ____ girls/boys in your class good at English?
11. Are ____ boys as clever as ____ girls? What do you think?

Der unbestimmte Artikel

Der unbestimmte Artikel bezeichnet einzelne Personen oder Dinge. Er hat im Englischen zwei Formen: *a* und *an.* Vor einem Vokal steht *an*, vor einem Konsonant *a.* Vor dem Halbvokal [j] (wie in *unit, uniform, yellow*) steht *a.*

Beispiele:

a book	**an a**pple
a good book	**an E**nglish book
a yellow car	**an e**mpty car
a nice uncle	**an u**ncle
a uniform	**an o**ld uniform

Wann benutze ich den unbestimmten Artikel?

Im Unterschied zum Deutschen steht der unbestimmte Artikel im Englischen bei Berufsbezeichnungen und bei bestimmten Ausdrücken wie *to have (got) a headache/a temperature* (Kopfweh, Fieber haben):

Tom has got **a** new girlfriend.
Her father is **a** taxi driver.
She's ill today; she's got **a headache** and **a temperature**.

5.

Tom's school bag

Packst du deine Schulmappe jeden Tag neu? Tom tut es nicht.

There are lots of things in Tom's school bag; there's 

__ English book, 

__ workbook,  __ exercise book,  __ German book and 

__ pencil case in it.

But there are other things, too. There's  __ apple,  __ empty bottle,  __ water pistol and  __ old sandwich in it.

6.
Who are they?

1. He brings the milk in the morning. He's a milkman.
2. He brings you letters and parcels. He's ...
3. You go to him when you want to buy sausages.
4. He sells you all kind of vegetables.
5. She helps you to find what you want when you are in a shop.
6. She works for a newspaper.
7. He comes when your house is on fire.
8. He helps animals when they are ill.
9. He gives you good or bad marks.
10. He breaks into your house to steal something.

7.
More persons and things
Setze alles in die Einzahl. Verwende *a* oder *an*.

Beispiel: an old woman, a young girl

___ old women	___ young girls	___ American cars
___ English children	___ silly answers	___ difficult questions
___ examples	___ bad ideas	___ school uniforms
___ yellow apples	___ afternoons	___ empty pages
___ wrong numbers	___ easy units	___ terrible teachers

8.
Boys and girls
Was kommt dir in den Sinn, wenn du die Wörter Mädchen oder Junge hörst? Verwende den unbestimmten Artikel und die folgenden Adjektive:

silly, interesting, boring, difficult, exciting, clever, strong, intelligent, nice, noisy, happy, unhappy ...

Beispiel: a good girl
a bad boy

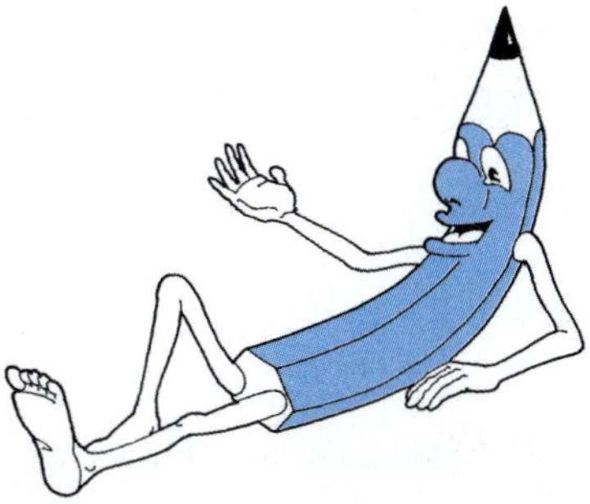

9.

Jenny is ill

Steht hier der bestimmte, der unbestimmte oder gar kein Artikel?

Jenny goes to ____ same school as ____ Tom. Sometimes Tom's father takes them to ____ school in ____ morning. ____ school they go to is ____ big school. There are a lot of ____ pupils at Jenny's school, and not all of them like ____ school. But Jenny does; she likes ____ school because ____ most of ____ teachers she has got are really nice. Today she can't go to ____ school; she must stay in ____ bed, but she hasn't got ____ temperature. She's got ____ cold and ____ bad headache. She feels terrible and she doesn't want to eat anything. She just wants to see ____ doctor and stay ____ bed. Poor Jenny!

Test

1.
Bestimmter, unbestimmter oder gar kein Artikel? Was ist richtig?

Tom has got ____ brother and ____ sister. They live in ____ York. That's in the north of ____ England. ____ Timmy is his baby brother and Kate is his sister.

Tom has got ____ grandpa and ____ grandma, too. His grandfather's name is Mr Mason. He has got ____ farm, so he is ____ farmer.

Tom and Kate go to ____ school, but Timmy doesn't. He's too young to go to ____ school. It's sometimes hard for Tom and Kate to get out of ____ bed when Timmy can still stay in it.

Tom usually goes to school by ____ bike. He only takes ____ bus when it's too cold or too windy. Kate goes to school by ____ bus. She mustn't go ____ bike; her mother says she is too young. Tom and Kate don't like everything about ____ school, but ____ most of their teachers are nice.

2.
Schreibe ein paar Zeilen über dich selbst und deine Familie.

- where you live
- what street or road you live in
- how old you are
- if you've got a brother or a sister
- if you've got a boyfriend/girlfriend
- what your father's and mother's job is
- if and why you like or don't like school
- what subject you like best
- what subject you hate
- if your teachers are okay or not
- how you get to school in summer/winter
- what you like better
- how your father and mother go to work

4 Substantive und ihre Begleiter

Die Possessivbegleiter

Englische wie deutsche Substantive stehen nicht immer allein. Sie werden häufig von anderen Wörtern „begleitet“, die sie näher bestimmen. In der deutschen Grammatik nennt man diese Wörter „Begleiter“; in der englischen Grammatik heißen sie *determiners*.

Die Possessivbegleiter *my, your* usw. drücken Besitz oder Zugehörigkeit aus. Mit Ausnahme von *their*, das sich auch auf Sachen beziehen kann, beziehen sich *my, your* usw. immer auf Personen.

Die Formen der Possessivbegleiter *(possessive determiners)* lauten:

	Singular	
This isn't	**my**	book.
Is it	**your**	book?
No, it isn't. It's	**her**	book.
No, it's	**his**	book.
	Plural	
Oh no. Is it	**your**	book, Tom and Kevin?
Let's see. No, it isn't	**our**	book. Perhaps it's the girls' book.
Yes, it is. It's	**their**	book.

Neben diesen Formen kommt auch *its* vor. *Its* bezieht sich immer auf eine Sache:
This is our school. **Its** classrooms are very nice.
This is Tom's bike. **Its** saddle is new.

1.
Everybody has got something

Verwende die Possessivbegleiter.

Beispiel: Timmy has got a teddy. It's his teddy.

1. Tom's grandparents have got a farm. It's ______________________
2. The Masons have got a flat. ______________________
3. Mr and Mrs Mason have got a car. ______________________
4. Tom has got a sister. ______________________
5. Kate has got a brother. ______________________
6. Timmy has got a lot of toys. ______________________
7. Mike has got a camera. ______________________
8. Jenny has got a boyfriend. ______________________
9. Jenny and Tom go to the same school. ______________________
10. Jenny's parents have got a house. ______________________

2.
Timmy's "toys"

Jüngere Geschwister „finden" manchmal Dinge, die ihnen nicht gehören. Das ist auch bei Timmy so. Er hat eine ganze Sammlung. Vervollständige, was Timmys Mutter sagt.

1. What have you got here, Timmy? What about these keys? Aren't they Dad's keys? I think they are ______ keys.

2. Look, Timmy, it's not ______ exercise book, it's Kate's. It's ______ exercise book.

3. Where have you got that from, Timmy?! Jenny's German book! How can Jenny do German tests when you keep it under ______ bed? What will ______ teacher say?

4. And look, Timmy. This is not ______ picture book. It's Kate's. It was ______ birthday present from Tom. So you can't keep it.

5. Don't cry, Timmy. Look, you've got so many things: Here's ______ teddy, here's ______ toy car, here's ______ telephone. So play with ______ things now.

Verwechsle nicht **you** mit **your**, **its** mit **it's**, **they** mit **their** und **they're** mit **there**!

1. **your**, **its**, **their** stehen nie allein. Sie stehen **immer vor** einem Substantiv.
2. **they** ist ein Personalpronomen und **steht für** ein Substantiv im Plural. **they're** ist die Kurzform von **they are**.
3. **there** (= da, dort, dahin, dorthin) steht entweder allein oder vor einer Form von *to be* (= es gibt, es sind). Nach **there is** muss das Substantiv im Singular stehen; nach **there are** folgt ein Substantiv im Plural:

   There **is a boy** over there and there **are some girls** there, too.

Vergleiche: Timmy, where are **you**?
Where is **your** teddy?
It's Tom's bike. **Its** saddle is new. **It's** got a new bell, too.
Are Tom and Mike **there**? No, **they** aren't. **They're** at school.
Where are **their** bikes? **They're** over **there**.

3.

Questions, questions ...

Setze *you* oder *your* ein und beantworte dann die Fragen.

1. What about _______ room? Do _______ like it?
2. Do _______ clean it or does _______ mother clean it?
3. What's in _______ room?
4. Is there anything under _______ bed?
5. Where do _______ keep _______ clothes?
6. Where do _______ do _______ homework?
7. Have _______ got a TV in _______ room?
8. Have _______ got posters and photos in _______ room, too?

4.

Tom's room

Füge *its, it's, they, their* oder *there* ein.

_______ are a lot of things in Tom's room. _______ are books and cassettes everywhere. _______ are on the chairs, on his bed and on the floor. And _______ is something under his bed. What is it? _______ an old pullover.

_______ are some socks under his bed, too. _______ are holes in them and _______ look dirty. And what's that on the wall? _______ are a lot of photos and posters on the wall over his bed. Look at that photo over _______. _______ a photo of Jenny. She is sitting on her bike. _______ not a new bike, but _______ handlebars and _______ saddle are new.

5.

A classroom

Beschreibe dieses Klassenzimmer. Verwende *there is, there are* in deinen Sätzen.

Die Demonstrativbegleiter

Die Demonstrativbegleiter *(demonstrative determiners) this/these* verweisen auf Personen oder Dinge, die in der Nähe des Sprechers sind; *that/those* verweisen dagegen auf Personen oder Dinge, die weiter entfernt sind.

Look at **this** book. **This** isn't my book.
And what about **that** book over there? Yes, **that's** my book.
And what about **these** pencils? Aren't they your pencils?
No, they aren't. But give me **those** pencils over there. They may be my pencils.

Ob du *this/that* oder *these/those* verwenden musst, hängt auch von dem folgenden Substantiv ab. Steht das Substantiv im Singular, steht immer *this/that*; steht das Substantiv im Plural, steht immer *these/those*.

This is my book and **that** is your book.
These are my pencils and **those** are your pencils.

6.

Timmy at school

Heute muss Frau Mason zum Arzt gehen. Da auch Herr Mason nicht zu Hause bleiben kann, nimmt Tom seinen kleinen Bruder in die Schule mit. Dort will Timmy alles wissen. Setze *this* oder *that* ein.

Timmy: Is _____ your classroom, Tom?

Tom: No Timmy, _____ isn't my classroom. My classroom is over there.

Timmy: Is _____ your class, Tom?

Tom: Yes, _____ is my class.

Timmy: And _____ class over there?

Tom: _____'s Kate's class.

Timmy: Is _____ your chair here?

Tom: Yes, it is. And look, Timmy, _____ chair over there, that's Jenny's.

Timmy: What's the name of _____ fat boy over there?

Tom: His name is John, but don't call him fat because he doesn't like it.

Timmy: Is _____ a teacher over there, Tom?

Tom: No, it isn't. It's a pupil, Timmy.

Timmy: But _____ is a teacher, Tom.

Tom: Where? Over there? Oh yes, _____'s our English teacher. You're right, Timmy.

Timmy: And the girl beside him is his daughter?

Tom: No, Timmy, it isn't. It's a girl in Kate's class.

7.

A pupil's work

In diesem Text gibt es 15 Fehler. Kannst du sie finden? Schreibe den Text noch mal, aber jetzt ohne Fehler.

This is my classroom. Their is room for 30 pupils. Their are 30 chairs and 15 desks in it and their is a desk and a chair for our teachers, too. Its a nice room. Their are many pictures on the walls and their is a map of England, too. Its on the back, over their.

The desk in front of the teacher's desk is my desk. My friend sits their. This is okay, but behind me, their are two girls … I don't like they. They always talk and throw things at my and my friend. And when they are quiet, they eat there sandwhiches and there chocolate pudding and there sweets. They …

much und *many*

Zu den Substantivbegleitern zählen auch *much* und *many*. Beide entsprechen, wenn sie vor einem Substantiv stehen, dem Deutschen „viel(e)". *Much* und *many* werden jedoch unterschiedlich gebraucht.

1. **many** kann nur bei einem Substantiv im Plural stehen:

   Are there **many girls** in your class? **How many teachers** have you got? How **many** tests do you have a week?

2. **much** steht nur bei einem Substantiv im Singular:

   How much homework do you get? **How much time** do you spend on your homework?

3. Bezieht sich **much** auf ein Verb, so bedeutet es meistens „sehr":

   Do you like **English** very **much**?

8.

A questionnaire

Füge *much* oder *many* ein.

1. How ________ homework have you got today?
2. How ________ time do you usually spend on it?
3. How ________ minutes do you spend on your English homework?
4. How ________ hours do you spend in front of the TV?
5. How ________ subjects have you got?
6. How ________ help do you get from your parents?
7. How ________ tests do you have a year?
8. How ________ good marks did you get last year?
9. How ________ tests have you written this week?

Test

1.
Übersetze bitte.

I've got ________________ (viel Zeit)
________________ (viele Freunde)
________________ (viele Hobbies)
________________ (viele Bücher)
but I haven't got ________________ (viel Geld)

2.
Ergänze mit *much* oder *many*.

School is too ____________ tests
too ____________ bad marks
too ____________ teachers
too ____________ homework
too ____________ work
too ____________ lessons
too ____________ questions
too ____________ boring subjects
too ____________ time indoors
That's why I love school so ____________.

3.
Trage in den Lehrerfragen ein, was fehlt.

a) Well, let me see __________ homework, John.

b) Is this __________ homework or did __________ neighbour do it?

c) When did __________ do it?

d) Where is Barbara's homework? Have I got __________ exercise book yet?

e) What about __________, Tom and Jenny? What are __________ doing there?

f) Are you doing __________ homework now?

g) Have you copied it from your neighbours? Then it's not __________ homework, but __________ homework!

5 Der Genitiv

Der *s*-Genitiv

Im Englischen gibt es zwei Möglichkeiten, den Genitiv zu bilden: den *s*-Genitiv *(s-genitive)* und den *of*-Genitiv *(of-genitive* oder *of-phrase)*.

Der *s*-Genitiv steht zumeist bei Personen. Wie die Possessivbegleiter *my, your* usw. gibt er an, wem etwas gehört oder wem etwas zuzuordnen ist.

Die Formen des *s*-Genitiv

Singular: ...'s	Kate**'s** book a child**'s** voice
Regelmäßiger Plural: ...s'	the girl**s'** books my parent**s'** house
Unregelmäßiger Plural: ...'s	children**'s** voices people**'s** ideas

Achtung:
Verwechsle den *s*-Genitiv nicht mit dem Plural-s. Beim Plural steht **nie** ein Apostroph!
Beispiel: My **parents** are not at home.

Auch bei der 3. Person Einzahl im *simple present* steht nie ein Apostroph.
Beispiel: He **works** in an office.

Verwechsle den *s*-Genitiv auch nicht mit den Kurzformen von *is* und *has*.
Beispiel: He's got a house. **It's** new.

1.

The s-genitive

Bilde den *s*-Genitiv.

Beispiel: Timmy's toys

Timmy
toys

the boys
teacher

the girls
school bags

our cat
food

Kate
friends

women
clothes

the man
boots

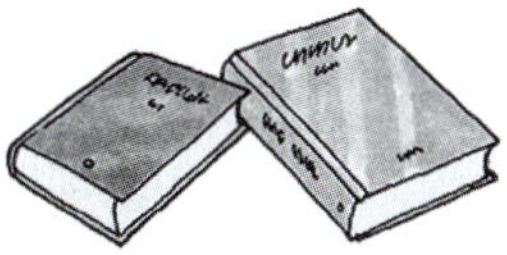

the children
books

girls
school uniforms

Jenny
dog

the Masons
house

my parents
car

2.
A dialogue

Stelle die Fragen und beantworte sie.

Beispiel: Are these your books, Mike? No, they aren't. They are Peter's.

Is this your .../Are these your ...

... toys, Tom?	No ________________ (baby brother)
... girlfriend, Kevin?	No, ________________ (Tom)
... magazine, Jenny?	No, ________________ (the girls)
... cat, Kate?	No, ________________ (my mother)
... homework, Joe?	No, ________________ (Kevin)
... house, Mr Mason?	No, ________________ (grandparents)
... your bike, Mrs Mason?	No, ________________ (Kate)
... your room, Tom?	No, ________________ (my sister)
... your teddy, Jenny?	No, ________________ (Timmy)
... your van, Timmy?	Yes, it is. It's my van!

3.
Timmy's treasures

Trage das fehlende Genitiv-s, das fehlende Plural-s, die fehlenden Apostrophe und Kurzformen ein.

Timmy is Tom______ baby brother. He is three years old. One of his favourite toy______ is his teddy; but he______ got other toy______, too. He keeps them in his cupboard; but there are other thing______ in his cupboard. Look! There______ one of Jenny______ letter______ to Tom; there______ an old German book and there______ Kate______ ruler. There are also some key______; are they his parent______ key______? There______ a tennis ball, too. Whose is it? Is it Kevin______ or Joe______? It can't be Kate______ or Tom______ because they don't play tennis.

4.

Jenny

Nimm zwei verschiedene Farbstifte und unterstreiche – jeweils in einer anderen Farbe – die *s*-Genitive und die Kurzformen, die du hier findest.

Jenny is Tom's girlfriend. She's twelve. She hasn't got a brother or a sister; she's only got her parents. Jenny is from York; her mother is from York, too, but her father is from Nottingham. They live in an old house; it's her grandparents' house. Jenny's other relatives live in London; she's got an aunt there who's over sixty and who's got a flat in London. She hasn't got any children, so Jenny is her only niece. In her summer holidays Jenny wants to see her: it will be Jenny's first visit to London.

Der *of*-Genitiv

Der ***of***-Genitiv drückt Zugehörigkeit und Mengenangaben aus. Im Unterschied zum ***s***-Genitiv steht er meist nur bei Sachen.

Zugehörigkeit	**Mengenangaben**
the pages **of** a book	a bottle **of** lemonade
the legs **of** the table	a pound **of** apples

5.
The *of*- or *s*-genitive?
Was ist richtig?

Beispiel: the boys' legs – the doors of my room

the boys/legs	the hands/girl	the car/windows
the doors/my room	the dog/feet	my neighbour/cat
Kate/books	the children/clothes	the end/school
on the evening/my birthday	the light/the moon	Jenny/story

6.
What goes together?
Bilde Paare.

Beispiel: a bar of chocolate

a bar	milk	a tin	cornflakes
lots	tea	a pound	crisps
a glass	food	a bag	cheese
a cup	strawberries	a packet	peas
a plate	chocolate	a plate	sausages

7.

Tom's shopping list

In ein paar Tagen hat Tom Geburtstag. Er möchte ein paar Freunde einladen und eine Party geben. Am Tag vor der Party geht er in ein Geschäft, um einzukaufen. Hier ist seine Einkaufsliste. Kannst du sie vervollständigen?

five ______________________________ crisps

three ____________________________ biscuits

five ______________________________ coke

five ______________________________ lemonade

a ________________________________ tomato ketchup

three ____________________________ sausages

five ______________________________ ice cream

8.

In the shop

Tom ist jetzt im Laden. Mrs White hilft ihm. Kannst du aufschreiben, was sie wohl sagen?

Mrs White: What can I do for you, Tom?

Tom: Can I have some crisps and some biscuits?

Mrs White: How many packets do you need?

Tom: I need three ______________________ and five ______________________.

Mrs White: Here you are. Anything else, dear?

Tom: I need some coke and some lemonade, too.

Mrs White: ____

Tom: ____

Schau dir den Einkaufszettel in Aufgabe 7 an und setze das Gespräch fort.

1. Der ***of***-Genitiv wird oft mit der Präposition **off** (von ... herunter/weg) oder mit **out of** (aus/heraus) verwechselt:

   Tom takes some money **out of** his purse.
   The purse falls **off** the table. Hands **off**! It's Tom**'s** purse. It's one **of** his birthday presents.

2. Verwechsle den ***of***- und den ***s***-Genitiv nicht mit der Präposition **from.** Die Präposition **from** gibt meist eine Richtung von einer Person oder von einem Ort her an:

   I've got a postcard **from** my father. It's **from** London. There are greetings **from** all the family on it.

9.

The s-genitive, *of*, *out of*, *off* or *from*?

Ergänze.

"Get _______ that bike," Tom said to Mike. "Let's put all the things on it. Then we needn't carry them." So they put all their things on Tom _______ bike. "Be careful, Mike, hold the bottles or they will fall _______ the bike." So Mike took one hand _______ his pockets and tried to hold them. It wasn't not very far _______ the corner shop to the Masons _______ flat – only a five-minute walk. But soon there was a loud crash and the bottles fell _______ the bike. Two lemonade bottles were broken. So they had to go back to Mrs White _______ shop. This time they got home all right. No bottles fell _______ the bike and Mike even took both hands _______ his pockets. At home, they carried everything into the kitchen. Then they went upstairs into Tom _______ room and talked about the party. Five minutes later there was a telephone call _______ Jenny _______ mother. "Jenny is ill, Tom. She's just come home _______ school and she looks really ill. I'm afraid she can't come to your party. But I nearly forgot to wish you all the best for your birthday. Greetings _______ Jenny and _______ my husband. You will hear _______ Jenny tomorrow. Bye, Tom, and have a nice party!"

Test

1.

Benutze den *of-* oder den *s*-Genitiv. Bilde mindestens 12 Paare.

Tom	milk	biscuits	legs
a packet	lemonade	my parents	comics
a bucket	computer	the legs	things
a pound	Jenny	the children	string
Timmy	trousers	magazines	people
a list	room	women	place

2.

In den folgenden Sätzen gibt es einige Fehler. Kannst du sie verbessern?

Do you like birthday parties? I like them. There are always lots of people's there. You can play games' and theres always some kind off fun. I hope Toms birthday party will be funny, too. There are some people's I know, too: Theres Jenny, theres Ann and theres his sister Kate, too. And perhaps Betty will be there, too. Shes a very nice girl, not as silly as the other girl's …

3.

Füge *out of, off, from, of* ein.

a) This plane is taking ______.

b) This is a letter ______ London. It's ______ Jenny's aunt.

c) This boy is taking ______ his clothes. He's taking the money ______ his pocket.

d) Where are you ______?

e) Turn the lights ______, please.

f) Is this one ______ your jokes?

6 *Have got, has got* und das *simple present* von *to be*

Have got und *has got*

Ob du *have got* oder *has got* verwenden musst, hängt vom Subjekt des Satzes ab:

Kate has got a bike.
My friends have got bikes, too.

Meist werden die Kurzformen verwendet, und zwar sowohl in bejahten als auch in verneinten Sätzen:

I've got a lot of books. **I haven't got** a pet.
Tom's got a baby brother. **He hasn't got** a baby sister.

Beachte:
has steht nur in der 3. Person Singular.
Bei **haven't** fällt das -**e** nicht aus. Der Apostroph steht hier für das ausgefallene „o“ von *not*. Bei **has** steht nie ein -**e**.

Wie verwende ich *have got* und *has got* in Fragen und Kurzantworten?

1. Bei Fragen stehen *have/has* vor dem Subjekt, *got* steht nach dem Subjekt.
2. Bei Kurzantworten musst du das Subjekt als Pronomen wiederholen.
3. Nach *yes* steht eine bejahte Langform, nach *no* eine verneinte Kurzform.
4. In der Kurzantwort steht kein *got.*

Has Kate got a brother? Yes, **she has**.
Has Kate got a sister? No, **she hasn't**.
Have her parents got a house? No, **they haven't**.
Have they got a flat? Yes, **they have**.

1.
The Masons' home

Füge die Formen von *have got* ein.

1. Tom's parents live in York. They __________ a flat there.
2. They __________ five rooms.
3. Tom __________ a room, and Kate __________ a room, too.
4. Timmy __________ a room. He is too young.
5. The Masons __________ a car.
6. Tom and Kate __________ a car, they __________ bikes.
7. Timmy __________ a bike because he's too young.
8. But he __________ two big toy cars and other toys in his room.

2.
What Kate has got

Bilde Sätze.

Beispiele:

1. Kate has got two brothers, but she hasn't got a sister.
2. What about you? I have got …, but I haven't got … .
3. What about your friend(s)? Have they got brothers, sisters, etc?

two brothers	boyfriend	bike	a teddy	a football	a radio
sister	a lot of friends	car	toy car	dog	TV set

3.
What about you? What have you got?

Stelle so viele Fragen, wie du kannst, und gib die entsprechenden Kurzantworten.

	you		a car		
	your parents		a lot of toys		
	your friends		a computer		
Has	your mother	got	a water pistol	**?**	Yes, …
Have	your grandmother	got	computer games		No, …
	your English teacher		a toy car		
	your boyfriend		a lot of friends		
	your father		a hamster		

Das *simple present* von *to be*

Bejahte Formen		**Verneinte Formen**	
Langformen	Kurzformen	Langformen	Kurzformen
I **am**	I**'m**	I **am** not	I**'m not**
you **are**	you**'re**	you **are** not	you **aren't**
he **is**	he**'s**	he **is** not	he **isn't**
she **is**	she**'s**	she **is** not	she **isn't**
it **is**	it**'s**	it **is** not	it **isn't**
we **are**	we**'re**	we **are** not	we **aren't**
you **are**	you**'re**	you **are** not	you **aren't**
they **are**	they**'re**	they **are** not	they **aren't**

Auch bei **to be** richtet sich die Form des Verbs nach dem Subjekt des Satzes:

I	**am**	ill.
They	**are**	my friends.

4.

Tom's birthday

Füge die Formen von *to be* ein.

Today, it _______ Tom's birthday. He _______ twelve years old today. All his friends _______ there. His sister _______ there, too. Her name _______ Kate. Only Jenny _______ not there. Where _______ she? She _______ ill. All the children _______ in the kitchen; it _______ full of children. They _______ all hungry and thirsty. There _______ a lot of sandwiches on the table; there _______ some bottles of lemonade, too. But one bottle _______ on the floor; it _______ broken and there _______ a pool of lemonade around it. And who _______ in the pool? It _______ Timmy, Tom's baby brother.

Wie verwende ich *to be* in Fragen und Kurzantworten?

1. Bei Fragen mit **to be** steht das Verb vor dem Subjekt.
2. Bei Kurzantworten (Antworten, die sich im Deutschen auf „Ja" oder „Nein" beschränken) musst du das Subjekt als Pronomen wiederholen.
3. Bei einer Antwort mit *yes* steht das Verb in der Langform, bei *no* in der Kurzform.

   Is it Kate's birthday? No, it **isn't**.
   Is Jenny there, too? No, she **isn't**.
   Is she ill? Yes, she **is**.
   Are Tom and Jenny unhappy? No, they **aren't**.
   Are the children hungry? Yes, they **are**.

4. Bei Fragen mit **is there/are there** ist **there** das Subjekt der Frage und muss in der Kurzantwort wiederholt werden:

   Are there sandwiches on the table? Yes, **there are**.
   Is there a bottle on the floor? Yes, **there is**.

5. Auf die Frage **is that** antwortet man mit **Yes, it is/No, it isn't**, auch wenn nach Personen gefragt wird:

   Is **that** Tom's baby brother? Yes, **it is**.

5.

Tom's birthday

Lies noch einmal die Aufgabe 4 durch und gib dann Kurzantworten.

1. Is it Timmy's birthday?
2. Is Jenny there?
3. Is Tom eleven years old?
4. Is Jenny Tom's mother?
5. Is Kate Tom's sister?
6. Is that Timmy in the pool of lemonade?
7. Are there sandwiches on the table?
8. Are the children in the bathroom?
9. Are they hungry and thirsty?
10. Is one bottle on the floor?

Der Gebrauch von *to be* in Fragen mit Fragewörtern

Das *simple present* von *to be* wird häufig in Fragen verwendet, die mit einem Fragewort beginnen. Die Fragewörter werden vor die Form von *to be* gestellt. Die übrige Wortstellung ändert sich nicht.

Who is Jenny?	**who** (= wer) fragt nach Personen.
What is on the table?	**what** (= was) fragt nach Sachen.
Where is Jenny?	**where** (= wo) fragt nach einem Ort.
Why isn't Jenny here?	**why** (= warum) fragt nach dem Grund.
How old is she?	**How** (= wie) fragt nach der Art und Weise und in Verbindung mit *old* nach dem Alter.

6.

Who or where?

Was ist richtig?

1. _______ is Timmy?	He's Tom's baby brother.
2. _______ is he?	He's at Tom's party.
3. _______ is Mike from?	He's is from Bristol.
4. _______ is Bristol?	It's in England.
5. _______ is Jenny?	She's Tom's friend.
6. _______ is she?	She's at home.
7. _______ are Joe and Kevin?	They are in the kitchen.

7.

Jenny

Auf der Party möchte Mike alles über Jenny wissen. Er stellt daher Tom eine Menge Fragen. Kannst du seine Fragen aufschreiben?

- who Jenny is
- if she is from York
- why she isn't here
- if her parents are at home
- how old she is
- if she is often ill

Test

1.

Vervollständige die Sätze mit den Formen von *to be* und von *have got*.

a) This __________ Kevin and that __________ Joe.

b) They __________ the best friends I __________.

c) And that boy over there __________ Bill.

d) He __________ in my class, too, and he __________ very good at maths.

e) And this __________ Ann. She __________ Jenny's friend.

f) She __________ very sorry that Jenny can't __________ here.

2.

Auf Toms Party spielen die Schüler ein Spiel. Tom denkt an seinen Englischlehrer. Die anderen müssen erraten, woran er denkt.

a) Is it a thing?	No, __________________
b) Is it an animal?	No, __________________
c) Is it in this room?	No, __________________
d) Have you got it at home?	No, __________________
e) Is it a person?	Yes, __________________
f) Is it a man?	Yes, __________________
g) Is it a teacher?	Yes, __________________
h) Is he a terrible teacher?	No, __________________
i) Has he got an old dirty car?	Yes, __________________
j) Is it our English teacher?	Yes, __________________

3.

Stelle einige Fragen an Jenny und gib ihre Antworten.

– why she isn't at Tom's party	(ill)
– if she is really ill	(yes)
– what she has got	(a cold)
– if she is unhappy that she can't come	(yes)
– if she has got a present for Tom	(yes)
– if it is a football	(no)
– what it is then	(a secret)

7

Das *present progressive*

Die Verlaufsform des Präsens, das *present progressive*, wird mit den Formen von *to be* und einer *ing*-Form gebildet. Das *present progressive* besteht daher immer aus zwei Teilen.

Es wird vor allem verwendet für Handlungen, die zur Zeit des Sprechens nicht vorbei sind, sondern noch andauern.

Bei verneinten Formen steht *not* oder die entsprechende Kurzform.

Die *ing*-Form *(present participle)* wird mit dem Infinitiv des Verbs + der Endung *-ing* gebildet.

What **are** they **doing**?

Tom's father	**is**	**cleaning**	his car.
Timmy	**is not**	**helping**	him.
Tom and Jenny	**are**	**doing**	their homework.
They	**aren't**	**playing**	in the garden.

Beachte bei der Bildung der *ing*-Form:

1. com**e** + ing   co**m**ing
   Ein auslautendes -**e**, das nicht gesprochen wird, entfällt.
2. si**t** + ing   si**tt**ing
   swi**m** + ing   swi**mm**ing
   Bei einsilbigen Verben mit kurzem, betontem Vokal wird der auslautende Konsonant verdoppelt.
3. l**ie** + ing   l**y**ing
   ie wird vor folgendem *-ing* zu **y**.

1.

At Tom's party

Auf der Party sind alle mit irgendetwas beschäftigt. Was tun sie gerade?

1. Mike/take/photos.
2. John/sit at the kitchen table/and drink/all the lemonade.
3. Kate/skip.
4. Tom/ring up/Jenny.
5. Betty/flirt/with Kevin.
6. Two boys/play/football in the kitchen.
7. Some girls/dance/in the kitchen.
8. Ann/lie on the floor/and watch/a film on TV.
9. Jim and Barbara/eat/sandwiches.
10. Susan/sit in a corner/and read a magazine.

2.

Timmy's report

Timmy ist auch auf der Party, aber er ist noch sehr klein und stört manchmal. Deshalb schickt ihn Tom zu seiner Mutter. Timmy erzählt ihr, was die anderen machen. Stimmt das, was Timmy sagt? Kannst du ihn korrigieren?

Beispiel: That's not right, Timmy. Mike isn't playing with his camera, he's taking photos.

1. Mike is playing with his camera.
2. John is eating all the sandwiches.
3. Kate is hopping around like a rabbit.
4. Tom is talking to his teacher.
5. Betty and Kevin are kissing.
6. Two boys are quarrelling about a ball.
7. Some girls are running around in the kitchen.
8. Ann is lying on the floor because she is ill.
9. Jim and Barabara are making sandwiches.
10. Susan is reading my picture book.

Wie verwende ich das *present progressive* in Fragen?

1. Bei Fragen im *present progressive* steht zunächst eine Form von **to be**, dann das Subjekt und schließlich das *present participle*.
2. Fragewörter wie *why, where, when, what* werden einfach vor die Form von **to be** gesetzt. Die Wortstellung ändert sich dadurch nicht.

   Beispiele:
   Are you talk**ing** to your teacher, Tom?
   Is Jenny ly**ing** in bed?
   Why is she ly**ing** in bed?
   What are her parents do**ing**?
3. Bei Kurzantworten wird das *present participle* ausgelassen:

   Is Jenny lying in bed? Yes, **she is**. (Pronomen + bejahte Langform)
   No, **she isn't**. (Pronomen + verneinte Kurzform)

3.
Timmy's answers

Timmys Mutter kann nicht ganz glauben, was Timmy ihr erzählt. Daher stellt sie ihm ein paar Fragen. Stelle erst diese Fragen und gib dann Timmys Antworten.

Beispiel: Is Tom really talking to his teacher? Yes, he is.
Is John really eating all the sandwiches? …

4.
Timmy is on the way again …

Timmys Mutter glaubt immer noch, dass Timmy manches nicht richtig begriffen hat. Sie schickt ihn daher mit einigen Fragen zurück, damit er nachfragt. Stelle du Timmys Fragen und lasse dir die Antworten geben.

Beispiel: What are you doing, Kate? – I'm skipping.

Timmy's mother wants to know

- what Kate is doing,
- if Tom is really talking to his teacher,
- what Mike is doing with his camera,
- if Susan is really reading his picture book,
- why Ann is lying on the floor,
- if Kate is playing a new game,
- what the boys are doing in the kitchen,
- what the girls are doing in the kitchen,
- if John is still hungry.

5.
In Timmy's room

First scene:
At 7.30 the party is over. The children are going home. They are all happy. Timmy is happy, too. He is in his room. He is lying on the floor, but he isn't crying. He's playing with Tom's birthday presents. They are in his room now. One parcel is open. There's a picture book and some chocolate in it.

Second scene:
Timmy is still lying on the floor. There is chocolate on his face and hands. He isn't playing any more. He's got a pencil in his hand and he is drawing a picture in Tom's picture book. What is Timmy drawing? He's drawing farm animals – red hens, blue dogs and green cows.

Third scene:
Somebody is coming upstairs. He is shouting a name. It is Timmy's brother. He is looking for his presents. He is angry. He is opening the door of Timmy's room. But the room is empty. Where is Timmy? Can you see him?

Schau dir den Text der drei Szenen an und frage dann nach den unterstrichenen Ausdrücken. Verwende dabei die richtigen Fragewörter: *who*? (wer?) – *where*? (wo, wohin?) – *what*? (was?) – *when*? (wann?)

Test

1.

Was machen die Schüler gerade? Stelle Fragen nach den unterstrichenen Wörtern.

- Betty/do/<u>her homework</u>.
- <u>Mark</u>/make/a paper plane.
- Tony and Tom/<u>fight</u> with each other.
- Jimmy/lie/<u>on the floor</u>/and/cry.
- Kate/clean <u>the board</u>.
- Pete and John/play/<u>a game.</u>
- <u>Jim</u>/have/<u>his second breakfast</u>.
- Mike/run/around <u>in the classroom</u>.

2.

Nicht bei allen Lehrern ist Ruhe, wenn sie ins Klassenzimmer kommen. So auch hier. Ergänze bitte.

Teacher: Hey, Bob? What ____________? *(do)* ____________ still ____________ with Sue? *(flirt)*

Bob: No, sir, ____________ just ____________ her a question. *(ask)*

Teacher: And what about you, Betty? ____________ still ____________ your homework? *(do)*

Betty: I ____________ not ____________ my homework, sir. I ____________ notes. *(do, take)*

Teacher: John, why ____________ still ____________? *(eat)*
You will get fat if you go on like this.

Teacher: And you Jimmy, why ____________ still ____________ *(cry)*? Look at the girls, they ____________ at you. *(laugh)*

Teacher: And Sam, can you stop singing now? ____________ you all ____________ now? *(listen)* Then we may start.

8 Modale Hilfsverben

Die Formen der modalen Hilfsverben

Modale Hilfsverben kennst du auch vom Deutschen. Es entsprechen dabei:

can	können, dürfen
can't/cannot	nicht können, nicht dürfen
must	müssen
mustn't	nicht dürfen
needn't	nicht müssen, nicht brauchen

Beachte: Die verneinte Form von **must** ist **needn't**!

Für „dürfen" bzw. „nicht dürfen" kann in Fragen und Kurzantworten auch **may** (statt *can*) bzw. **may not** (statt *mustn't, can't*) stehen:

May I help you? Yes, you **may**. – No, you **may not**.

Englische Hilfsverben weisen folgende Eigenschaften auf:

1. Sie haben keinen Infinitiv und kein *-s* in der 3. Person Singular.
2. Ihre Formen sind für alle Personen gleich.
3. Hilfsverben können im Englischen nicht alleine stehen; ihnen muss immer ein Verb folgen (eine Ausnahme bilden die Kurzantworten).

Vergleiche: Er **kann** English. He **can speak** English.

4. Wie im Deutschen folgt einem Hilfsverb immer ein Infinitiv.
5. Objekte und andere Ergänzungen stehen im Englischen immer nach der Verbgruppe.

Vergleiche: Er kann **sie** sehen. He can see **her.**

1.

After the party

Unterstreiche im folgenden Text die modalen Hilfsverben.

After the party Kate can go to her room. It isn't her birthday, so she needn't help. But Tom must. He must help his mother wash up the dishes and clean the kitchen floor. Then they must tidy up the living room.

Must Timmy help, too? No, he needn't. He must go to bed because it's already late. He is very unhappy. "Why can't I help you? Why must I always go to bed?" he cries. "Look, Timmy," his mother says, "it's already 8 o'clock; you must go to bed now. You can stay up longer next year." But Timmy is still unhappy. "I can wash the dishes, too." "OK, Timmy, you can help Tom with the dishes, but you mustn't drop them," his mother says. "Fetch the dirty plates from the living room," Tom says to him. Timmy is happy now. He is big and strong and he can help. But what's that? There is a loud noise in the living room, then everything is quiet again. When Tom opens the door, Timmy is gone, but there are three plates on the floor …

2.

Right or wrong?

Lies den Text in Aufgabe 1 noch einmal und verbessere dann, was falsch ist.

1. Kate must go to her room.
2. She mustn't help Tom.
3. Tom must clean Kate's room.
4. He needn't wash up the dishes.
5. He must clean the kitchen floor.
6. He must clean the kitchen windows, too.
7. Timmy can help him.
8. Timmy must clean the kitchen floor, too.
9. Timmy must drop the plates.
10. Timmy can stay up a little longer.

3.

A phone call

Am nächsten Tag ruft Tom Jenny an. Jennys Mutter ist am Telefon.
Ergänze die modalen Hilfsverben.

Tom:	*Jenny's mother:*
________ I talk to Jenny, please?	Sorry, Tom, you ______________________. Jenny's in the bathroom.
________ Jenny come tomorrow?	No, she ______________________ get up.
________ she stay in bed all day?	Yes, she ______________________.
________ she take medicine?	No, she ______________________.
________ I see her this afternoon?	No, you ________________ see her today.
________ I see her tomorrow?	Well, let's see what the doctor says.
	But you ___________ ring her up again in the evening.

4.

What Jenny must do

Endlich ist Jenny am Telefon. Sie erzählt Tom, was sie tun muss oder nicht tun darf. Kannst du aufschreiben, was sie sagt? Fang so an: I must/mustn't …

2. Stay in bed for three days.

3. Take your medicine.

1. Don't go to school.

4. Don't play with your friends.

5. Don't watch too much TV.

6. Tell your mum to take your temperature every morning.

7. Come to my surgery again on Monday at 4 o'clock.

5.

Jenny is really ill

Was kann, darf, muss, braucht Jenny nicht zu tun? Bilde Sätze.

take her medicine
watch TV
ride on her bike
read a book
clean her room
go to school
help her mother in the kitchen
do her homework
listen to music
ring up her friends
play football
write letters
wash her clothes
kiss her doctor

Der Gebrauch modaler Hilfsverben in Fragen und Kurzantworten

Bei Fragen steht das Hilfsverb vor dem Subjekt; nach dem Subjekt steht immer der Infinitiv.

Bei Kurzantworten wird nur das Hilfsverb wiederholt, für das Subjekt steht ein Pronomen.

Hilfsverb	**+ Subjekt**	**+ Infinitiv**
Can	Kate get up?	Yes, she can. No, she **can't.**
Must	she stay in bed?	Yes, she **must.** No, she **needn't.**

6.

At the doctor's

Wenn du krank bist, wirst du deinem Arzt gewiss ein paar Fragen stellen. Kannst du seine Antworten geben?

1. Must I go to school? — No, ______________.
2. Must I stay in bed? — Yes, ______________.
3. Must I do my homework? — No, ______________.
4. Must I stay in bed all day? — Yes, ______________.
5. Can I get up? — No, ______________.
6. Can I ring up my friends? — Yes, ______________.
7. Must I take my temperature? — Yes, ______________.
8. May my friends come to see me — Yes, ______________, but not on the first day.
9. Can I watch TV? — Yes, ______________.
10. Must I take all that medicine? — Yes, ______________.

7.

Your questions

Dein Freund oder deine Freundin ist krank. Du besuchst ihn/sie.
Bilde die entsprechenden Fragen und gib die Kurzantworten.

- if he/she is very ill (Yes)
- if he/she must stay in bed (Yes)
- if he/she must stay indoors all day (Yes)
- if he/she may get up for an hour or two (Yes)
- if he/she has got a temperature (Yes)
- if he/she can go to school on Thursday (No)
- if he/she is happy that she needn't go to school (Yes)
- if his/her teachers are happy, too (No)

8.

Timmy

Vervollständige die Sätze.

1. Timmy is three. He ____________ go to school. (Er braucht nicht …)
2. He ____________ go to kindergarten. (Er kann …)
3. He ____________ play with other children there. (Er kann …)
4. ____________ he go there every day? (Muss er …?)
5. No, he ____________. (Nein, er muss nicht.)
6. ____________ he go there alone? (Darf er …?)
7. No, he ____________. (Nein, er darf nicht.)
8. ____________ he take his bike? No, he ____________. (Darf er …? Nein, er darf nicht.) It's too dangerous.
9. ____________ Tom fetch him in the afternoon? (Muss Tom …)
10. Yes, he ____________ on Thursdays and Fridays. (Ja, er muss …)

Zu den modalen Hilfsverben, die häufig in Fragen verwendet werden, gehört auch **shall**. Mit **Shall I/Shall we** ...? kann man einen Wunsch erfragen oder ein Angebot machen. Dies ist allerdings nur mit **I** und **we** möglich.

Shall	**+ Subjekt**	**+ Infinitiv**
Shall	**I open**	the window for you? Soll ich ...?
Shall	**I give**	you your medicine? Soll ich ...?
Shall	**we call**	the doctor again? Sollen wir ...?

9.

Helping people

Deine Mutter ist krank. Was kannst du für sie tun? Hier sind ein paar Ideen. Bilde Fragen mit "Shall I ..."?

Beispiel: Shall I do the shopping for you?

do the shopping
do the washing up
clean the rooms
make your bed
go to the chemist's
buy you some lemonade
get your medicine
open the window
cook the meals
ring up the doctor
make an appointment
look after my sister/brother

Test

1.
Bilde Sätze. Gib auf die Wortstellung Acht.

a) A doctor must/his patients/examine.
b) Their temperature/must/he/take.
c) Listen/he/must/what they tell him/to.
d) A prescription/give/them/must/he.
e) Go and see/must/he/his patients.
f) Ask/them/how they feel/must/he.
g) He/his patients/to hospital/must send/when they are seriously ill.

2.
Stimmt das, was hier steht? Wenn nicht, korrigiere, was nicht richtig ist.

a) A good patient can do what the doctor tells him/her.
b) A good patient mustn't take his/her medicine.
c) A good patient needn't stay in bed when he/she is ill.
d) A good patient mustn't forget his/her appointment.
e) A good patient mustn't be late at the doctor's surgery.
f) A good patient mustn't listen to his/her doctor.

3.
Einige Leute helfen gerne. Gehörst du auch dazu? Was sagst du dann?

Jenny: I can't understand this exercise. You: Shall I explain it to you?

Kate: My school bag is so heavy. You: ____________________

Timmy: I'm so hungry. You: ____________________

Tom: I can't find my English book. You: ____________________

Mike: I can't do this exercise. You: ____________________

Sarah: My windows are so dirty. You: ____________________

Kevin: I' m not very good at German. You: ____________________

Paul: It's so cold in here. You: ____________________

Susan: It's Ann's birthday tomorrow. You: ____________________

9 Das *simple present* von Vollverben

Das *simple present* in bejahten Sätzen

Vollverben sind Verben, die eine Tätigkeit oder einen Zustand nennen oder beschreiben. Sie kommen im Englischen wie im Deutschen in verschiedenen Zeiten *(tenses)* vor. Eine dieser Zeiten ist das *simple present*.

Bis auf die 3. Person Singular hat das *simple present* die gleiche Form wie der Infinitiv (ohne *to*).

In der 3. Person Singular *(he, she, it)* wird ein *-s* angehängt.

Formen

I	**like**	ice cream.
You	**like**	sweets.
My father	**likes**	tennis.
My mother	**likes**	English.
A cat	**likes**	mice.
We	**like**	Tom.
You	**like**	us.
They	**like**	TV.

Bei der Schreibung der 3. Person Singular gibt es folgende Besonderheiten:

1. Bei Verben, die auf die Laute [s], [ʃ], [tʃ] enden, hängt man ein **-es** [iz] an:

   He always catch**es** the bus at six o'clock.
   He sometimes miss**es** it.
   He never push**es** other people.

2. Wie bei der Pluralbildung der Substantive ändert sich das **-y** nach einem Vokal nicht; nach einem Konsonant wird es jedoch zu **-ie**:

to f**ly**	He fl**ies** to France.
to t**ry**	He tr**ies** to be helpful.
Aber: to st**a**y	He st**ays** with his friends.

3. Auch bei *to go* und *to do* wird in der 3. Person Singular ein **-es** angehängt:

He go**es** home.
He do**es** his homework.

1.
What Tom does
Verwende das *simple present*.

1. He ____________ at 7 o'clock every morning *(get up)*.
2. Then he ____________ *(wash)* and ____________ on his clothes *(put)*.
3. Then he ____________ down to the dining room *(go)*.
4. There he ____________ breakfast *(have)*.
5. Then he ____________ for his school bag *(look)*.
6. After that he ____________ the house *(leave)*.
7. Then he ____________ to the bus stop *(go)*.
8. He usually ____________ the bus when it is cold *(take)*.
9. He ____________ at school at a quarter to nine *(arrive)*.
10. He ____________ hello to his friends *(say)*.

2.
What they usually do after lessons
Bilde die folgenden Sätze.

- Tom/go home/do his homework with Jenny/play games/watch TV
- Kate/go to her room/listen to music/ring up her friends/play
- Mike/sit in front of his computer/play computer games/often forget his homework
- Ann and Barbara/send SMS messages/listen to music/read magazines
- John/have tea/eat a lot of sandwiches/lie down on his bed/have a nap

Das *simple present* in verneinten Sätzen

Bei der Verneinung musst du eine Form von *to do* gebrauchen. Diese Form lautet in der 3. Person Singular *does not* bzw. *doesn't*, in den anderen Personen *do not* bzw. *don't*. Das folgende Verb steht im Infinitiv; d. h. du darfst dann in der 3. Person kein *-s* oder *-es* anhängen.

Formenübersicht

I	**don't**	**like**	maths.
You	**don't**	**like**	biology.
Tom	**doesn't**	**like**	maths.
Jenny	**doesn't**	**like**	English.
We	**don't**	**like**	our teacher.
You	**don't**	**like**	geography.
They	**don't**	**like**	their teacher.

Beachte:
Ist *to do* ein Vollverb, so heißt die Verneinung **don't do/doesn't do**:

He **doesn't do** his homework.
They **don't do** their homework.

3.
A strange family
Die Browns wohnen ganz in der Nähe. Sie haben vier Kinder. Was tun sie nicht?

1. They ________________ in the morning. *(get up)*
2. They ________________ an early breakfast. *(have)*
3. Mr Brown ________________ his car. *(wash)*
4. Mrs Brown ________________ the cooking. *(do)*
5. Often, their children ________________ school. *(go)*

6. They ________________ school. *(like)*

7. Helen ________________ her teachers. *(like)*

8. She ________________ her homework. *(do)*

4.
People are different
Bilde Sätze nach dem folgenden Muster.

Beispiel: Tom likes bananas, but he doesn't like oranges.

Tom		Jenny + Kate		Timmy		Mike		The Browns	
bananas	+	volleyball	+	cornflakes	+	photos	+	work	–
oranges	–	tennis	–	tea	–	comics	–	sleeping	+
Jenny	+	sports	+	dogs	+	music	+	books	–
Ben	–	all sports	–	cats	–	singing	–	TV	+

5.
Over to you
Was magst du, was magst du nicht? Was mögen deine Freunde/Freundinnen, deine Eltern? Was mögen sie nicht? Schreibe 10 Sätze auf.

Beispiel: I like football, but my father doesn't. He likes tennis.

Das *simple present* in Fragen und Kurzantworten

Bei Fragen mit einem Vollverb musst du immer eine Form von *to do* verwenden. Wie bei der Verneinung steht das Verb im Infinitiv.

In der Kurzantwort steht für das Vollverb immer eine Form von *to do.*

Do you **like** football?	Yes, **I do**.
	No, **I don't**.
Does your mother **like** football, too?	Yes, **she does**.
	No, **she doesn't**.

Beachte: Wenn **to do** ein Vollverb ist, muss es auch bei Fragen wiederholt werden.

Do you always **do** your homework?	Yes, I **do.**
Do you often **do** it in the morning?	No, I **don't**.

Die Wortstellung *form of to do + subject + infinitive* bleibt auch dann erhalten, wenn die Frage mit einem Fragewort beginnt.

When	**does**	Mike	**get**	up?
When	**do**	his parents	**get**	up?
What	**do**	they	**do**	then?
Why	**does**	Mike	**get**	up at 7?
How	**does**	his sister	**go**	to school?
When	**do**	his parents	**take**	him there?
What subjects	**doesn't**	he	**like?**	

Beachte: to do muss wiederholt werden, wenn es ein Vollverb ist.

What **does** Mike **do** in the evenings?
What **do** you **do** at school?

6.
Mike

Mike ist neu in Toms Klasse. Am ersten Tag stellen ihm seine Klassenkameraden viele Fragen. Stelle die Fragen und gib Mikes Antworten.

1. __________ you like your new school? (Yes)
2. __________ you play football? (Yes)
3. __________ your sister go to our school? (Yes)
4. __________ she play tennis? (No)
5. __________ you and your sister go to school by bike? (Yes)
6. __________ play an instrument? (No)
7. __________ your father work in York? (Yes)
8. __________ your mother like York? (Yes)
9. __________ your parents like it here? (Yes)

7.
An interview

Frage deinen Freund/deine Freundin und gib seine/ihre Antworten.

1. Where/you/live?
2. When/get up/in the morning?
3. When/your mother/get up?
4. What/have/for breakfast?
5. Why/not like/cornflakes?
6. When/your parents/leave the house?
7. When/they/come home again?
8. How/get/to school?
9. Why/not take/the bus?
10. What/do/in the afternoon?
11. What games/do/like?
12. What/do in the evening?
13. When/go/to bed?
14. When/switch off/the light?
15. When/your parents/go to bed?

8.
Mike

Frage nach den unterstrichenen Wörtern. Benutze das richtige Fragewort.

Mike lives in York now. He likes his new school, but he doesn't like all his subjects. He goes to school by bike. In winter and when it rains, his mother drives him to school. The first lesson begins at 8.45, so he gets up at 7. He leaves the house at a quarter to eight and usually arrives at school at 8.30. He has lunch at school because his parents don't come home until the evening. After school he often goes to see Tom. They play games together until 6 or 7 o'clock or do their homework. Then Mike goes home.

9.

Mike's father

Kannst du ihn interviewen?

1. He gets up at 5.30 o'clock in the morning.

   When ____ you ____________________?

2. He starts work at 7 o'clock.

   When____________________________?

3. He leaves his house at 6.30.

   When____________________________?

4. He drives a school bus.

   What ____________________________?

5. He collects the children from the villages.

   Who_____________________________?

6. He takes them to school.

   Where ___________________________?

7. School starts at a quarter to nine.

   When____________________________?

8. In the afternoon he fetches them from school.

   When____________________________?

9. He takes them home again.

   Where ___________________________?

10. Then he cleans the bus.

    What ____________________________?

11. He often finds things in the bus.

    What ____________________________?

Test

1.
Bilde Sätze mit den folgenden Verben. Verwende nur die 3. Person Singular.

Beispiel: to fetch My brother fetches a chair.

to go, to carry, to wear, to write, to lose, to want, to use, to sound, to take, to teach, to throw, to tie, to do, to love, to miss, to see, to brush, to choose, to close, to empty, to fly

2.
Füge bitte die richtigen Verben ein.

know	listen	find	do	make
talk	show	try	have	

When the pupils ___________ lessons with Mr Cummins, they all ___________. He ___________ a lot of things to ___________ his lessons interesting. He ___________ to them about foreign countries, and even ___________ them how to use the Internet. Here they often ___________ a lot of information about the subjects they ___________ about. But he can be very funny, too. He ___________ a lot of jokes and when they ___________ a problem, he always ___________ and ___________ to help.

3.
Es gibt vielleicht ein Mädchen oder einen Jungen in deiner Klasse, die/den du viel besser kennen möchtest. Also stellst du ihr/ihm die folgenden Fragen ...

- when he/she usually gets home
- what he/she usually does after school
- if he/she likes going to the cinema
- what kind of films he/she likes
- if he/she often goes to the cinema
- when he/she does her homework
- how much time he/she needs for it

10 *Simple present* und *present progressive*

Look! The boy **is doing** his homework. He**'s doing a** German exercise now.

1. Wann benutze ich das *present progressive*?

Wie dir das obige Beispiel zeigt, gebraucht man das *present progressive* für Handlungen, die zur Zeit des Sprechens nicht vorbei sind, sondern noch andauern.

Signalwörter dafür sind zum Beispiel: *now, at this moment, look, listen, today, this morning (afternoon, evening).*

2. Wann benutze ich das *simple present*?

Das *simple present* gebraucht man für wiederholte, gewohnheitsmäßige und lang andauernde Handlungen:

He usually **does** his homework after school.
He **goes** to a comprehensive school.

Signalwörter sind hier: *always, often, sometimes, never, usually, seldom (= selten), every day (week, month, year), in the morning (afternoon, evening).*

Beachte:
Always, often, usually, never stehen im *simple present* immer vor dem Verb:

He **usually** does his homework after school.
He **often** does it in his room.

Sometimes kann auch am Satzanfang stehen:

Sometimes he forgets it, too.

1.
Mike's photos
Mike fotografiert gern. Hier sind ein paar seiner Fotos. Kannst du den Text vervollständigen?

This is Dad.
sit/bus

This is Dad again.
clean/bus

This is our house.
live/there

This is Mum.
leave the house/
always leave at 8

This is our garden.
Look! Mum/work in it/
like her garden

This is our corner shop.
Mum/work there/
sell something

2.

Things are different today

Setze das *simple present* oder *present progressive* ein.

1. Mike usually ____________ up at 7, but today he is still in bed. *(get)*

   He ____________. *(still sleep)*

2. He usually ____________ breakfast at 7. 30, but today he ____________ in bed. *(have; still lie)*

3. He often ____________ no time to wash, but this morning he ____________ a bath. *(have; take)*

4. He usually ____________ his school uniform, but today he ____________ different clothes *(put on; wear)*

5. He usually ____________ lunch at school, but today he ____________ lunch at home. *(have)*

6. Mike usually ____________ mother with the dishes, but today he needn't. His

   father ____________ the dishes. *(help; wash)*

7. His parents usually ____________ the house in the morning, but things are

   different today. They ____________ for a walk. *(leave; go)*

   Do you know why? Well, it's ____________.

3.

What about your Sundays?

Was tust du oft, nie, selten, manchmal usw. am Sonntag? Hier sind ein paar Ideen:

		get up late
		play football
		watch TV
	always	play computer games
	never	clean my room
On Sundays I	usually	help Mum and Dad
	sometimes	listen to CDs
	often	brush my shoes
	seldom	learn English
		go for a walk
		write letters
		go to Church

Das *simple present* steht im Englischen auch für aufeinander folgende Handlungen. Solche Handlungen kommen vor allem in Erzählungen und Berichten vor.

Signalwörter sind unter anderem: *first, then, after that, next, soon, at last.* Schau dir dazu diesen Text an:

After school Mike often goes to see Tom. **When** they arrive at Tom's, they **first** put their school bags in a corner. **Then** they go to the kitchen and look for something to drink. **Then** they go to Tom's room. There they play for an hour or two. **After that** they do their homework together. **Then** Mike goes home.

4.

Mr Mason

Toms Vater ist Tierarzt. So sieht ein normaler Arbeitstag bei ihm aus:

7.00	get up at seven o'clock
7.00–7.30	wash
7.30	have breakfast
8.00	get in his car
8.30	open his surgery
9.00–12.00	examine sick animals
12.30	have lunch at a restaurant
17.00	have a cup of tea
17.30	close the door of the surgery
18.00	come home

Schreibe auf, was Toms Vater jeden Tag tut. Verwende dabei Signalwörter wie *first, then, after that.*

5.

What you do

Schreibe auf, was du jeden Tag machst. Verwende dabei alle Signalwörter, die du kennst.

6.
Scrambled eggs

Heute sind Toms Eltern nicht zu Hause. Die Kinder haben Hunger und gehen in die Küche, um etwas zu essen. Aber der Kühlschrank ist leer. Es sind nur ein paar Eier drin. Also machen sie Rühreier. Bilde Sätze und bringe sie in die richtige Reihenfolge.

add some milk, salt and pepper
eat them
put fat in the frying pan
put the scrambled eggs on a plate
stir the eggs
put everything in the frying pan
break the eggs
put the eggs in a bowl
cook the eggs in the frying pan

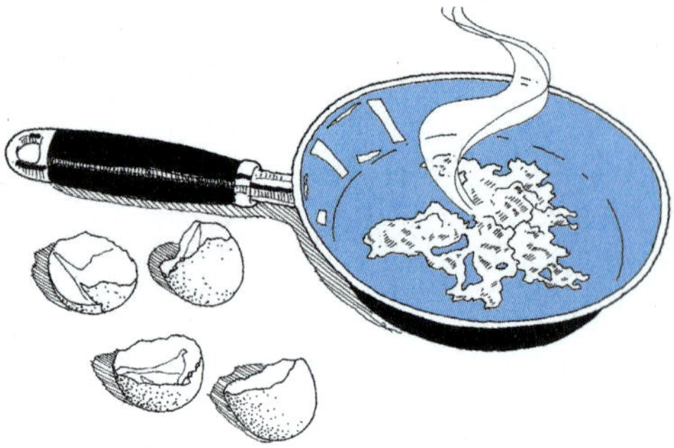

7.
Another breakfast

Simple present oder *present progressive*? Setze die richtigen Formen ein.

1. The weather is fine and the sun __________ *(shine)*. It is already ten o'clock, and the Masons ______ still __________ *(sit)* at the breakfast table.
2. It's Sunday. The Masons always __________ *(have)* a late breakfast on Sundays. But somebody ______ still __________ *(miss)*. It's Kate. She is still in her room; she __________ *(sleep)*.
3. So Timmy __________ *(go)* to Kate's room. He __________ *(open)* the door and __________ *(see)* that Kate is still in her bed. He __________ *(try)* to wake her up, but Kate __________ *(not listen)*, so Timmy __________ *(go)* back and __________ *(tell)* his dad that Kate ______ still __________ *(sleep)*.
4. Mr Mason __________ *(say)*: "Come on, Timmy. Get Tom's water pistol and ask your sister if she __________ *(not want)* to get up now."
5. So Timmy __________ *(fetch)* Tom's water pistol and __________ *(go)* to Kate's room. Suddenly there is a loud noise in Kate's room and somebody __________ *(shout)* in an angry voice: "You just wait, Timmy. When I get you, I ..."

Test

1.

Simple present oder *present progressive*? Vervollständige die Sätze.

a) Mike ___________ a picture of his new school. He ___________ taking pictures. He often ___________ pictures. *(take; like)*

b) He ___________ only ___________ pictures of schools, he ___________ pictures of everything. Here he ___________ a picture of Tom and Jenny. *(take)*

c) He always ___________ his pictures in an album. Look! He ___________ a picture in his album now. *(put)*

d) He ___________ already ___________ a lot of albums. He ___________ them in his room. *(have got; keep)*

e) He often ___________ his pictures to his friends. Here he ___________ an album to Tom. *(show)*

2.

Fülle die Lücken mit den angegebenen Verben aus.

Anne _____________ *(like)* music. She _____________ *(learn)* to play the piano. Anne's baby sister Jane _____________ *(like)* the piano, too, because she can make a lot of noise on it. One night when everybody is already in bed, Anne _____________ *(wake)* up. What is it? She _____________ *(sit)* up in her bed and _____________ *(listen)*. It's the piano. Somebody _____________ *(play)* it. Who can that be? Oh, Jane of course! Anne _____________ *(jump)* out of bed, _____________ *(rush)* downstairs and _____________ *(switch)* on the lights. But there is nobody there. "Jane, come here! I know that you are there!" There is no answer. Anne _____________ *(turn)* off the lights and _____________ *(go)* upstairs to Jane's room. Jane is in her bed and she _____________ *(sleep)*. Anne _____________ *(hear)* the piano again …

11 Verneinung, Fragen und Kurzantworten

Die Verneinung

Tom schreibt manchmal auch in der Schule Briefe an seine Freundin Jenny. Hier ist einer davon, aber jemand hat den Brief gefunden und Tom einen Streich gespielt. Der Brief ist nämlich verändert. Kannst du die Stellen herausfinden?

Dear Jenny,
I hope we **can't see** each other this afternoon. **I haven't got** a lot of homework to do, but I **don't think** I can come at 4 o'clock. Can you wait for me at the bus stop? I hope I **can't come.** I really **don't want** to see you again. You **aren't** the nicest girl I know. I **am not** always thinking of you. You know I **don't like** you.

Love, **(ha! ha!)**
Tom

Wenn du den Brief anschaust, siehst du, dass die Verneinung im Englischen nur bei den Vollverben im *simple present* mit einer Form von *to do* – mit **do not/does not** bzw. **don't/doesn't** – gebildet wird.

Bei den Formen von *to be, have got,* den Hilfsverben *can, may* usw. und dem *present progressive* wird die Verneinung nur mit *not* gebildet.

Beispiele:

Jenny **isn't** the nicest girl.	**to be**
He **isn't thinking** of her.	**present progressive**
He **can't** see her.	**auxiliary**
He **hasn't got** a lot of homework.	**have got**

Vergleiche aber:

He **doesn't like** her.	**simple present**

1.

What is right?

Was denkst du, dass Jenny tut, wenn sie den Brief erhält? Bilde die folgenden Sätze.

Beispiel: I think Jenny doesn't begin to cry.

1. She begins to cry.
2. She is very unhappy.
3. She must leave the classroom.
4. She must laugh.
5. She writes a letter, too.
6. She shows it to her teacher.
7. She reads it to the class.
8. She goes home immediately.
9. She falls ill.
10. She kicks Tom.
11. She is very angry with him.
12. All her neighbours begin to laugh.

2.

Good pupils

Was sind gute Schüler für dich? Hier sind ein paar Ideen. Verwende auch verneinte Formen.

1. Good pupils are silly.
2. Good pupils work too much.
3. Good pupils are bad at sports.
4. Good pupils always do their homework.
5. Good pupils never forget anything.
6. Good pupils never make their teachers angry.
7. Good pupils never talk in lessons.
8. Good pupils have got a lot of friends.
9. Good pupils always talk to their teachers.
10. Good pupils are unhappy.
11. Good pupils are only interested in school.
12. Good pupils never go out with boys/girls.
13. Good pupils always talk about school.
14. Good pupils know everything.

Die Fragebildung

Auch Fragen werden im *simple present* mit **to do** gebildet. Wie bei der Verneinung steht das entsprechende Vollverb dann im Infinitiv:

Does	Tom	**like** Jenny?
Do	Tom's parents	**like** her, too?

Bei den Formen von *to be, have got* und den Hilfsverben wie *can, must* darfst du **to do** nicht verwenden. Dies gilt auch für das *present progressive.*

Is	Tom		happy?
Has	he	**got**	a girlfriend?
Is	he	**writing**	her a letter?
Can	he	**see**	her?

3.

An article for the school magazine

Tom schreibt einen Artikel über Schüler, die sich an der Schule nicht wohl fühlen. Er möchte eine Art Fragekatalog aufstellen, um die Gründe dafür herauszufinden. Kannst du seine Fragen formulieren?

Beispiel: Are you often alone?

Tom wants to know if

- they are often alone,
- they like their parents,
- they have got any friends,
- they have got any hobbies,
- their parents often play with them,
- they have got anybody to talk to,
- they watch a lot of TV,
- most of their teachers are nice,
- they are often afraid when they are alone
- their parents are often out in the evening.

4.

Pupils, pupils ...

Wie du weißt, sind nicht alle Schüler gleich. Frage deinen Nachbar/deine Nachbarin und versuche herauszufinden, was für ein Schüler/eine Schülerin er/sie ist.

There are pupils who

- can't sit still,
- talk all the time,
- can't listen,
- listen only when the teacher gets angry,
- often forget things,
- don't do their homework,
- find everything boring,
- often sleep during lessons,
- are often late,
- are often ill for tests,
- only like sports.

5.

You and your school

Bilde Fragen.

1. _____ you _____________ school? *(like)*
2. _____ you often _____________ your homework? *(forget)*
3. _____ you _____________ your homework now? *(do – present progressive)*
4. _____ your mum _____________ you now? *(help – present progressive)*
5. _____ your parents often _____________ you? *(help)*
6. _____ you _____________ nice teachers? *(have got)*
7. _____ they _____________ you? *(like)*
8. _____ they _____________ you a lot of homework? *(give)*
9. _____ you _____________ during lessons? *(can talk)*
10. _____ you _____________ chewing gum in the English lessons? *(may eat)*
11. _____ you _____________ a school magazine at your school? *(have got)*
12. _____ you _____________ it? *(read)*
13. _____ you _____________ it interesting? *(find)*

Entscheidungsfragen und Kurzantworten

Bei Fragen musst du zwischen zwei Grundtypen unterscheiden, nämlich zwischen Entscheidungsfragen und Ergänzungsfragen.

Bei Entscheidungsfragen will man wissen, ob sich eine Sache so oder so verhält. Man antwortet daher immer mit Ja oder Nein. Im Englischen entspricht diesem Ja oder Nein eine Kurzantwort. Vergleiche:

to be	**Is** Kate ill?	Yes, **she is**. No, **she isn't.**
present progressive	**Is** she **sleeping?**	Yes, **she is.** No, **she isn't.**
auxiliary	**Must** she **see** a doctor?	Yes, **she must.** No, **she needn't.**
have got	**Has** she **got** a cold?	Yes, **she has.** No, **she hasn't.**
simple present	**Does** she **go** to school?	Yes, **she does.** No, **she doesn't.**
	Do her friends **look** after her?	Yes, **they do.** No, **they don't.**

Beachte:

1. Für Vollverben im *simple present* tritt eine Form von **to do** ein.
2. Das Subjekt der Kurzantwort ist immer ein Pronomen (*I, you* usw.).
3. Nach *yes* steht eine Langform, nach *no* die Kurzform.
4. Ist **this** oder **that** das Subjekt des Fragesatzes, so steht in der Kurzantwort immer **it**.

   Is **this** your brother? Yes, **it** is.
   Is **that** your mother? Yes, **it** is.

6.

Timmy's new picture book

Während Tom in seinem Zimmer schreibt, kommt Timmy herein. Er hat sein neues Bilderbuch dabei und den Kopf voller Fragen. Kannst du sie beantworten? Gib Kurzantworten bitte.

1. Look at that house, Tom. Is that a church?
2. The man with the hat – is that a postman?
3. And what is he doing? Is he trying to get into the house?
4. And what about those men? Are they climbing the ladder?
5. Or are they running away?
6. Is the man running after the two other men?
7. Does he want to catch them?
8. Are they afraid of him?
9. Is he a policeman?
10. Do they want to steal the bike?
11. Do they want to ride away on it?
12. Is that a bike, too?

Ergänzungsfragen

Im Unterschied zu Entscheidungsfragen will man bei Ergänzungsfragen eine zusätzliche Information über eine Sache oder eine Person. Sie beginnen daher immer mit einem Fragewort. Kurzantworten mit *yes* oder *no* sind nach Ergänzungsfragen nicht möglich.

Bei Ergänzungsfragen musst du beachten, ob du nach dem Subjekt eines Satzes oder nach anderen Satzteilen fragen willst.

1. Fragen nach dem Subjekt

Bei der Frage nach dem Subjekt nimmt das Fragewort die Stelle des Subjekts ein. Das Verb steht – wie im Deutschen – immer in der 3. Person Singular. Die Umschreibung mit **to do** wird nur in verneinten Fragen verwendet.

Who	has got	a new pet?	**Jenny** has.
Who	must look	after it?	**Jenny** must.
Who	is looking	after it?	**Jenny** is.
Who	buys	its food?	**Jenny** does.
Who	doesn't pay	for its food?	**Jenny** doesn't.
Whose dad	pays	for it?	**Jenny's dad** does.

2. Fragen nach dem Objekt

Bei Fragen mit den Formen von **to be** und **have got** oder mit den Hilfsverben **can, must** usw. wird keine Form von **to do** gebraucht. **To do** steht nur bei Vollverben im *simple present.*

Where	are	you?	
What	are	you	doing?
Who	are	you	ringing up?
What	has	she	got?
What	must	she	do?
Where	must	she	go?
What	does	she	say?
Who	does	she	help?
Where	does	she	go?

Beachte:
Mit ***who*** (wer/wen) und ***what*** (was) kannst du sowohl nach dem Subjekt als auch nach dem Objekt fragen:

Who likes Tom?
Who does Tom like?

What happens?
What does she do?

7.
Some questions for you
Schau dir noch mal Timmys Bilderbuch an. Trage das richtige Fragewort ein. Manchmal sind auch zwei verschiedene Fragewörter möglich.

1. _________ building can you see in this picture?
2. _________ high are the walls?
3. _________ is behind the walls?
4. _________ are these people there?
5. _________ is leaning against one wall?
6. _________ many people can you see?
7. _________ are they doing?
8. _________ is running away?
9. _________ are they running away?
10. _________ are the two men?
11. _________ is the bike?
12. _________ is running after them?
13. _________ is the man trying to do?

what	(was)	fragt nach Sachen
who	(wer/wen)	fragt nach Personen
whose	(wessen)	fragt nach dem Besitzer
why	(warum)	fragt nach dem Grund
where	(wo/wohin)	fragt nach dem Ort oder der Richtung
when	(wann)	fragt nach der Zeit
how	(wie)	fragt nach dem Wie

8.

Your questions

Frage nach dem Subjekt der folgenden Sätze.

1. Timmy doesn't know the building in his picture book.
2. Its walls are very high.
3. A ladder is leaning against the wall.
4. Two people are running away.
5. They are running to a bike.
6. A policeman is running after them.
7. He wants to catch them.
8. He hasn't got a uniform on.
9. The two men are afraid of him.

9.

Jenny

Frage nach den unterstrichenen Wörtern oder Ausdrücken.

1. Jenny is Tom's girlfriend.
2. Her parents are from Leeds.
3. They have got a car.
4. Sometimes her parents are strict (= streng).
5. She can't always see Tom.
6. She must tell her parents where she is going.
7. She must be back early.
8. She mustn't be out after 8 o'clock in the evening.
9. Listen! The telephone is ringing.
10. Tom is at home.
11. Jenny is ringing up Tom.
12. She's very excited.

10.

A phone call

Jenny möchte Tom etwas sagen, aber die Verbindung ist sehr schlecht. Daher muss Tom dauernd fragen, was sie gesagt hat.

Beispiel: *Jenny:* "I've got a new pet." *Tom:* "What have you got?"

Jenny:	*Tom:*
"I have got a new pet."	"What ____________________?"
"A new pet. It's a hamster."	"What ____________________?"
"I like it."	"What ____________________?"
"I must buy some food for it."	"What ____________________?"
"Food. Can you come to the pet shop?"	"Where must ______________?"
"Can you lend me some money?"	"What must _______________?"
"I want to buy a book about hamsters, too."	"What ____________________?"
"A book about hamsters. I don't know anything about hamsters."	"I can't understand you. The line is very bad."
"_____________________________"?	"The line. I can't understand you."
"_____________________________"?	"You. Let's meet at the pet shop then."
"At the pet shop? Yes, OK, at three o'clock."	"OK. See you then."

11.

Bingo

Jenny und Tom treffen sich in der Tierhandlung. Sie kaufen ein Buch und Futter für Jennys Hamster. Dann gehen sie im Park spazieren. Dort sehen sie zwei Mädchen und einen Mann mit einem Hund. Die Mädchen stellen dem Mann viele Fragen über seinen Hund. Hier sind seine Antworten. Wie lauteten die Fragen?

1. How old ____________________? He's nearly two years old.
2. Where ____________________? He sleeps in the hall.
3. When ____________________? I usually get up at six.
4. What ____________________? Then I make him his breakfast.
5. What ____________________? Usually, he has some dog food.
6. When ____________________? Well, I take him for a walk after breakfast.
7. When ____________________? I go to work at half past eight.
8. Where ____________________? I take him to my neighbour's house.
9. How long ____________________? He stays there until I come home.
10. Where ____________________? We play in the garden.
11. What ____________________? I try to teach him some tricks.
12. What ____________________? In the evening? Well, we watch TV together.
13. What films ____________________? He likes westerns.
14. Why ____________________? Well, he likes horses.
15. What ____________________? He always barks when he sees them.
16. Why ____________________ now? Look! There is a girl over there. She is riding a horse.

Test

1.
Verneine die folgenden Sätze.

Beispiel: Jenny hasn't got a cat, she has got a hamster.

a) Jenny has got a cat.	(a hamster)
b) She keeps it in her bedroom.	(a cage downstairs)
c) It sleeps in her bed.	(its cage)
d) Jenny must talk to it a lot.	(it's not a budgie)
e) Tom must catch mice for it.	(it's not a cat)
f) She takes it to school.	(teachers not like that)

2.
Gib Kurzantworten.

a) Have you got a cat?	______________________
b) Do you like cats?	______________________
c) Has any of your friends got a cat?	______________________
d) Do they like pets?	______________________
e) Must you buy food for your pet?	Yes, you ________________
f) Must you keep it in a cage?	No, ___________________
g) Must your pet sleep in your bed?	No, ___________________

3.
Stelle Fragen mit *who, whose, what* und *where*.

a) Jenny has got a boyfriend.	(who/what)
b) His photo is on the wall.	(whose/where)
c) He likes her.	(who/who)
d) She likes him.	(who/who)
e) Her parents like him, too.	(who/who)
f) They are in the same class.	(who/where)
g) They often go home together.	(who/where)
h) Tom often rings her up.	(who/who)
i) Sometimes they are happy.	(who/what)

12

Zeitformen zur Wiedergabe der Zukunft

Das *will*-Futur

Im Deutschen gebrauchen wir für zukünftige Handlungen meist nicht das Futur, sondern das Präsens. Im Englischen muss dagegen fast immer ein Futur stehen, wenn eine Handlung in der Zukunft stattfindet.

1. Formen

Das *will*-Futur *(will-future)* wird mit *will* + Infinitiv (bei Kurzformen: *'ll* + Infinitiv) gebildet. Verneinte Formen bildet man mit *will not* (Kurzform: *won't*) + Infinitiv, Fragen durch Umstellung von Subjekt und Prädikat. Bei Kurzantworten steht nur *will* oder *won't*.

What **will happen** next year?	Kate **will be** twelve.
When **will** she **be** twelve?	She'**ll be** twelve in May.
Will she **be** happy then?	Yes, she **will**.
Will she **be** unhappy?	No, she **won't**.

2. Gebrauch

Das *will*-Futur wird verwendet

1. für neutrale zukünftige Handlungen oder Ereignisse und Vorhersagen:

   Kate **will be** twelve in May.
   All her friends **will come**.

2. für Vermutungen und um eine Hoffnung auszudrücken. Dies ist besonders nach *perhaps* und Verben wie *I think, I believe, I'm sure, I hope* der Fall:

   I **hope** the weather **will be** nice.
   Perhaps she'**ll have** a big party, too.
   I think I'**ll go**.

3. bei spontanen Entschlüssen:

   "I must buy a present for her." "Oh, then **I'll buy** her a present, too."

4. im Hauptsatz von Nebensätzen der Bedingung:

   If you go to her party, **I'll go**, too.
   But **I'll go** only if she invites me.

5. im Hauptsatz von Nebensätzen der Zeit:

   When I see her, **I'll ask** her.
   I'll tell you when we see each other again.

Beachte:
Eine Form von **to do** ist bei **will** nicht möglich.

1.
An excursion
Kates Klasse macht einen Ausflug ans Meer. Vervollständige bitte, was ihr Englischlehrer sagt, bevor sie losfahren.

1. I think/the weather be nice
2. I don't think/it rain again
3. I hope/we spend a nice day together there
4. I hope/water not too cold
5. If the water isn't too cold/we go for a swim
6. I hope/you have a good time

2.
What will happen if ...
Bilde Sätze.

Beispiel: If the coach is late, they won't leave at 8 o'clock.

What will happen	if the coach is late? if it rains all day? if the sun doesn't shine? if some of the children are late? if their teacher is ill? if there is too much traffic?

3.
Questions

a) Die Kinder haben viele Fragen. Schreibe sie auf.
b) Stelle dir vor, du wärst der Englischlehrer. Was würdest du antworten?

Jenny:
when we be there?
we need a warm pullover?
you buy us an ice cream?

Peter:
what games we play?
we be allowed to walk around on our own?

Kevin:
lunch on the beach?
play games on the beach?
go back bus/train?

Susan:
have time enough to go shopping?
when back?
our maths teacher come with us?

4.
Kate's hopes

Kate freut sich auf diesen Ausflug. Sie hofft, dass ...

lots of fun
not rain
interesting things to see
weather/nice
enough pocket money
her friends go, too
not ill
no homework for the next day
not too many teachers
not get a cold

a) Bilde Sätze mit *she hopes, thinks, she's sure, perhaps* usw.
b) Was würdest du von einem solchen Ausflug erwarten? Beginne so: I hope ...

5.

On the beach

Was tun die Kinder, wenn sie am Strand sind?
Bilde Sätze mit den folgenden Angaben.

When they are on the beach,	take off their clothes play games go for a swim look for shells* splash* their teacher with water have a picnic be very noisy run around rush into the water

*shell – Muschel
*to splash – bespritzen

6.

There are nice people

Bevor sie ans Meer gehen, machen sie eine Stadtbesichtigung. Vervollständige bitte, was sie dabei sagen.

Kate: My bag is very heavy. There are too many things in it.

Ben: I'll carry it for you.

Christine: I must buy something to drink.

Catherine: ______________________.

Jane: Look at these postcards. I need some.

Helen: ______________________.

Susan: Look at that girl. I'll talk to her.

Jim: No problem. ______________________.

Kevin: Im so hungry. I think I'll have a sandwich.

Ronny: Well, then ______________________.

Das *going to*-Futur

1. Formen

Das *going to*-Futur *(going to-future)* wird mit dem Präsens von *to be + going to* gebildet. Dem *to* folgt ein Infinitiv. Verneinte Formen werden mit *not* gebildet, Fragen durch Umstellung von Subjekt und Prädikat.

"What **are** you **going to** do on your birthday, Kate?"
"**I'm going to** have a party and **I'm going to** invite all my friends."
"**Are you going to** invite Ben, too?" Yes, I am."
"And what about Ronny? **Are you going to** invite him, too?"
"No, I'm not. **I'm not going to** invite him."

Beachte: Verwechsle das *going to*-Futur nicht mit dem *present progressive*:

He**'s going** home.	He**'s going to** go home.
(Er geht gerade nach Hause.)	(Er hat vor, nach Hause zu gehen.)

2. Gebrauch

Wenn du ausdrücken willst, dass jemand etwas in der Zukunft plant oder tun will, musst du das *going to*-Futur gebrauchen. Dies gilt vor allem dann, wenn diese Absicht schon seit längerem besteht.

7.

Plans, plans, plans ...

Alle haben sich etwas vorgenommen. Trage bitte die richtigen Verben ein.

write help buy do spend go invite clean work

1. Kate's tests aren't very good, so she is going to ________________ harder.
2. Jenny thinks that Kate's tests aren't very nice. So ________________.
3. Kate doesn't like Ben. So she isn't ________________.
4. Helen likes Ben. She ________________ this afternoon.

5. Linda's bike is very old. Her parents ________________.

6. Betty's room is very dirty. What ________________? Well, she ________________.

7. Mary is looking forward to the holidays. She ________________ to the seaside.

8. She ________________ her holidays there.

8.

Asking the others about their plans

Schau dir die Aufgabe 7 noch einmal an. Frage bitte Kate, Jenny und die anderen nach dem, was sie vorhaben.

Beispiel: What are you going to do about your tests?
Are you going to work harder?

9.

The *will-* or *going to*-future?

Kate hat bald Geburtstag. Dazu gehen ihr einige Gedanken durch den Kopf.

1. If the weather is fine, we ________________ play in the garden.
2. I think everybody ________________ like that.
3. But I hope Ben ________________ come (not). I ________________ to invite him (not).
4. There are still so many things to do. Perhaps Jenny ________________ help me.
5. Where is my shopping list? I hope Tom ________________ help me with the lemonade. I ________________ ask him when I see him.
6. And who ________________ buy all the rest?
7. What can I do with Timmy? Well, I ________________ ask Mum if she can take him for a long, long walk. Perhaps he ________________ tired when he gets back.

10.

Planning a test

Dein Lehrer hat euch gesagt, dass ihr nächsten Montag eine Klassenarbeit schreiben werdet. Verwende das *going to*- oder das *will*-Futur in den folgenden Sätzen.

1. "Well, there's no need to hurry. We ________________ write it before next Monday. There's plenty of time to prepare it. I think I ________________ start next Sunday."
2. "Why bother? I ________________ ask my father if he has the time to help me. He's always happy when he gets good marks."
3. "A test next Monday? What ________________ it ________________ be about, by the way? I think I ________________ have to ask John about it."
4. "All right, all right, I don't think it ________________ be very difficult. And I've got a good neighbour. We are a good team. And I'm quite sure he ________________ help me this time, too."
5. "I'm always a bit nervous before tests, so I always take my time to prepare them. If I don't start to prepare it today, I ________________ be terribly nervous on Monday."
6. "A test? Okay, but why on Monday? Doesn't he know that there is an important football match next weekend? I ________________ (not) miss it. And if I don't find the time to prepare the test, well, then I ________________ (not go) to school."

Test

1.
Hilfst du gern anderen Leuten? Dann sage ihnen, was du tun willst.

a) "I don't like my English homework." "Then I'll do it for you."

b) "My room is so dirty." ____________________

c) "My school bag is so heavy." ____________________

d) "I haven't got any money." ____________________

e) "Where's my pen? I can't find it." ____________________

f) "Where are my shoes? Are they in my room?" ____________________

g) "I don't want to kiss my girlfriend." "Oh, ____________________"

2.
Übersetze die folgenden Sätze. Achte auf die Zeiten, die du verwendest!

a) Morgen schreiben wir einen Englisch-Test.
b) Ich hoffe, er ist nicht zu schwer.
c) Ich hoffe, meine Nachbarin hilft mir.
d) Vielleicht bekomme ich dann eine gute Note.
e) Ich frage sie heute Abend, ob sie mir helfen will.
f) Wenn sie mir hilft, gebe ich ihr eine Tafel Schokolade.
g) Ich gebe sie ihr aber nur, wenn ich eine gute Note habe.
h) Wenn ich keine gute Note habe, esse ich die Tafel Schokolade selbst *(= myself)*.

3.
Was willst du am nächsten Wochenende machen? Schreibe auf, was du tun und was du nicht tun willst.

help Mum
go to school
play computer games
play football
play with my teddy
get up late
go for a walk
go and see my friends
go mountain climbing
go to the beach
tidy up my room
clean my bike
work for school
go for a walk with my friend
see my teacher
eat a lot of ice cream
play with my parents

13 Das *present perfect*

Die Formen des *present perfect*

Look, the boy **hasn't finished** his homework, but his friends **have** already **arrived**. **Have** they **played** with him yet? No, they **haven't.** They **haven't played** with him yet.

Das *present perfect* wird mit dem Präsens von *have* (in der 3. Person Singular *has*) und dem *past participle* (Partizip der Vergangenheit) gebildet. Die Kurzformen von *have ('ve/'s)* sind natürlich auch möglich.

Verneinte Formen bildest du mit *not*, Fragen durch die Umstellung von Subjekt und *has/have.* Wie bei allen zusammengesetzten Zeiten sind Formen von *to do* bei der Frage und Verneinung nicht möglich.

Die regelmäßige Form des *past participle* wird durch Anhängen der Endung -**ed** an den Infinitiv gebildet:

to finish	he has finish**ed**
to talk	she has talk**ed**
to play	they have play**ed**

Besonderheiten bei der Bildung des *past participle*

1. Ein auslautendes **-e**, das nicht gesprochen wird, entfällt:
   to arrive — he has arriv**ed**
2. Bei einsilbigen Verben mit kurzem, betonten Vokal wird der auslautende Konsonant verdoppelt:
   to stop — he has sto**pped**
3. Nach Konsonant wird **-y** zu **-i**:
   to cry — he has cr**ied**

Beachte:
Neben den regelmäßigen Formen des *past participle* gibt es im Englischen genau wie im Deutschen auch unregelmäßige Formen. Diese musst du auswendig lernen. Die unregelmäßigen Verben findest du in deinem Lehrbuch und in jedem guten Wörterbuch.

1.
The past participle
Bilde die Partizipien der Vergangenheit mit den folgenden Verben.

to live	*lived*	to give	
to carry		to play	
to say		to lie	
to show		to feel	
to catch		to think	
to bring		to tell	
to leave		to buy	
to spend		to stand	
to write		to take	
to keep		to find	
to speak		to know	
to read		to make	
to hear		to begin	

2.
The infinitive
Wie lautet der Infinitiv der folgenden Verben?

paid		taught	
chosen		fallen	
lost		dropped	
thrown		tried	
fed		bought	
slept		met	
worn		run	

3.
Holiday plans
Dieses Jahr wollen die Masons mit ihrem Wohnwagen zum Lake District fahren. Notiere anhand der Liste in Sätzen, was sie bereits erledigt haben.

- book a place for July
- write to the local tourist office
- have a look at the road map
- try to find out the best route
- begin to check their caravan
- buy a new bottle of gas
- check the tyres
- repair the rear window

4.
Preparations
Die Masons richten ihren Wohnwagen für die Reise zum Lake District her. Sie haben sich eine Liste der Dinge gemacht, die noch zu tun sind. Schreibe auf, was sie bereits getan und was sie noch nicht getan haben.

Beispiel: We have washed the caravan, but we haven't cleaned the floor yet.

- wash the caravan ✔
- clean the floor
- clean the windows ✔
- make the beds
- put in some food ✔
- buy a new frying pan
- put in Timmy's toys ✔
- buy a new picture book
- take Tom's tennis racket ✔
- buy new tennis balls
- tell the neighbours to look after the flowers ✔
- give them a key

5.

Timmy's questions

Timmy ist sehr aufgeregt. Er möchte wissen, was mit seinen Sachen passiert ist. Stelle Timmys Fragen.

Beispiel: Have you seen my potty?

- buy a new picture book for me
- put it in the caravan
- pack my swimming things
- take away my pencils
- find my red toy car
- put my telephone in the caravan
- see my teddy
- buy some chocolate

Merke

Für die Kurzantworten im *present perfect* gelten die üblichen Regeln: Das Subjekt wird durch ein Pronomen wiederholt; bei bejahten Kurzantworten steht die Langform des Hilfsverbs; bei verneinten Kurzantworten steht die Kurzform des Hilfsverbs.

6.

A last check

Bevor sie abfahren, fragt Herr Mason noch einmal alle:

1. "Let me see … Have we shut all the windows?" *Mrs Mason:* Yes, we have ______.
2. "Have you been to the neighbours, Jane?" *Mrs Mason:* Yes, ______.
3. "Have you locked the back door, Kate?" *Kate:* No, ______.
4. "Have you all been to the toilet?" *All:* Yes, ______.
5. "Have you lost your teddy again, Timmy?" *Timmy:* No, ______.
6. "Have we forgotten anything?" *All:* No, ______.
7. "Can we go now?" *Timmy:* No, we ______. I've left my teddy upstairs.

Die Wortstellung beim *present perfect*

Wie bei anderen zusammengesetzten Zeiten steht das Objekt im Englischen immer hinter der Verbgruppe und nicht – wie im Deutschen – vor dem Verb.

Vergleiche:

I	have	**done**	**my homework**.
Ich	habe	**meine Hausaufgaben**	**gemacht.**

Von den **Signalwörtern**, die häufig mit dem *present perfect* gebraucht werden, stehen:

1. unmittelbar vor dem Verb: **never** (niemals), **ever** (jemals) und **already** (schon)
2. am Satzende: **yet** (schon), **not … yet** (noch nicht)

   Beispiele:

   Have you **already** packed your things?
   Have you **ever** been late?
   I have **never** been late.

   I have**n't** packed my clothes **yet.**
   Have you finished **yet**?

7.
Questions and answers

Stelle die folgenden Fragen und beantworte sie.

Beispiel: Have you ever driven a caravan? No, I haven't. I've never driven a caravan.
Or: No, I haven't driven a caravan yet.

				to a caravan site?
			be	a caravan?
	you		clean	to England?
Have	your father	ever	go	on a caravan holiday?
Has	your sister	already	have	an accident?
	your friends	never	drive	a caravan?
			sleep	in a caravan?
			play	lunch in a caravan?

8.
Let's put it right

Hier stimmt etwas mit der Wortstellung nicht. Korrigiere die folgenden Sätze.

1. Everything/the Masons/packed have/already.
2. They/to their neighbours/the key of their house/given/have/they.
3. They/in the caravan/all their things/have put.
4. York/have/they left/today.
5. They/already/done/100 kilometres/have.
6. But they/not arrived/have/yet/at their camping site.
7. All/they/enjoyed/have/so far*/their trip.
8. They are sure/never/had/they/such a nice trip/had.
9. Not/yet/been/Timmy/sick*/has.
10. He is hungry. He/yet/not/has/for lunch/anything/had.
11. But he/already/been/on his potty/four times/has.

*so far – bisher
*to be sick – sich übergeben

Der Gebrauch des *present perfect*

Das *present perfect* benutzt man für Handlungen, die zwar vorbei sind, die aber ein Ergebnis haben, das in der Gegenwart noch wirksam oder sichtbar ist:

"We **have washed** the caravan. It's clean now."
"Where are my car keys? I hope I **haven't lost** them."
"**Have** you **seen** them? Do you know where they are?"

9.
What has happened?
Kannst du die folgenden Sätze ausschreiben?

Beispiel: There's lipstick on Tom's face. Jenny has kissed him goodbye.

There's lipstick
on Tom's face.
(Jenny – kiss him goodbye)

Here are Mr Mason's
car keys.
(find again)

Here are the Masons
in front of their caravan.
They are ready to leave now.
(pack everything)

Look at that window.
It's not shut.
(somebody forget to shut it)

Test

1.
Was hast du heute schon gemacht? Bilde Sätze und benutze das *present perfect.*

Beispiel: I have done my homework.

I/wake up
I/get out of bed
I/not wash
I/have breakfast
I/take my dog for a walk
I/hurry to school
I/not be late
I/try to listen
I/not make much noise
I/come here

2.
Mike ist heute sehr traurig. Daher stellen ihm seine Freunde viele Fragen.

Beispiel: What has happened, Mike? Have …

what happen	have an accident	you lose your money	write a bad test
see your English teacher	get up on the wrong side of the bed		
your girlfriend leave you	not have breakfast	Sandra try to kiss you	

3.
Bilde Sätze im *present perfect* und korrigiere die Wortstellung.

a) Mike/never/a good worker/be.
b) Never/he/working/like.
c) Two left hands/he/have/always.
d) He/his room/nearly never/clean himself.
e) He/already/his room/clean/today?

14 Das *simple past*

Die Formen des *simple past*

Wie im Deutschen gibt es auch im Englischen regelmäßige und unregelmäßige Formen des *simple past*. Die unregelmäßigen Verben *(irregular verbs)* musst du dir gut einprägen; eine Liste von ihnen findest du in jedem guten Wörterbuch.

Die Formen des *simple past* sind für alle Personen gleich. Dies gilt sowohl für die regelmäßigen wie die unregelmäßigen Verben.

Bei den regelmäßigen Formen wird das *simple past* wie das *past participle* mit dem Infinitiv + -**ed** gebildet. Dabei gelten für die Schreibung folgende Regeln:

1. Bei regelmäßigen Verben, die auf -**e** enden, entfällt das -e.
2. Bei regelmäßigen Verben, die mit Konsonant + **y** enden, verändert sich das **y** zu **i**.
3. Bei regelmäßigen Verben, die auf einen Konsonanten nach einem kurz gesprochenen Vokal enden, verdoppelt sich der Konsonant.

to liv**e**	liv**ed**	to tr**y**	tr**ied**	to sto**p**	sto**pp**ed

Beachte:
Die Formen des *simple past* von *to be* sind unregelmäßig. Sie lauten:

I	**was**	we	**were**
you	**were**	you	**were**
he, she, it	**was**	they	**were**

1.

Back at school

Die Kinder sind aus den Ferien zurück und erzählen sich, was sie erlebt haben. Unterstreiche im folgenden Text die regelmäßigen und die unregelmäßigen Formen des *simple past* mit verschiedenen Farben.

Mike:

We visited the Isle of Wight and did quite a lot of things there. I even tried to talk to some Germans there, but they just laughed when I tried to say something in German to them. I think my German sounded a bit funny to them. So I stopped speaking German to them and laughed at their English.

Tom:

We went to the Lake District. We found a fantastic camping site and had a great time there. Only Timmy wasn't very lucky. One day he … but I' ll tell you about that later.

2.

Mind the spelling and the pronunciation

Welche dieser Verben sind regelmäßig, welche nicht? Unterstreiche die unregelmäßigen Verben.

say buy stop lead write read
play sit feel
cry catch set hear ride
carry swim
think feed leave
fall meet
fly bring let lose get break
teach pay

3.
Regular and irregular verbs
Setze die folgenden Verben in das *simple past*.

say		lead	
play		sit	
carry		lose	
fly		write	
buy		set	
catch		feed	
fall		meet	
stop		read	
leave		feel	
think		ride	
let		make	
teach		hear	
pay		break	

4.
Going on holidays
Vor den Ferien müssen du und deine Eltern viele Dinge erledigen.

You must

- check your car
- put a good map in it
- pack your things
- lock the doors
- shut the windows
- switch off all lights
- say goodbye to your neighbours
- look up the route you want to take

Das hat die Familie Mason bereits alles erledigt. Schreibe auf, was sie getan haben. Verwende das *simple past*.

Beispiel: Before they left, they checked their car, they …

5.

The Masons are leaving

Trage die fehlenden Verben ein. Verwende das *simple past*.

know	want	arrive	be	leave	carry	see
come	see	go	run	hear	get	shut

The Masons __________ to leave early, but as usually it __________ quite late when they __________ off. Kate __________ still tired and Tom __________ to finish a letter. Then Timmy's potty __________ missing and nobody __________ where it __________. When they __________ all in the car again, somebody __________ that a window __________ still open. So Mr Mason __________ out of the car, __________ into the house again and __________ it. When he __________ back, Timmy __________ to go to the toilet again. So Mr Mason __________ out of the car again and __________ Timmy to the bathroom. When they __________ back, they __________ the telephone ringing. So Tom __________ out of the car and __________ into the house again. But he __________ not fast enough. When he __________, the line __________ dead. But finally they __________ all in the car and ready to leave.

6.

The Masons' trip

Erzähle, was auf der Fahrt zum Campingplatz alles geschah. Verwende das *simple past*.

finally leave at 10 o'clock
first stop at 11.30
Timmy sick*
lunch at 1 p.m.
forget Timmy's teddy
get into car at 2 p.m.

arrive at 6 p.m. at the camping site
try to put up tent* for Tom
tent collapse
had supper at 8
go to bed at 9
all very tired

*to be sick – sich übergeben
*tent – Zelt

Das *simple past* in verneinten Sätzen, Entscheidungsfragen und Kurzantworten

1. Vollverben werden im *simple past* mit *did not* bzw. der Kurzform *didn't* verneint. Danach steht immer der Infinitiv.
   Was/were werden mit *not* verneint. Statt *was not/were not* sind auch die entsprechenden Kurzformen *(wasn't/weren't)* möglich.

Subjekt	**did not**	**(didn't)**	**+ Infinitiv**
Timmy	**did not**	**(didn't)**	**enjoy** the trip.
He	**did not**	**(didn't)**	**feel** fine.
Timmy	**was not**	**(wasn't)**	happy.
Tom and Kate	**were not**	**(weren't)**	sick.

2. Das gilt auch für Fragen und Kurzantworten.
   Wenn du eine Frage im *simple past* mit Vollverben bilden willst, musst du *did* bzw. *didn't* gebrauchen. Danach steht immer ein Infinitiv.
   In Kurzantworten wird das Vollverb durch *did* bzw. *didn't* ersetzt.

Did	you **have** a nice holiday?	Yes, I **did**.
Didn't	you **go** swimming?	No, I **didn't**.

3. Bei *to be* ist keine Form von *to do* möglich. Du bildest die Frage allein durch Umstellung von Subjekt und Prädikat. Bei Kurzantworten stehen die entsprechenden Formen von *to be.*

Were	you	on the beach?	No, I **wasn't**.
Was	the water	cold?	Yes, it **was**.
Weren't	you	unhappy?	No, I **wasn't**.

7.

The first night

Setze die folgenden Sätze ins *simple past.* Verwende die verneinten Formen.

The first night Timmy not sleep very well – not have his teddy – not quiet enough at the camping site – at home not sleep in the same bed with Kate – his sister not leave him enough room – she not want him in "her" bed – Timmy not warm enough – not have nice dreams – not happy that night.

8.

The next morning

Am nächsten Morgen fragt Timmys Mutter, wie seine erste Nacht im Wohnwagen gewesen ist. Stelle ihre Fragen und antworte für Timmy. (Schau dir dazu Aufgabe 7 an).

1. _______ you sleep well tonight, Timmy?
2. _______ you miss your teddy?
3. _______ it quiet enough?
4. _______ you sleep with all that noise?
5. _______ Kate leave you enough room?
6. _______ you warm enough?
7. _______ you have nice dreams?
8. _______ you like your first night here?

9.

What the Masons did the first day

Formuliere die folgenden Sätze.

Beispiel: The first day they didn't get up early. They had a late breakfast.

	not cook in the caravan	write a letter to Jenny
Timmy	not sick any more	have a late breakfast
Tom	not do any work	go for a walk
Kate	not get up early	buy a new teddy for Timmy
Mr Mason	not do any homework	have lunch in a restaurant
Mrs Mason	not lie on the beach	look for new friends
	not stay in the caravan	feel better

Das *simple past* in Ergänzungsfragen

Auch bei Ergänzungsfragen, d. h. Fragen mit Fragewörtern, musst du *did* oder *didn't* gebrauchen. Bei Fragen nach dem Subjekt ist *didn't* dagegen nur in verneinten Fragen möglich.

1. Fragen nach dem Subjekt

Who was on the beach?
What happened?
Who didn't come back?
Who broke his arm?

2. Fragen nach allen anderen Satzteilen

Where was Timmy?
What did he **do** there?
Why didn't he **come** back?
What did he **break**?

Beachte: Bei Fragen mit **to be** steht **nie** ein **did**!

10.
Tom's letter
Lies den folgenden Bief. Schreibe auf, was die Eltern Kate wohl gefragt haben.

Dear Mike,
Something terrible happened yesterday. I wanted to go to the beach with Timmy and Kate. Timmy had his teddy and his picture book in his hands, so perhaps he didn't see where he was going. Anyway – suddenly Timmy cried and fell over a big stone. I turned round and saw Timmy. He was lying on the ground. He still had his teddy in his hand; but his arm looked strange. Timmy didn't cry at first, but his face looked very white. I didn't know what to do, so I told Kate to run home and to fetch Mum or Dad. Kate did what I told her and five minutes later Mum and Dad were there. They carried Timmy back to the caravan and phoned a doctor. When she came, she examined Timmy …

11.

What Mike's parents wanted to know

Als Mike Toms Brief bekam, erzählte er seinen Eltern von Timmys Unfall. Sie wollten viel wissen. Stelle du ihre Fragen.

- why Timmy didn't see the stone
- where the accident happened
- if Timmy broke his arm
- if Timmy cried a lot
- how he looked
- if he was sick
- if they called a doctor
- when the doctor came
- what she told them
- if Timmy had to go to hospital

12.

At the hospital

Timmy musste ins Krankenhaus. Dort untersuchte ihn ein Arzt, der ihm einige Fragen stellte. Was fragte er? Was antwortete Timmy?

Beispiel: Did it hurt, Timmy? Yes, it did.

- hurt?
- how?
- why?
- fall on your arm?
- cry?
- when?
- his teddy all right?
- who help you?
- anybody with you?

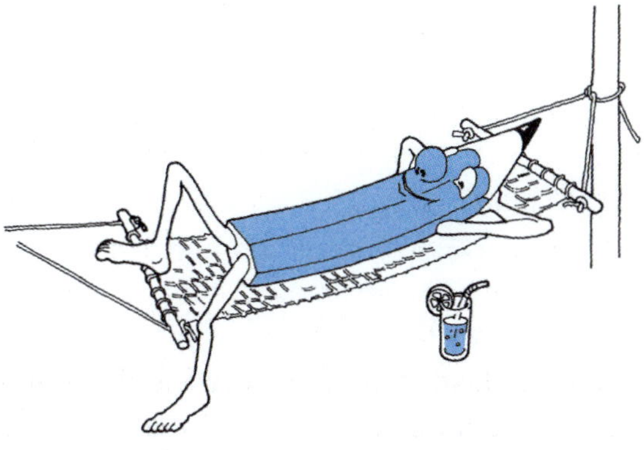

Die Vergangenheitsform einiger Hilfsverben

Von den englischen Hilfsverben hat nur *can* (können) eine Vergangenheitsform: *could/could not* bzw. die Kurzform *couldn't*. Für die anderen Hilfsverben musst du Ersatzverben *(substitutes)* verwenden.

Hilfsverb		Ersatzverb
may	(dürfen)	**was/were allowed to**
may not/mustn't	(nicht dürfen)	**wasn't/weren't allowed to**
must	(müssen)	**had to**
needn't	(nicht müssen)	**didn't have to**

Beachte:
Nach Hilfsverben und Ersatzverben steht immer ein Infinitiv. Bei Hilfsverben steht jedoch – im Unterschied zu Ersatzverben – kein **to** vor dem Infinitiv!

13.
At the hospital
Füge die Vergangenheitsformen der Hilfsverben ein.

1. When the doctor examined Timmy, he found out that Timmy's arm was broken. So Timmy ________________ go home. *(konnte nicht)*
2. He ________________ stay in hospital for some days. *(musste)*
3. He ________________ stay in bed all the time. *(musste nicht)*
4. His parents ________________ to visit him. *(durften)*

5. His parents ________________ take him home. *(konnten nicht)*

6. He ________________ to get up the first day. *(durfte nicht)*

7. But he ________________ to get up the next day. *(durfte)*

14.
Timmy's "jobs"
Die ersten Tage im Krankenhaus durfte Timmy bestimmte Dinge nicht tun. Was konnte, durfte er tun, was nicht? Was musste er tun? Was nicht?

- make his bed
- play with his teddy
- draw pictures with his right arm
- cook his meals
- clean the room
- stay in bed all day
- play in the corridor
- look at his picture book
- be careful with his arm
- talk to the nurses
- run around in the room
- stand on his right arm
- eat his meals
- keep his arm still (= ruhig)

15.
Questions
Frage Timmy, was er tun musste und was nicht, und gib seine Antworten.

Beispiel: Did you have to stay in bed all the time? – No, I didn't.

16.
Prescriptions
Setze die fehlenden Ersatzverben ein.

After three days the Masons ________________ to take Timmy home. They ________________ leave the camping site and break off their holidays, the doctors told them, but there were some things that Timmy ________________ to do. He ________________ to stay in the caravan all day, but he ________________ to be very careful with his arm; he ________________ to play any wild games and above all, he ________________ to swim. He ________________ to take his medicine, and they ________________ to worry, but they ________________ to look after Timmy.

17.

When I was ill ...

Du bist doch sicher schon einmal krank gewesen? Was konntest du, durftest du, musstest du tun und was nicht? Schreibe acht Sätze dazu. Beginne so: The last time I was ill, I ...

18.

Questions

Als Tom aus den Ferien zurück war, fragten ihn seine Freunde viel. Stelle du ihre Fragen und verwende dabei das *simple past.*

- if he had to go there with his parents
- if they stayed at a hotel
- if he had to sleep in a tent
- if he had to take his German books with him
- if he was allowed to stay up late
- when he had to go to bed
- if he had to help his parents
- what he had to do
- if he made any friends there
- if there were other girls
- why he didn't kiss them
- if they were nicer than Jenny
- what the weather was like
- if he was happy that he was back.

Test

1.
Setze Timmys Bericht über seine erste Nacht im Wohnwagen ins *simple past*.

a) I (not sleep) very well.
b) My sister always (take) my blanket away.
c) She always (kick) me.
d) I (be) very tired, but I (can't) sleep.
e) And it (be) very cold.
f) Some people (be) very loud outside.
g) They (shout) and (play) games.
h) I (miss) my teddy.
i) And I (have) a bad dream.
j) It (be) about my teddy.

2.
Wie du noch weißt, träumte Timmy schlecht. Hier ist sein Traum. Erzähle du ihn, aber verwende das *simple past*.

Beispiel: My teddy was all alone in the house.

His teddy is all alone in the house. Everybody is gone. He feels very lonely and there are big tears in his eyes. Why have they all left him? And why under the bed? It's dark and dusty there and he can't see a thing. And there are noises in the room, noises he doesn't know. And they come nearer and nearer. He feels that there is somebody or something watching him. What is it? Suddenly he sees two green eyes and feels something touching him, something that is cold and slimy. He tries to run away, but something keeps him back …

3.
Es passierten aber auch viele schöne Dinge in den Ferien. Frage nach den unterstrichenen Wörtern. Verwende das *simple past*.

They went <u>to the beach</u> and enjoyed <u>the sea and the sun</u>. <u>They</u> played a lot of games or found the time to read a book or two. Timmy read <u>his new picture book</u>, too. <u>When the weather was fine</u>, they went for long walks <u>in the countryside</u>. They watched <u>the fishermen</u> and their boats. One day, Mr Mason and Tom <u>went fishing</u>, too, and came back with a big fish. "<u>We caught it this morning</u>," they told everybody, but nobody really believed them.

15 *Simple past* oder *past progressive*?

Der Gebrauch des *simple past*

Das *simple past* steht

1. bei Handlungen, die in der Vergangenheit stattfanden und abgeschlossen sind. Es findet sich daher nach **Signalwörtern** wie *yesterday, a (week, a month, year) ago, last Friday (month usw.), in + Jahreszahl*. Oft steht es auch nach *when*:

   Mr Mason **had** an accident, too.
   But this **was** *many years ago.*
   When **did** he **have** the accident?
   It **was** *in 1975, when he was much younger* than today.

2. nach wiederholten und gewohnheitsmäßigen Handlungen, die in der Vergangenheit stattfanden. **Signalwörter** sind hier – wie schon beim *simple present* – *always, usually, often, sometimes* usw.:

   He **played** in a football team *then.*
   They **played** *every Saturday.*
   His team **wasn't** a good team, so they *often* **lost**.
   But *sometimes* they also **won**.

3. für abgeschlossene, aufeinander folgende Handlungen der Vergangenheit. **Signalwörter** sind hier *first, then, after that, the next moment, the next morning, last night, when, suddenly* usw.:

   One day they **were** on their way home, when their bus *suddenly* **ran off** the road. He **felt** a pain in his left leg, and things **went** black before his eyes. *Then* he **didn't feel** anything else. *Afterwards,* they **told** him that his left leg **was** broken.

1.
After the accident

Erzähle Timmys Geschichte. Verbinde die Sätze mit *first, then, after that, so, when* usw.

1. Tom send Kate back to parents
2. Kate run to caravan/Kate tell parents all about Timmy's accident
3. Mrs Mason phone a doctor
4. doctor arrive/examine Timmy/call an ambulance
5. ambulance arrive/the ambulance men put Timmy on a stretcher*/carry him inside the ambulance/drive him to the hospital

*stretcher – Bahre

2.
Timmy at the hospital

Im Krankenhaus fragt eine Krankenschwester Timmy, wie es zu dem Armbruch gekommen ist. Erzähle, wie es dazu kam. Verwende das *simple past*.

Tom and Kate – want to go – to the beach – I ask Mum – if I can go there, too. First not want, but then say yes. So I tell Tom to wait for me – I go into the caravan – fetch my teddy – They walk very fast – so I must run – a big stone in my way – not see it – fall over it – break my arm – not let go my teddy – hold it in my hand – I feel pain in my leg – then Tom and Kate come – but I not know what happen then …

Der Gebrauch des *past progressive*

Das *past progressive* wird mit *was/were* und der -ing-Form, dem *present participle*, gebildet. Zur Bildung des *present participle* vergleiche Kapitel 7.

Bei Fragen wird umgestellt: Hilfsverb – Subjekt – Verb. Verneinte Formen werden mit *not* gebildet. Die Umschreibung mit *to do* ist bei Fragen und bei der Verneinung nicht möglich.

Wann benutze ich das *past progressive*?

Im Unterschied zum *simple past* musst du das *past progressive* für Handlungen verwenden, die zu dem Zeitpunkt noch nicht vorüber waren, als eine neue Handlung einsetzte. Handlungen im *past progressive* bilden den Hintergrund für neu einsetzende Handlungen.

Beispiele:
What **were** the Masons **doing** when Timmy had his accident?
Were they **going** to the beach, too? No, they **weren't**.
Mr Mason **was talking** to a neighbour.
They **were having** a coke and **talking** about football.
Mrs Mason **was reading** a book.
She **wasn't listening** to what they **were talking** about.

3.
Bad talk
Ein Nachbar der Familie Mason erzählte allen Leute schlechte Dinge.
Bilde ganze Sätze.

When poor Timmy broke his arm,	his parents his mother his father nobody	just get up not look after Timmy lie in the sun smoke and talk still lie in bed write a letter just have breakfast

4.

What people were doing

Schau dir das Bild an und sage, was die Leute gerade taten, als Timmy sich den Arm brach. Beginne so: When Timmy had his accident, …

a woman reading a magazine
a man lying in a deckchair
some people swimming
two children playing with a ball
a boy listening to the radio
a girl putting on her clothes
a family having a picnic

Simple past und *past progressive* im Vergleich

Wie du bereits weißt, steht das *simple past* für Handlungen, die vorüber sind und aufeinander folgen. Solche Handlungsketten kommen vor allem in Erzählungen und Berichten vor. Deshalb musst du das *simple past* in einer Geschichte oder einem Bericht für jede neu einsetzende Handlung verwenden.

Wann benutze ich das *simple past* und wann das *past progressive*?

Um das zu entscheiden, musst du dich fragen:

1. Welche Handlung ist neu? *(simple past)*
2. Was passierte gerade zu dieser Zeit? *(past progressive)*
3. Welche Handlung setzt neu ein? *(simple past)*
4. Was war zu dieser Zeit noch nicht vorbei? *(past progressive)*

Beispiele:
When the ambulance **arrived**, Timmy **was** still **lying** on the beach. He **was crying**.
The ambulance men **examined** Timmy, while a lot of people **were standing** around them.
Then the ambulance men **put Timmy** on a stretcher and **drove** him off to hospital.
When the ambulance **left**, the people **were** still **standing** there.

Signalwörter für die Verwendung des *past progressive* sind **still** und **while.**

Beachte:
Nicht alle Verben können im Englischen eine *progressive form* bilden. Verben wie

to be, to belong, to see, to feel, to hear, to want, to like, to know, to think, to sound

haben im Englischen meist keine *progressive form.* Hier musst du die *simple forms* gebrauchen.

5.

At the doctor's

Nach ein paar Tagen im Krankenhaus durfte Timmy wieder nach Hause. Aber er musste sich beim Hausarzt untersuchen lassen. Im Wartezimmer waren viele Patienten. Warum waren sie hier? Bilde Sätze.

play football/
fall to the ground/
broke my arm

climb a rock/
slip

I slip/have a shower
broke three ribs*

* rib – Rippe

I clean the windows/
ladder break/
fall onto the floor

I lie in my deckchair/
it collapse

I do my homework/
fall asleep/
fall off the chair

6.
A ghost story

Simple past oder *past progressive?*

Timmy still ____________ *(have)* to be very careful with his arm and he ____________ *(can't)* go for a swim, of course. So everybody ____________ *(must)* to keep him busy. Tom often ____________ *(read)* ghost stories to him.

Timmy's favourite story ____________ *(be)* about an American family who ____________ *(want)* to buy an old castle in England. When they ____________ *(come)* to the castle, the sun ____________ *(not shine)*. It ____________ *(rain)* and thunder ____________ *(sound)* again and again. When they ____________ *(enter)* the castle, a flash of lightning* ____________ *(fill)* the hall and there ____________ *(be)* thunder all through the night.

When they ____________ *(come)* down the next morning, they ____________ *(see)* some blood* on the floor. The next night they ____________ *(hear)* strange noises in the corridor outside their bedrooms. When Mr Otis ____________ *(open)* the door, he ____________ *(see)* a terrible old man. Long hair ____________ *(fall)* from his head, his eyes ____________ *(be)* like fire and …

*flash of lightning – Blitz
*blood – Blut

7.
Timmy's dream

Eines Nachts träumte Timmy erneut schlecht, nachdem ihm Tom eine Gruselgeschichte vorgelesen hatte. Erzähle Timmys Traum. Pass auf die Zeiten auf!

Timmy lie in his bed – his teddy sleep beside him
Suddenly the door open – somebody come into his room
When open his eyes – he see that a dark figure stand in front of his bed/look at him/then sit down on his bed
A cold hand touch his face – he wake up with a loud cry
The lights go on – his mother stand in front of him –
"You dream, Timmy?" she said.

Test

1.

In dem Augenblick, in dem Timmy sich den Arm brach, geschahen noch andere Dinge. Bilde Sätze.

– the sun shine/not rain
– some people play games
– other people talk to each other
– people eat or have something to drink
– children laugh and shout
– some people swim in the sea
– others lie in the sun
– people put on or take off their clothes
– some people go home.

2.

Trage die folgenden Verben ein. Pass auf, ob du das *simple past* oder das *past progressive* verwenden musst.

take	lie	open	unpack	put	dream	sleep
come	begin	wake	wait	see	carry	

a) When Timmy ______________ home, a big suprise ______________ for him.

b) A new picture book ______________ on the table.

c) When Timmy ______________ it, he immediately ______________ it and ______________ to “read”.

d) While he ______________, his parents ______________ his things.

e) When they ______________ back, Timmy ______________.

f) Mr Mason ______________ him in his arms and ______________ him upstairs into his room.

g) There he ______________ him in his bed.

h) Timmy ____ not ______________ up; he ______________ of doctors, ghosts and other things.

16 *Simple past* und *present perfect*

Perfekt im Deutschen und *simple past* im Englischen

Wenn du das *present perfect* und das *simple past* im Englischen verstehen willst, musst du umdenken, da die Verwendung beider Zeiten vom Deutschen stark abweicht.

Verwechsle das *simple past* und *present perfect* nicht mit dem Perfekt im Deutschen!

Vergleiche:

„Gestern **sind** wir **heimgekommen;** wir **haben** unser Gepäck aus dem Auto **geholt** und **haben** dann zu Abend **gegessen.** Dann **sind** wir ins Bett **gegangen** und **sind sofort eingeschlafen**."

"Yesterday we **came** home; we **fetched** our luggage from the car; then we **had** supper. After that we **went** to bed and **fell** asleep immediately."

In der deutschen Umgangssprache gebraucht man das Perfekt vor allem dazu, eine Geschichte zu erzählen oder über etwas zu berichten, das vorbei ist. Dies ist im Englischen mit dem *present perfect* nicht möglich.

Wenn man im Englischen etwas erzählen oder berichten will, gebraucht man das *simple past.* Es ist die eigentliche Erzählzeit im Englischen und findet sich daher auch nach **Signalwörtern** wie *first, then, after that, at that moment, suddenly* usw.

1.
The first lesson

Tom und seine Klasse lernen Deutsch. In der ersten Stunde nach den Ferien mussten sie ihrem Deutschlehrer über ihre Ferien berichten. Kannst du übersetzen, was sie sagten?

1. Wir sind gestern zurückgekommen.
2. Ich bin oft schwimmen gegangen.
3. Ich habe Mike in den Ferien getroffen.
4. Ich habe einen deutschen Jungen kennen gelernt.
5. Ich habe sehr viel Deutsch gesprochen.
6. Wir haben einen Unfall gehabt.
7. Ich habe keine Hausaufgaben in den Ferien gemacht.
8. Ich habe in den Ferien zu viel gegessen.
9. Ich bin richtig dick geworden.
10. Wir haben in den Ferien viele Schlösser besichtigt. *(to visit)*

2.
Mike's story

In einer der ersten Stunden nach den Ferien mussten Tom und seine Mitschüler einen Aufsatz über ihre Ferienerlebnisse schreiben. Hier sind Mikes Notizen für seinen Aufsatz. Kannst du ihn schreiben? Pass auf die Zeiten auf!

In the holidays we visit Carisbroke Castle – old castle – famous, too, because Charles I prisoner there some hundred years ago before his execution. People say – he not found peace yet – his ghost still walk there.

When we come there, the sky very dark – when walk through the entrance – begin to rain – so go into the castle – very dark in there, too; lots of strange noises – suddenly a door open – when I look there – I see something green – come towards me – run out of the building and tell everything to my parents – not believe me – just laugh at me.

After the holidays over – we must go home again – The first night I go to bed early, but wake up at midnight – strange noise – see something green – it sit at my desk – it write something in an exercise book – I very afraid, not move – five minutes later it gone. I get up – go to the desk – there see my German exercise book – open – a note in the book – it run: DON'T DO ANY HOMEWORK TOMORROW OR YOU'LL DIE! This is what the ghost tell me – that's why I not do any homework last Tuesday.

Der Gebrauch von *simple past* und *present perfect*

1. Das *simple past* steht für Handlungen, die abgeschlossen und daher vorüber sind. (Siehe dazu auch Kapitel 15.)
2. Das *present perfect* steht für Handlungen, die zwar vorbei sind, aber für die Gegenwart noch Folgen haben. In dieser Funktion steht das *present perfect* immer ohne eine Zeitangabe der Vergangenheit.

   Mit dem *present perfect* oft benutzte **Signalwörter** sind:
   already (schon), **yet** (schon), **not ... yet** (noch ... nicht), **never** (niemals) und **ever** (jemals).

Vergleiche:

The Mason **have packed** everything.	They **packed** already yesterday.
They **have turned** off the gas.	They **turned** the gas off after breakfast.
They **have already locked** the door.	When **did** they **lock** the door?
They **have paid** for the camping site, too.	They **paid** ten weeks ago.

3.
Mike's photos
Während der Ferien hat Mike viele Fotos gemacht. Hier zeigt er sie Tom und Jenny. Vervollständige die Sätze. Verwende dabei die richtigen Zeiten *(simple present, simple past, present perfect)*.

Look! This our hotel/
stay there for two weeks

That is the beach in front
of our hotel/always go
swimming there

This is our car/accident/
we not repair it yet

This is Carisbrooke Castle/ visit the castle/you know that Charles I prisoner here?

That is Tim. I play with him a lot/we often go to the beach/have a swim together

And that girl over there – his sister/we play with her sometimes

4.

Back at school

Alle Schüler sind wieder von den Ferien zurück. Sie stellen einander viele Fragen. Stell du diese Fragen. Entscheide dabei, ob du das *simple past* oder das *present perfect* verwenden musst.

1. When ________ you ________ come back?
2. Where ________ you ________ go?
3. ________ you ________ *(like)* your stay there?
4. ________ ever ________ *(be)* to Italy?
5. ________ you ________ *(do)* anything for school as our teacher ________ *(tell)* you?
6. ________ you ________ *(play)* tennis in the holidays?
7. How many postcards ________ you ________ *(write)*?
8. Where ________ you ________ *(buy)* these shoes?
9. What ________ *(be)* the weather like? ________ it ________ *(rain)* a lot?
10. ________ you already ________ *(see)* Mike? Is he late again?

5.

So sorry, but …

Nicht alle Schüler mögen Hausaufgaben. Gehörst du auch dazu? Dann findest du hier einige Entschuldigungen, die du deinem Lehrer sagen kannst, wenn du sie nicht gemacht hast. Achte auf die Zeiten!

I couldn't do my homework,
I can't show you my homework,

B
E
C
A
U
S
E

my neighbour (be) ill.
I (not remember) where I (put) it.
I (leave) my book at school.
I (leave) it on the bus/at home.
my mother father/sister (be) ill yesterday.
I (feel) so ill in the afternoon.
my pen (not work).
I (forget) my school bag.
my baby brother/baby sister (ruin) it.
my computer (break) down.
my printer (not) work.
my exercise book (be) full.
my baby brother (make) a plane out of it.
I (must) repair my bike.
my mother (not have) time to help me.
somebody (steal) it.
I (cannot) open my school bag.

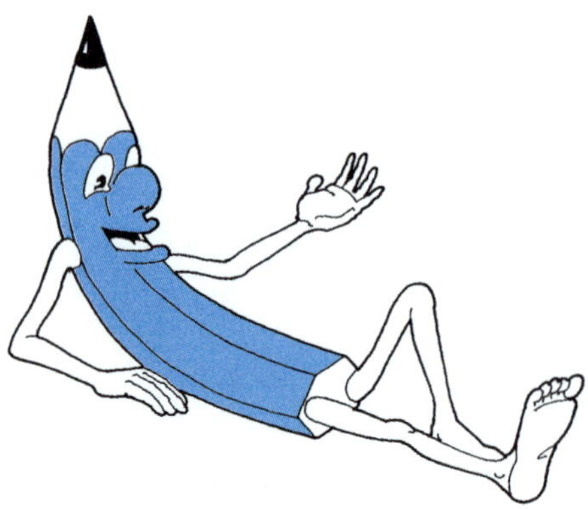

Test

1.
Übersetze bitte.

a) Ich habe das Gepäck ins Auto getan.
b) Dann sind wir alle eingestiegen.
c) An einer Verkehrsampel mussten wir halten.
d) Da ist uns jemand in unser Auto gefahren *(= crash into).*
e) Wir sind alle ausgestiegen.
f) Verletzt *(= injured)* war niemand.
g) Aber unser Auto war beschädigt *(= damaged).*
h) Dann mussten wir auf die Polizei warten und konnten nicht weiterfahren.

2.
Trage die richtigen Zeiten (*simple past* oder *present perfect*) im folgenden Telefongespräch ein.

Tom: Guess who it is? Well, it's me, Tom. ________ you __________ *(get)* my letters? I __________ *(write)* the last one two days ago.

Jenny: Hi, Tom. Nice to hear your voice again. I __________ *(get)* your other letters, but I __________ *(get)* the last one yet. How many __________ you __________ *(write)*?

Tom: I think about ten. But tell me, when ________ you __________ *(come)* back?

Jenny: I __________ *(come)* back two days ago.

Tom: How ________ you __________ *(like)* London?

Jenny: Well, I __________ *(like)* it, but my aunt __________ *(be)* terrible sometimes. She just __________ *(think)* that I __________ *(be)* a small baby. She always __________ *(say)* that I __________ *(be)* too young to look after myself. And she __________ *(not like)* your letters, Tom.

Tom: But why? __________ she __________ *(not like)* my handwriting?

Jenny: Don't be stupid, Tom. She thinks it's not good for a girl of my age to talk to boys.

17 Adjektive

Der Gebrauch der Adjektive

Adjektive beziehen sich immer auf Substantive oder Pronomen. Dabei geben sie Eigenschaften der jeweiligen Sachen oder Personen an.

Wie im Deutschen steht das Adjektiv unmittelbar vor dem Substantiv *(a nice boy).* Nach bestimmten Verben wie z. B. *to be* steht es auch nach dem Substantiv: *Tom is nice.*

Are there any **nice** and **clever girls/boys** in your class?
Or are **they** all **silly** and **stupid?**

1.
What's your English teacher, friend, brother, sister like?
Wähle drei Adjektive für jede Person, die du beschreibst, von der folgenden Liste aus:

Beispiel: What's your English teacher like? Let me see – he/she is clever and intelligent, but he/she can be strange, too. And what about your …

bad, beautiful, good, boring, busy, careful, crazy, exciting, fantastic, noisy, fat, loud, modern, poor, powerful, quick, slow, strange, tall, small, thin, strong, worried, nice, clever, intelligent, funny, heavy, dangerous, interesting, wonderful, difficult

2.

And what about your dream girl/dream boy?

Wie sollte er/sie sein? Was für ein Mädchen/Junge möchtest du als Freund/Freundin haben? Schreibe dazu fünf Sätze. Benutze die Adjektive in Aufgabe 1.

3.

Your idea again

Wähle nochmals drei Adjektive von der Liste in Aufgabe 1 aus und schreibe, was du über die folgenden Dinge oder Personen denkst:

Beispiel: Girls are nice, clever and intelligent.

English tests
boys
comics
TV
computers
books
books
baby brothers/sisters
teachers
films
pop music
football
TV
girls

4.

What's the opposite?

Stelle Gegensatzpaare auf.

Beispiel: A good teacher – a bad teacher

a funny girl ____________________

an old town ____________________

a small boy ____________________

a good mark ____________________

a boring film ____________________

a fast runner ____________________

a bad driver ____________________

a slow worker ____________________

a clever pupil ____________________

a quiet boy ____________________

a happy child ____________________

a difficult text ____________________

a silly person ____________________

a terrible story ____________________

a rich man ____________________

a dirty room ____________________

Die Steigerung der Adjektive

Die Grundform oder Grundstufe, also die ungesteigerte Form eines Adjektivs, heißt Positiv *(positive)*, die 1. Steigerungsstufe Komparativ *(comparative)* und die Höchststufe der Steigerung Superlativ *(superlative)*.

Adjektive werden im Englischen wie folgt gesteigert:

Positiv	**Komparativ**	**Superlativ**
poor	poor**er**	the poor**est**
fin**e**	fin**er**	the fin**est**
bi**g**	bi**gger**	the bi**ggest**
funn**y**	funn**ier**	the funn**iest**
angr**y**	angr**ier**	the angr**iest**
clev**er**	clever**er**	the clever**est**
famous	**more** famous	the **most** famous
terrible	**more** terrible	the **most** terrible
difficult	**more** difficult	the **most** difficult

1. Adjektive mit einer Silbe *(poor, fine)* und zweisilbige Adjektive auf -**y** und -**er** *(funny, angry, clever)* bilden den Komparativ mit -**er** und den Superlativ mit -**est**. Dabei entfällt ein auslautendes -**e**.
2. Bei Adjektiven, die auf -**y** enden, wird das -**y** zu -**i** (happier, the happiest).
3. Einsilbige Adjektive mit einem kurzen, betonten Vokal, die auf Konsonant enden, verdoppeln den auslautenden Konsonanten (bigger, the biggest).
4. Zweisilbige Adjektive, die nicht auf -**y** und -**er** enden sowie alle Adjektive, die mehr als zwei Silben haben, bilden den Komparativ mit **more** und den Superlativ mit **most**.

Beachte:
Die folgenden Adjektive haben unregelmäßige Steigerungsformen:

good	**better**	**the best**
bad	**worse**	**the worst**

5.

Comparatives and superlatives

Bilde die Komparative und Superlative der Adjektive, die du in Aufgabe 1 findest.

6.

Tom's family

Schau dir die Personen an und vergleiche sie. Verwende die Komparative von *tall* und *small*.

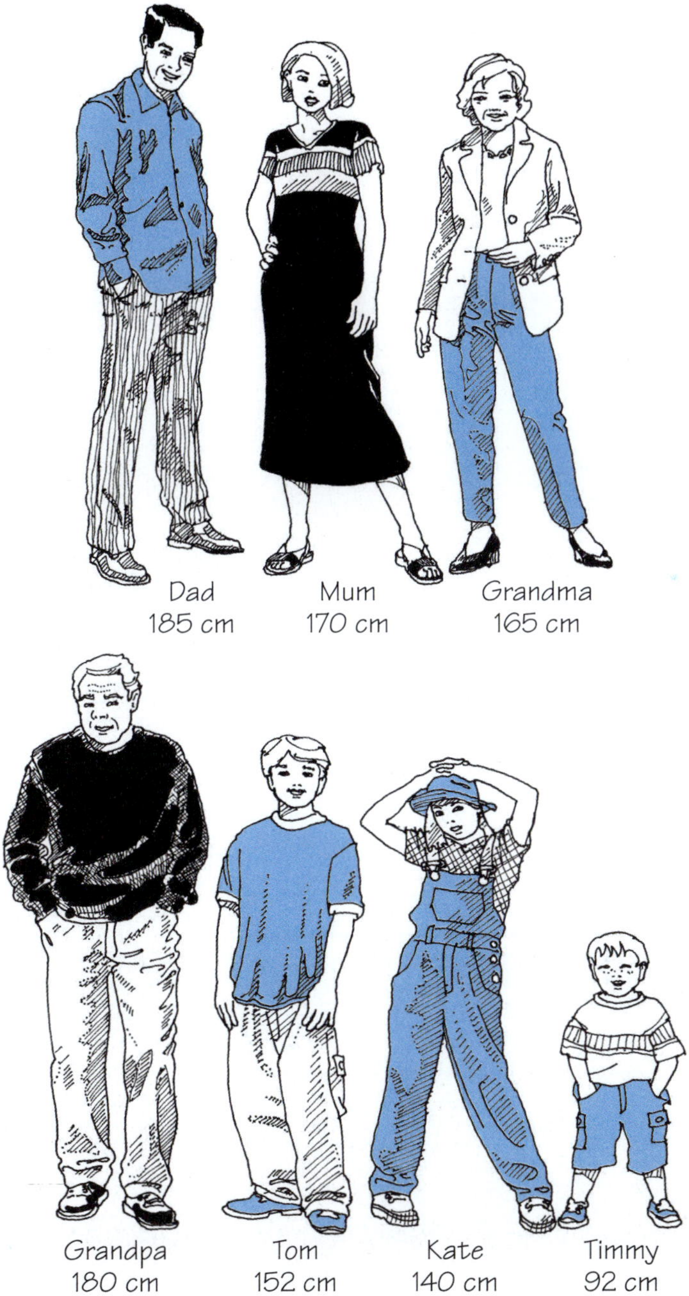

Der Vergleich im Satz

Die verschiedenen Formen der Adjektive benutzt man oft dazu, Vergleiche zu ziehen. Gleichheit bzw. Ungleichheit werden dabei folgendermaßen ausgedrückt:

	Gleichheit:	
Mike is **as** tall **as** Tom. Is he also **as** intelligent?	(eben)so … wie … (eben)so …	**as** + **positive** + **as**
	Ungleichheit:	
Tom's sister is**n't as** tall **as** Mike.	… nicht so … wie…	**not as** + **positive + as**
She is small**er than** Mike. But she is **more intelligent than** Mike.	… kleiner als … … intelligenter als …	**comparative** + **than**

Beachte:
Vor und nach der Grundform des Adjektivs steht immer **as**, nach dem Komparativ dagegen immer **than**.
Achtung: Verwechsle *than* (als) nicht mit *then* (dann, damals).

7.
Comparisons
Susan und Betty, zwei Mädchen aus Toms Klasse, mögen einander nicht besonders. Daher sind sie oft verschiedener Meinung.

Beispiel: *Susan:* I think football is more exciting than volleyball.
Betty: No, it isn't, but it's more dangerous.
Susan: More dangerous? I think volleyball is as dangerous as football.

tennis	difficult	English	nice	comics	funny
swimming	expensive	German	useful	books	interesting

8.

What girls whisper

Schau dir diese Mädchen an. Sie reden über Mike, aber er kann nicht alles hören. Kannst du einfügen, was sie sagen? Benutze die Adjektive *tall, strong, silly, bad, good, nice* in ihren verschiedenen Formen.

He is very tall. I think he's ______________ boy in our class.

Is he? No, I think David is ______________ him.

And he's so strong. He must be ______________ boy in our class.

He is very nice. I think he is even ______________ than Tom.

Look at his hair. It has got the same colour ______________ your hair. Have you got the same shoes, too?

Oh, don't be stupid; or you'll get a prize for ______________ question.

Is he good at maths? Do you think he can help me? I need somebody who is ______________ Tom. You know, at maths Tom is even ______________ me.

Why don't you go and ask him? He looks a bit silly, but perhaps he is ______________ at maths ______________ he looks.

Have you seen any of his photos? Anne told me his photos are ______________ photos she has ever seen.

Did he take any photos of Anne? Then they must be ______________. She always thinks she's ______________ girl in our class.

9.

What about your training?

Du bist bald fertig mit diesem Buch. Kannst du ein paar Fragen beantworten?

1. Has your English become _______________ *(good)*?
2. Let's hope it hasn't become _______________ *(bad)*.
3. Is the number of mistakes in your English tests _______________ or _______________ *(small/big)* than before?
4. Were the exercises very _______________ *(boring)*?
5. Were they _______________ *(interesting)* than in your textbook?
6. Were they _______________ *(boring)* as in your textbook?
7. Or were they _______________ *(bad)*?
8. Was the grammar _______________ *(clear)* enough?
9. Or was the grammar in your textbook _______________ *(easy)*?
10. We hope that you didn't find things too _______________ *(difficult)*.

Test

1.
Welche Form hat das Adjektiv?

a) York is one of the ______________ cities in England. *(old)*

b) It was, together with London, the ______________ town in Roman times. *(important)*

c) York has many monuments. It has, for example, the ______________ medieval* Cathedral in Northern Europe. *(large)*

d) It has many good museums, too. The Jorvic Viking Centre is one of the ______________ museums about Viking history. *(interesting)*

e) There is the railway museum, too. It is ______________ *(big)* railway museum in the world.

f) The countryside around York is very beautiful. It offers one of ______________ sights in Northern England. *(beautiful)*

*medieval – mittelalterlich

2.
Vergleiche bitte "the two Yorks".

a) New York is much ______________ York. *(big)*

b) York's population isn't ______________ *(mixed)* ______________ New York's population.

c) York is much ______________ ______________ New York. *(old)*

d) New York's history isn't ______________ old ______________ York's, but it is certainly ______________. *(interesting)*

e) New York's climate is different. It's much ______________ in summer and much ______________ in winter *(hot/cold)*.

f) There is more money in New York today ______________ in York. Most people are ______________, but there are also many people who are ______________. *(rich/poor)*

18

Adverbien

Adverbien der Art und Weise

Wenn du sagen willst, wie man etwas tut – ob schnell, langsam, gründlich usw. –, verwendest du ein Adverb, und zwar ein Adverb der Art und Weise. Solche Adverbien gibt es auch im Englischen *(adverbs of manner)*.

Im Deutschen haben die Adverbien oft die gleiche Form wie das entsprechende Adjektiv. Im Englischen musst du dagegen zwischen zwei verschiedenen Formen unterscheiden.

Adverb	**Adjektiv**
Sie singt **schön**.	Ihre Stimme ist **schön**.
She sings **beautifully**.	Her voice is **beautiful**.

Du bildest die Adverbien, indem du an das Adjektiv ein -**ly** anhängst:

bad + **ly**	→ bad**ly**
careful + **ly**	→ careful**ly**
nice + **ly**	→ nice**ly**

Beachte:

1. Bei Adjektiven, die auf Konsonant + **y** enden, wird das **y** zu **i**:

happ**y** + **ly**	→ happ**ily**
nois**y** + **ly**	→ nois**ily**

2. Adjektive, die auf -**ble** enden, verlieren das -**le**:

terri**ble** + **ly**	→ terri**bly**

3. **Good, hard, fast** haben unregelmäßige Adverbformen:

Tom is a good singer.	He sings **well**.
Mike is a fast runner.	He runs **fast**.
Jenny is a hard worker.	She works **hard**.

1.

Tom's class

Trage die Adverbien ein.

1. Betty is a good dancer. She dances _______________.
2. Kevin is a fast runner. He runs _______________.
3. Ann has a beautiful voice. She sings _______________.
4. Susan is a quiet girl. She does everything _______________.
5. Jim is a very noisy boy. He always runs around _______________.
6. Barbara is a hard worker. She works _______________.
7. Kate is a clever girl. She always answers _______________.
8. John is a happy boy. He always laughs _______________.
9. Jane is a terrible dancer. She dances _______________.
10. Matthew is very good at German. He speaks German very _______________.

2.

What can you do, what can your friends do?

Zähle auf, was du tun kannst. Dann berichte, was dein Freund/deine Freundin oder sonst jemand aus deiner Klasse ist oder tun kann. Verwende Adjektive und Adverbien.

Beispiel: a) I am good at English. I can speak English very well.
b) My friend ...

noisy fast slow hard easy careful intelligent excellent bad clever quick exciting nice wonderful boring

Adjektiv oder Adverb?

Um diese Frage zu beantworten, solltest du dir folgende Grundregeln einprägen.

1. Adjektive beziehen sich immer auf Pronomen und Substantive. Vor einem Substantiv steht daher immer ein Adjektiv und nie ein Adverb:

   He is a **careful** worker.
   He is a **dangerous** driver.

2. Adverbien der Art und Weise geben an, wie etwas getan wird. Sie beziehen sich daher immer auf ein Verb:

   He works **carefully**.
   He drives **dangerously**.

3. Ist *to be* das Verb eines Satzes, steht immer ein Adjektiv:

   She **is clever** and **intelligent**.

4. Ein Adverb steht dagegen, wenn *to be* Teil einer *progressive form* ist:

   She is answering **cleverly**.

3.
A fire at school
Adjektiv oder Adverb? Was ist richtig?

All the children were ____________ *(quiet)* sitting in the classroom when suddenly they heard a siren. What was it? Could it be one of those ____________ *(silly)* fire alarms? Then they all saw it. Smoke was coming out in ____________ *(thick)* clouds from the main building and in one room they saw ____________ *(red)* flames. They were all very ____________ *(excited)* and immediately wanted to leave the class-room. "Be ____________ *(quiet)* and sit down," the teacher shouted ____________ *(angry)*. "You needn't be ____________ *(afraid)*. Remember what you must do when there is a fire alarm. You Pete, you get up ___________ *(quick)* and shut these windows. Then let's leave the room, but don't run: let's leave it ___________ *(slow)* and in ___________ *(good)* order. Keep together and remember to shut the door ___________ *(careful)*. Leave your things in the room if you can't pack them ___________ *(quick)*. Are you all ___________ *(ready)*? So let's get out ___________ *(slow)* now. Jane, don't forget the register. Jimmy, you are the last; be ___________ *(sure)* to shut the door behind you."

4.

Chaos at school

Als alle im Flur waren, sahen die Lehrer viele Dinge, die ihnen nicht gefielen. Adjektiv oder Adverb? Was gehört in die Lücken?

1. Lots of windows and doors were still _______________ *(open)*.
2. Some pupils were running around _______________ *(excited)* in the corridor.
3. Others were still _______________ *(quiet)* packing their things.
4. One pupil was _______________ *(busy)* copying his homework from his friend's exercise book. He wasn't even writing very _______________ *(fast)*.
5. Another pupil was reading a comic. He didn't think it was _______________ *(dangerous)* to remain in the building.
6. Some were _______________ *(excited)* watching the smoke from the windows of their classrooms.
7. Others were _______________ *(happy)* that there was a fire at their school.
8. A _______________ *(good)* fire is less _______________ *(boring)* than an English lesson, one of them said _______________ *(excited)*.
9. And there will be no English tomorrow, somebody else added _______________ *(quick)*.

Die Stellung von Adverbien der Art und Weise

Wenn du Adverbien der Art und Weise verwendest, musst du auf die Satzstellung aufpassen.

1. Adverbien der Art und Weise stehen nach dem Verb, wenn kein Objekt vorhanden ist:

   They talked **quickly**.
   He listened **excitedly**.
   He smiled **happily**.

2. Ist ein direktes Objekt vorhanden, so steht das Adverb meist nach diesem Objekt:

   They left the room **quietly**.
   They shut the door **quickly**.

3. Ist das Adverb weniger betont, kann es auch vor dem Verb stehen:

   They **quietly** left the room.

Beachte:
Im Unterschied zum Deutschen darf im Englischen **nie** ein Adverb zwischen dem Verb und dem direkten Objekt stehen!

5.
Helping hands ...
Bald hörten die Schüler ein anderes Geräusch. Es war die Sirene eines Feuerwehrautos, das in den Schulhof einbog. Setze die Adverbien an die Stelle, an die sie hingehören.

1. Four men jumped out of it.
2. Two of them ran into the building.
3. They raised a ladder.
4. One man climbed up the ladder.
5. Another man fetched the water hose.
6. “Where can we take the water from?” one man asked.
7. “Where do we begin?” one man asked.

quick
careful
nervous
worried
excited
busy
fast

Test

1.
Adjektiv oder Adverb? Trage die richtige Form ein.

a) When there is a fire, don't be ______________ *(nervous)*, don't run around ______________ *(excited)*, but keep cool and pack your things ______________ *(quick)*, or better leave them where they are.

b) Shut all windows and doors ______________ *(careful)*, see that nobody is left behind and leave the room as ______________ as you can. *(fast)*

c) Don't panic when you see the smoke or the fire, but try ______________ not to get excited *(hard)*.

d) Follow the instructions of the firemen ______________ *(careful)* and leave the building immediately.

e) Make a ______________ job out of a ______________ thing. *(good/bad)*

2.
Am nächsten Tag musste Toms Klasse über das Feuer schreiben. Hier sind ein paar Auszüge aus den Aufsätzen. Wähle ein passendes Adjektiv aus, bilde das Adverb und schreibe die Sätze neu mit den Adverbien.

excited	nervous	bad	deep
fast	loud	hard	
stupid	quiet	terrible	quick

a) I was sitting in the classroom when suddenly the alarm bell rang. First I didn't know what do do, but then I understood the danger we were in.
b) The firemen did a good job and managed to put out the fire.
c) Teachers and pupils were running around.
d) There were quite a lot of pupils who behaved …
e) I ran along the corridor with the other pupils of my class; we shouted, "Fire, fire!"
f) My neighbour coughed when the smoke got into his lungs.

19 Die Wortstellung im Englischen

Die Stellung des Subjekts im Aussagesatz

Da englische Substantive außer der Pluralendung keine Endungen haben, liegt die Wortstellung im Englischen fest. Du kannst sie daher nicht einfach ändern, ohne dass sich auch der Sinn des Satzes ändert:

The dog bites the postman. The postman bites **the dog**.

Wie du aus diesem Beispiel siehst, bestimmt im Englischen die Wortstellung die Funktion eines Substantivs (oder Pronomens): Steht es in einem Aussagesatz vor dem Verb, ist es Subjekt. Steht es nach dem Verb, ist es Objekt des Aussagesatzes. Aus diesem Grunde sind auch andere Umstellungen, die du vom Deutschen her kennst, im Englischen nicht möglich.

Im englischen Aussagesatz steht das Subjekt **immer** vor dem Verb. Es wird auch dann nicht umgestellt, wenn ihm ein anderer Satzteil vorausgeht.

Heute **habe ich** Kopfweh. Today **I have got** a headache.
Heute **bin ich** krank. Today **I am** ill.

1.

A week in Jenny's life

Jenny trägt immer in ihren Kalender ein, was passiert oder was sie vorhat. Schau dir ihren Kalender an und frage sie dann nach ihren Eintragungen.

Beispiel: What are you going to do on Monday, Jenny? Well, let me see ... On Monday, I ...

Monday:	4 p.m. table tennis with Tom
Tuesday:	8.15 p.m. watch film on TV
Wednesday:	after school learn for German test with Tom
Thursday:	6 p.m. help Kate with maths homework
Friday:	5 p.m. buy birthday present for Sarah/ring up Sarah
Saturday:	Sarah's birthday party at 2 p.m.
Sunday:	ring up Tom/go for a walk with Tom at 4 p.m.

2.

Tom's homework

Als Hausaufgabe in Deutsch musste Tom acht Sätze schreiben. Hier sind sie. Kannst du sie ins Englische übersetzen?

1. Heute bin ich krank.
2. Heute muss ich nicht aufstehen.
3. Heute kann ich im Bett bleiben.
4. Heute muss ich nicht in die Schule gehen.
5. Heute muss ich keine Hausaufgaben machen.
6. Heute habe ich kein Deutsch.
7. Heute habe ich Fieber.
8. Heute ist ein schöner Tag.

Die Stellung von Objekten, Orts- und Zeitangaben

1. Wenn das indirekte Objekt (wem?) nicht besonders betont ist, steht es gewöhnlich vor dem direkten Objekt (wen oder was?). Folgt es dem direkten Objekt, muss ein *to* vor das indirekte Objekt gestellt werden.

Subjekt	**Verb**	**(ind. Objekt)**	**dir. Objekt**	**(ind. Objekt)**
Tom	has got		a sister.	
He	likes		her.	
She	likes		ice cream.	
He	gives	her	an ice cream.	
He	gives		an ice cream	to his sister.
He	gives	Timmy	an ice cream.	

Beachte:

Objekte stehen im Englischen **immer nach** dem Verb oder der Verbgruppe. Im Englischen dürfen keine Satzteile zwischen dem Verb und dem Objekt stehen.

2. Zeitangaben stehen meist am Ende des Satzes. Wenn sie am Satzanfang stehen, sind sie stärker betont. Auch Ortsangaben können am Satzanfang stehen.

   Wenn Zeit- und Ortsangaben zusammentreffen, steht die Ortsangabe **immer vor** der Zeitangabe:

Zeit/Ort			**Ort**	**Zeit**
	Tom	gets up		at 6.30.
	He	goes	to school	after breakfast.
Today	he	walks	to school.	
In England	school	starts		at 8.30.

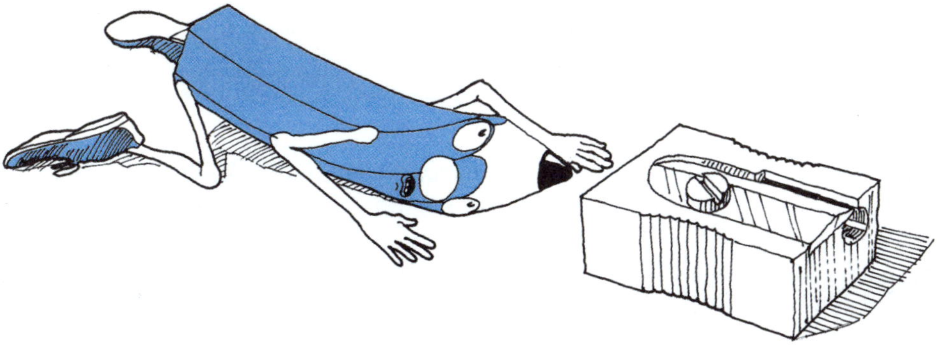

3.

Where's my money?

Als Sarah ihre Pommes frites bei Mrs Owen bezahlen will, stellt sie fest, dass sie kein Geld dabei hat. Sie fragt ihre Freundinnen, ob sie ihr welches leihen können. Setze bitte ein, was sie sagen.

Mrs Owen: So, here you are. That's £ 2.30.
Sarah: Oh, dear. Where have I put my purse?
Did I give ______________, Christine?
Christine: No, you didn't. But perhaps you gave ______________ Sandra. Sandra, have you got it?
Sandra: No, I haven't. Perhaps you left it at home.
Sarah: Maybe. Can any of you lend ______________ some money?
Christine: Sorry, I can't. I've already lent ______________ Tom and he hasn't given it back yet.
Sandra: Sorry, Sarah. I've just got enough money on me to pay for my chips.
Sarah: Well then, no lunch for me today. Sorry, Mrs Owen.
Mrs Owen: No need to worry, Sarah. I know you. You can have your chips and bring ______________ tomorrow.
Sarah: Thanks, Mrs Owen. I won't forget to ______________ back ______________ you.

Die Stellung von Adverbien der Häufigkeit

Unter Adverbien der Häufigkeit versteht man Ausdrücke wie *often, always, sometimes, never, usually, seldom, mostly* u. a. Sie geben an, wie oft man bestimmte Dinge tut.

Im Unterschied zum Deutschen stehen Adverbien der Häufigkeit im Englischen **nie** zwischen Verb und Objekt.

Die Adverbien der Häufigkeit stehen:

1. im *simple present* und im *simple past* vor dem Verb.

   Last year Mike **often did** his homework at school.
   This year he **usually does** it at home.

2. bei Hilfsverben, denen ein Infinitiv oder ein *past participle* folgt, nach dem Hilfsverb.

   He **must always** help his sister.
   She **has never** done his homework.
   She **will never** do it.

3. im *simple present* und *simple past* nach den Formen von *to be*, sonst nach dem Hilfsverb.

   Timmy **isn't often** ill.
   He **was sometimes** ill last year.
   But he **has never** been really ill.

Beachte:
Sometimes kann auch am Satzanfang stehen, wenn es besonders betont ist:

Sometimes Tom forgets his homework.

4.
Homework

Bilde Sätze mit *often, usually* usw.

There are pupils

- who forget their homework. (usually)
- who have forgotten their homework. (never)
- who do their homework at school. (often)
- who have copied it from their neighbours. (never)
- who know what they must do. (never)
- who write down what they must do. (never)
- who forget their homework at home. (always)
- who do it on the way to school. (usually)
- who leave their exercise book at home. (sometimes)
- who forget it on the bus. (sometimes)

5.
You and your homework

Antworte in ganzen Sätzen. Verwende dabei *always, often* usw.

1. What about your homework? Do you usually do it?
2. When do you usually do it?
3. Where do you do it?
4. Do you often forget it?
5. Why do you sometimes forget it?
6. Do you often copy it from your neighbour?
7. Are you usually busy in the breaks?
8. Must your neighbour/your mum/your dad often help you with your homework?
9. In what subjects must he or she often help you?
10. Has your teacher ever helped you?

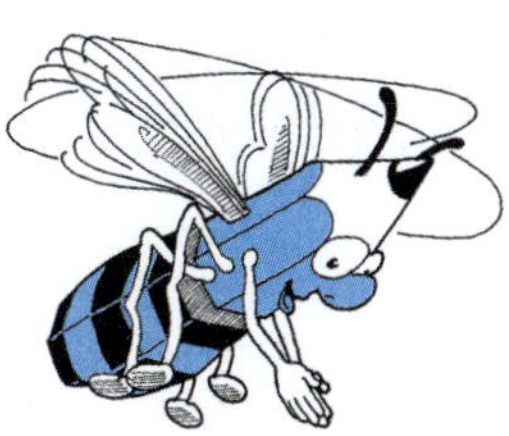

6.

Schools in England

Englische Schulen sind zum Teil anders. Lies dir die folgenden Sätze durch und schreibe sie richtig aus. Beachte dabei die Wortstellung!

1. go already/English pupils/when they are five/to school
2. go to a comprehensive school/most English pupils/when they are eleven.
3. when they are 16/school/they can leave
4. school uniforms/in many schools/they must wear
5. are blue and grey/the school colours/in Tom's school
6. the school uniforms/in special shops/can buy/the pupils' parents
7. later than in Germany/in most English schools/begin lessons
8. lessons/in the afternoon/most English pupils have/also
9. school cafeterias/many English schools/so/there are lessons also in the afternoon/ have
10. lunch/pupils/can have/during lunch break/at the school cafeteria
11. In many English schools/learn/pupils/to cook

7.

What you can do or say

Schreibe zehn Sätze. Beginne mit dem Nebensatz.

Beispiel: Before I go to school, I usually do my homework.

		before you go to school?
		when you don't want to go to school?
		when it's too cold to get up?
		when you are late?
	say	when you must do your homework?
What do you	do	when you must go to bed?
	think	before you get up?
		before you have breakfast?
		when you go to bed?
		when you can't find your homework?

Test

1.

Trage die fehlenden Adverbien ein.

a) Today, I'll play football. I ________________ on Friday. *(usually)*
b) On Mondays, I go to the cinema. *(sometimes)*
c) After school, I go to Tom. *(often)*
d) What we do there? We play games or do our homework. *(usually)*
e) Do you play with Kate, too? No, we ________________. *(seldom)*
f) What I do in the evening? When I'm at home, I watch TV. *(often)*
g) If I watch TV with my parents? Yes, I do. *(usually)*
h) If my parents are out? *(often)* You can't tell; they are or they aren't. *(sometimes)*
i) When I go to bed? I go to bed at 10. *(always)*
j) When I get up? I get up at 7. *(usually)*
k) If I am late? *(often)* No, I'm not. I'm late *(never)*.

2.

Verbessere die Wortstellung in den folgenden Sätzen.

a) As you know, are German schools from English schools different.
b) Pupils start usually school at the age of 6 or 7.
c) In Germany start lessons earlier than in England.
d) In most cases are German schools no all-day schools.
e) Usually German pupils have at home lunch.
f) No school cafeterias have most German schools.
g) So spend German pupils not so much time at school.
h) They usually are in the early afternoon at home.

Überblick über die Zeiten im Englischen

Zeit	Beispiel	wird benutzt für	Signalwörter
simple present	1. He lives in London. 2. He often forgets his homework. 3. He comes home, switches on the lights and sits down.	1. lange andauernde Handlungen 2. wiederholte oder gewohnheitsmäßige Handlungen 3. aufeinanderfolgende Handlungen	2. seldom, always, never, sometimes, every morning 3. then, after that, the next day, the next morning
simple past	1. I saw her yesterday. 2. I often saw her at school. 3. I came home, opened the door and switched on the lights. 4. I was writing a letter when the door opened.	1. Handlungen, die vorbei sind 2. wiederholte oder gewohnheitsmäßige Handlungen 3. aufeinanderfolgende Handlungen 4. neu einsetzende Handlungen	1. yesterday, last, ago, in + year, when 2. often, usually, sometimes, never 3. then, after that, the next day 4. suddenly, when
present perfect	I have read that book.	das gegenwärtige Ergebnis einer Handlung, die vorüber ist	never, ever, already, just, yet, not ... yet

Zeit	Beispiel	wird benutzt für	Signalwörter
will-future	1. I'll be 13 next Monday. 2. I hope it won't rain. 3. When/if I see him, I'll talk to him. 4. "Oh, then I'll come, too."	1. Handlungen/ Ereignisse, die auf jeden Fall eintreten 2. zukünftige Handlungen nach bestimmten Verben/Ausdrücken 3. im Hauptsatz von Bedingungssätzen und adverbialen Nebensätzen der Zeit 4. plötzliche Entschlüsse	2. to hope, think, be sure, perhaps
going to-future	I'm going to have a party.	geplante zukünftige Handlungen	
present progressive	I'm singing. I'm playing football today.	Handlungen, die im Augenblick oder in einem gegenwärtigen Zeitraum noch nicht vorüber sind	now, at this moment, look!, listen!, this morning/afternoon, today
past progressive	I was writing a letter when she came in.	Handlungen, die zu einem bestimmten Zeitpunkt der Vergangenheit noch nicht vorüber sind	

Lösungen

Allgemeiner Hinweis:

In den Lösungen wurde bei den Hilfsverben und den Formen von *to be* und *to do* nur eine mögliche Antwort angegeben. Sowohl die Langformen (*she is, cannot, is not, does not* usw.) als auch die Kurzformen (*she's, can't, isn't, doesn't* usw.) sind als richtig zu betrachten.

1 Substantive

1.

a) There are Mr Mason, his wife and a farmworker on the farm. There are a cock and a few geese, some hens, a cat, a dog and some pigs on the farm, too.

b)

nouns in the singular	*nouns in the plural*
a farmhouse	some farmhouses
a wife	some wives
a dog	some dogs
a pig	some pigs
a cock	some cocks
a hen	some hens
a goose	some geese
a chimney	some chimneys
an apple tree	some apple trees

2.

a cat – a bull – a cow – a dog – a horse – a pony – a mouse – a goose

3.

There are a lot of men, women and children – presents – two boys – hand – present – teddy – one foot – one arm – one eye – mice – cake

4.

1. This is a boy and these are boys, too.
2. That is a car and those are cars, too.
3. This is a street and these are streets, too.
4. That is a house and those are houses, too.

5. This is a brush and these are brushes, too.
6. That is a baby and those are babies, too.
7. This is a foot and these are feet, too.

5.

trousers – shoes – clothes – clothes – jeans – tights

6.

are – them – They are – It is – are

7.

a) I'm wearing ...

b) I like ... best.

Test

1.

singular	*plural*
a horse	some horses
a hen	some hens
a goose	some geese
a duck	some ducks
a rabbit	some rabbits
a boy	some boys
a girl	some girls
a child	some children
a teddy	some teddies
a man	some men
a woman	some women
a house	some houses
a brush	some brushes
an apple	some apples
a sandwich	some sandwiches

2.

these old things – this old pullover – it – They – they – They – them

3.

presents – photos – people – those two big boxes – homework

2 Das Personalpronomen

1.

1. He is on the farm.
2. She is in the house.
3. He is at school.
4. It is at school, too.
5. He is on his potty.
6. They are on the floor.
7. They are on his bed.
8. She is not at home.
9. She is with her.
10. They are in the park.

2.

1. I can't find them.
2. I can't find it.
3. I can't see/hear you.
4. I can't see him.
5. I can't see them.
6. I can't find them.
7. I can't find them.
8. I can't find/see it.
9. I can't find him.
10. I can't see it.
11. I can't see/find it.
12. I can't see/find them.

3.

Kate: me – them – they
Timmy: they – they
Kate: they – me – they
Timmy: they – They are

Kate: it
Timmy: It's
Kate: they
Timmy: them

Test

1.

	Lösungsvorschläge:
Where are Tom and Mike?	They are in the classroom/here/on the bus/at school.
Where is your homework?	It's here/on the bus/at home/in my schoolbag …
Where is your English book?	It's on the desk/here/at home …
Where is your book?	It's in my schoolbag/at home/here …
Where is Christine?	She's in the classroom/here/at home/not here …
Where is the register?	It's on the desk/in my schoolbag/on the bus …
Where are they from?	They're from York.
Where are you from?	I'm from …
Where is Kate?	She's not here/at home/in the classroom …

2.

When I've got a dog, I must wash it/brush it/talk to it/look after it.
When I've got a lot of homework, I must forget it.
When I've got dirty clothes, I must wash them.
When I've got a silly neighbour, I must talk to him/her.
When I've got a baby, I must look after him/her.
When I've got a friend, I must be nice to him/her.
When I've got a new computer game, I must try it.
When I've got problems, I must talk about them.
When I've got a good book, I must read it.

3 Bestimmter und unbestimmter Artikel

1.

[ðɪ]
old women
English children
examples
afternoons
easy units
American cars
empty pages

[ðə]
yellow apples
wrong numbers
young girls
silly answers
bad ideas
difficult questions
school uniforms
terrible teachers

2.

Jenny isn't Tom's sister, she is Tom's friend – in Apple Street – Apple Street is – in the north of York – to school by bus – to school by bike – Tom is – all the girls and boys – she likes Tom – the nicest boy – like Tom – likes maths – Maths is the subject – Before tests – helps Tom

3.

Lösungsvorschläge:

I can go to Germany by plane/by train …
I can go to New York by plane/by boat …
I can go to Scotland by train/by car/by taxi/by bike/by motorbike/on foot …
I can go to Ireland by plane/by boat …
I can go to Denmark by plane/by boat …
I can go to France by plane/by train/by ferry …
I can go to the Isle of Wight by boat/by train …
I can go to Wales by train/by plane/by bus/by car …
I can go to California by plane.

4.

1. Boys like girls.
2. Tom likes Jenny.
3. Do you like the boys in your class?
4. Do you usually like girls more than boys?
5. What about the girls in your class?
6. Which of the boys/girls do you like best?

7. Who is the nicest boy/girl in your class?
8. What's the name of the girl/boy you like best?
9. Which boy/girl do most of you like best?
10. Are the boys/girls in your class good at English?
11. Are boys as clever as girls?

5.

an English book – a workbook – an exercise book – a German book – a pencil case – an apple – an empty bottle – a water pistol – an old sandwich

6.

1. He's a milkman.
2. He's a postman.
3. He's a butcher.
4. He's a greengrocer.
5. She's a shop assistant.
6. She's a reporter/journalist.
7. He's a fireman.
8. He's a vet.
9. He's a teacher.
10. He's a burglar.

7.

an old woman – a young girl – an American car – an English child – a silly answer – a difficult question – an example – a bad idea – a school uniform – a yellow apple – an afternoon – an empty page – a wrong number – an easy unit – a terrible teacher

8.

Lösungsvorschläge:

a silly boy
a boring boy
a clever boy
a strong boy
a nice boy
a noisy boy
an unhappy boy

an interesting girl
a difficult girl
an exciting girl
a nice girl
an intelligent girl
a happy girl
…

9.

Jenny goes to the same school as Tom – takes them to school in the morning – The school they go to is a big school – a lot of pupils – like school – she likes school – most of the teachers – she can't go to school – stay in bed – she hasn't got a temperature – a cold – a bad headache – a doctor – stay in bed

Test

1.

Tom has got a brother and a sister. They live in York. That's in the north of England. Timmy …
Tom has got a grandpa and a grandma, too. – He has got a farm, so he is a farmer.
Tom and Kate go to school. – He's too young to go to school. It's sometimes hard for Tom and Kate to get out of bed …
Tom usually goes to school by bike. He only takes the bus … Kate goes to school by bus. She mustn't go by bike … Tom and Kate don't like everything about school, but most of their teachers are nice.

2.

Lösungsvorschläge:
I live in …
I live in … Street.
I'm …
I've got/I haven't got …
My father/mother is a …
I like school/I don't like school because …
I like … best.
I hate …
My teachers are …
In winter/summer I get to school by …
I like better to go to school by …
My father/mother goes to work by …

4 Substantive und ihre Begleiter

1.

1. It's <u>their</u> farm.
2. It's <u>their</u> flat.
3. It's <u>their</u> car.
4. It's <u>his</u> sister.
5. It's <u>her</u> brother.
6. They are <u>his</u> toys.
7. It's <u>his</u> camera.
8. It's <u>her</u> boyfriend.
9. It's <u>their</u> school.
10. It's <u>their</u> house.

2.

1. I think they are <u>his</u> keys.
2. It's not <u>your</u> exercise book, it's Kate's. It's <u>her</u> exercise book.
3. How can Jenny do Geman tests when you keep it under <u>your</u> bed? What will <u>her</u> teacher say?
4. This is not <u>your</u> picture book, it's Kate's. It was <u>her</u> birthday present from Tom.
5. Here's <u>your</u> teddy, here's <u>your</u> toy car, here's <u>your</u> telephone. So play with <u>your</u> things now.

3.

1. your – you
2. you – your
3. your
4. your
5. you – your
6. you – your
7. you – your
8. you – your

4.

There are a lot of things – There are – They are on the chairs – there is something – It's an old pullover – There are some socks – There are holes in them and they look dirty – There are a lot of photos – that photo over there – It's a photo – It's not a new bike, but its handlebars and its saddle are new.

5.

Lösungsvorschläge:

Look at this classroom. There are ten desks. One of them is the teacher's desk. It is in front of the blackboard. There are a lot of exercise books, pencils and other things on the desks. There are some school bags on the floor. There is a map on the wall. It is a map of Great Britain and Ireland.

6.

Timmy:	*Tom:*
Is this your classroom?	This isn't my classroom.
Is this your class?	Yes, this is my class.
And that class over there?	That's Kate's class.
Is this your chair here?	... that chair over there, that's Jenny's.
What's the name of that fat boy over there?	
Is that a teacher over there?	
But that is a teacher, Tom.	Oh yes, that's our English teacher.

7.

There is room for 30 pupils. There are 30 chairs ... and there is a desk. ... It's a nice room. There are many pictures on the walls and there is a map of England, too. It's on the back, over there.

My friend sits there. ... but behind me, there are two girls ... I don't like them. They ... throw things at me and my friend. ... they eat their sandwiches and their chocolate pudding and their sweets ...

8.

1. How much homework ...
2. How much time ...
3. How many minutes ...
4. How many hours ...
5. How many subjects ...
6. How much help ...
7. How many tests ...
8. How many good marks ...
9. How many tests ...

Test

1.

- much time
- many friends
- many hobbies
- many books
- much money

2.

- too many tests
- too many bad marks
- too many teachers
- too much homework
- too much work
- too many lessons
- too many questions
- too many boring subjects
- too much time indoors
- so much.

3.

a) your; b) your – your; c) you; d) her; e) you – you; f) your; g) your – their

Der Genitiv

5

1.

Timmy's toys
our cat's food
the man's boots
Jenny's dog

the boys' teacher
Kate's friends
the children's books
the Masons' house

the girls' school bags
women's clothes
the girls' school uniforms
my parents' car

2.

	Mögliche Antworten:
Are these your toys, Tom?	No, they aren't. They are my baby brother's.
Is this your girlfriend, Kevin?	No, it isn't. It's Tom's.
Is this your magazine, Jenny?	No, it isn't. It's the girls'.
Is this your cat, Kate?	No, it isn't. It's my mother's.
Is this your homework, Joe?	No, it isn't. It's Kevin's.
Is this your house, Mr Mason?	No, it isn't. It's my grandparents'.
Is this your bike, Mrs Mason?	No, it isn't. It's Kate's.
Is this your room, Tom?	No, it isn't. It's my sister's.
Is this your teddy, Jenny?	No, it isn't. It's Timmy's.

3.

Tom's baby brother – one of his favourite toys – he's got (he has got) other toys, too – other things – there's (there is) one of Jenny's letters – there's (there is) an old German book and there's (there is) Kate's ruler – some keys – his parents' keys – there's (there is) a tennis ball – Is it Kevin's or Joe's – It can't be Kate's or Tom's ...

4.

s-Genitiv	*Kurzform*
Tom's girlfriend	She's (she is) twelve. She hasn't got ... she's only got (she has only got) got her parents it's (it is) her ...
her grandparents' house	
Jenny's other relatives	she's got (she has got) an aunt who's (who is) over sixty and who's (who has got) got a flat ... She hasn't got
Jenny's first visit to London	

5.

the boys's legs
the doors of my room
Kate's books
on the evening of my birthday
the girl's hands
the dog's feet
the children's clothes
the light of the moon
the windows of the car
my neighbour's cat
the end of school
Jenny's story

6.

Lösungsvorschläge:

a bar of chocolate
a glass of milk/tea
a cup of tea/coffee
lots of chocolate/food
a plate of strawberries
a tin of peas
a pound of cheese/sausages
a bag of food/crisps
a packet of cornflakes
a piece of cheese

7.

five bags of crisps
three packets of biscuits
five bottles of coke
five bottles of lemonade
a bottle of tomato ketchup
three pounds of sausages
five packets of ice cream

8.

Lösungsvorschläge:

Mrs White	*Tom*
	I need three packets of biscuits and five bags of crisps.
	I need some lemonade and some coke, too.
How many bottles do you want?	I need five bottles of lemonade and five bottles of coke.
Anything else?	Can I have some sausages, too?
How many do you need?	I need three pounds of sausages.
Anything else?	I need some ice cream, too.
How much do you want?	I need five packets of ice cream.

9.

Get off that bike – on Tom's bike – they will fall off the bike – Mike took one hand out of his pockets – not very far from the corner shop to the Masons' flat – the bottles fell off the bike – to Mrs White's shop – no bottles fell off the bike – both hands out of his pockets – into Tom's room – a telephone call from Jenny's mother – she has just come home from school – Greetings from Jenny and from my husband – you will hear from Jenny tomorrow.

Test

1.

Lösungsvorschläge:

Tom's trousers/comics
Jenny's computer/room
Timmy's trousers/legs
women's magazines
my parents' room/computer
people's legs/magazines
children's magazines
a list of things
a bucket of milk
a packet of biscuits

2.

lots of people – play games – there's always– some kind of fun – Tom's birthday party – some people – There's Jenny, there's Ann and there's his sister Kate – She's a very nice girl, not as silly as the other girls.

3.

a) This plane is taking <u>off</u>.
b) This is a letter <u>from</u> London. It's <u>from</u> Jenny's aunt.
c) This boy is taking <u>off</u> his clothes. He's taking the money <u>out of</u> his pocket.
d) Where are you <u>from</u>?
e) Turn the lights <u>off</u>, please.
f) Is this one <u>of</u> your jokes?

6 *Have got, has got* und das *simple present* von *to be*

1.

1. They have got a flat there.
2. They have got five rooms.
3. Tom has got a room, and Kate has got a room, too.
4. Timmy hasn't got a room.
5. The Masons have got a car.
6. Tom and Kate haven't got a car, they have got bikes.
7. Timmy hasn't got a bike ...
8. But he has got two big toy cars ...

2.

1. Kate hasn't got a sister/a boyfriend/a car/a toy car/a TV set, but she has got two brothers, a lot of friends/a bike/a teddy/a football/a radio.
2. I have got ..., but I haven't got ...
3. My friend has got .../My friends have got .../He, she has got .../They have got ...

3.

Lösungsvorschläge:

Have you got a car? No, I haven't.
Has your mother got a water pistol? No, she hasn't.
Has your English teacher got a toy car? No, he hasn't.
Have your friends got a lot of toys? Yes, they have.

4.

Today, it is Tom's birthday – He is twelve – All his friends are there – His sister is there – Her name is Kate – Only Jenny is not there – Where is she? – She is ill – All the children are – it is full of children – They are all hungry – There are a lot of sandwiches – there are some bottles – But one bottle is on the floor – it is broken – there is a pool – And who is in the pool? – It is Timmy ...

5.

1. No, it isn't. It's Tom's birthday.
2. No, she isn't. She is ill.
3. No, he isn't. He's twelve.
4. No, she isn't. She's Tom's friend/girlfriend.
5. Yes, she is. She's his sister.
6. Yes, it is. It's Timmy.
7. Yes, there are. There are lots of sandwiches ...
8. No, they aren't. They are in the kitchen.
9. Yes, they are. They are hungry and thirsty.
10. Yes, it is. One bottle is on the floor.

6.

1. Who is Timmy?
2. Where is he?
3. Where is Mike from?
4. Where is Bristol?
5. Who is Jenny?
6. Where is she?
7. Where are Joe and Kevin?

7.

Who is Jenny?
Is she from York?
Why isn't she here?
Are her parents at home?
How old is she?
Is she often ill?

Test

1.

a) This is Kevin and that is Joe.
b) They are the best friends I have got.
c) And that boy over there is Bill.
d) He is in my class, too, and he is very good at maths.
e) And this is Ann. She's Jenny's friend.
f) She is very sorry that Jenny can't be here.

2.

a) Is it a thing ? No, it isn't.
b) Is it an animal? No, it isn't.
c) Is it in this room? No, it isn't.
d) Have you got it at home? No, I haven't.
e) Is it a person? Yes, it is.
f) Is it a man? Yes, it is.
g) Is it a teacher? Yes, it is.
h) Is he a terrible teacher? No, he isn't.
i) Has he got a dirty old car? Yes, he has.
j) Is it our English teacher? Yes, it is.

3.

Why aren't you at Tom's party? I'm ill.
Are you really ill? Yes, I am.
What have you got? I've got a cold.
Are you unhappy that you can't come? Yes, I am.
Have you got a present for Tom? Yes, I have.
Is it a football? No, it isn't.
What is it then? It's a secret.

7 Das *present progressive*

1.

1. Mike is taking photos.
2. John is sitting at the table and drinking all the lemonade.
3. Kate is skipping.
4. Tom is ringing up Jenny.
5. Betty is flirting with Kevin.
6. Two boys are playing football in the kitchen.
7. Some girls are dancing in the kitchen.
8. Ann is lying on the floor and watching a film on TV.
9. Jim and Barbara are eating sandwiches.
10. Susan is sitting in a corner and reading a magazine.

2.

1. That's not right, Timmy. Mike isn't playing with his camera, he's taking photos.
2. John isn't eating all the sandwiches, he's drinking all the lemonade.
3. Kate isn't hopping around like a rabbit, she's skipping.
4. Tom isn't talking to his teacher, he's talking to Jenny.
5. Betty and Kevin aren't kissing, they are talking.
6. They aren't quarrelling, they are playing football.
7. The girls aren't running around in the kitchen, they are dancing.
8. Ann isn't lying on the floor because she is ill. She's lying on the floor because she is watching a film on TV.
9. Jim and Barbara aren't making sandwiches, they are eating them.
10. Susan isn't reading your picture book, she is reading a magazine.

3.

– Is John really eating all the sandwiches?	Yes, he is.
– Is Mike really playing with his camera?	Yes, he is.
– Is Kate really hopping around like a rabbit?	Yes, she is.
– Are some girls really running around in the kitchen?	Yes, they are.
– Is Susan really reading your picture book?	Yes, she is.
– Is Ann really lying on the floor because she is ill?	Yes, she is.

...

4.

– What are you doing, Kate?	I'm skipping.
– Are you talking to your teacher, Tom?	No, I'm talking to Jenny.

- What are you doing with your camera, Mike? I'm taking photos.
- Are you reading my picture book, Susan? No, I'm reading a magazine.
- Why are you lying on the floor, Ann? I'm watching a film.
- Are you playing a new game, Kate? No, I'm not. It's an old game.
- What are you doing in the kitchen? We are playing football.
- And what are you doing in the kitchen? We are dancing.
- Are you still hungry, John? Yes, I am.

5.

First scene:

When is the party over?
What is over at 7.30?
Where are the children going?
What are they?
Who is happy, too?
Where is he?
Who is lying on the floor?
Where is he lying?
What isn't he doing?
Who is playing with Tom's birthday presents?
Where are they now?
What is in the parcel?

Second scene:

Where is Timmy still lying?
What has he got in his hand?
Where is he drawing a picture?
What is he drawing?

Third scene:

Who is coming upstairs?
What is he shouting?
Who is it?
What is he doing?
What is he?
What is he opening?
What is empty?

Test

1.

What is Betty doing?
Who is making a paper plane?
What are Tony and Tom doing?
Where is Jimmy lying?
What is Kate cleaning?
What are Pete and John playing?
Who is having his second breakfast?
What is Jim having?
Where is Mike running around?

2.

What are you doing? Are you still flirting with Sue?
No, sir, I'm just asking her a question.
Are you still doing your homework?
I'm not doing my homework, sir. I'm taking notes.
John, why are you still eating?
And you Jimmy, why are you still crying? Look at the girls, they are laughing at you.
Are you all listening now?

8 Modale Hilfsverben

1.

can – needn't – must – must – must – must – needn't – must – can't – must – must – can – can – can – mustn't – can

2.

1. No, that's wrong. Kate can go to her room.
2. No, that's wrong. She needn't help.
3. No, that's wrong. Tom must help his mother to wash the dishes and to clean the kitchen floor, but he needn't clean Kate's room.
4. No, that's wrong. He must help to wash them up.
5. That's right.
6. That's wrong. He needn't clean them.
7. That's right. Timmy can help him with the dishes.
8. That's wrong. He needn't clean it.
9. That's wrong. He mustn't drop them.
10. That's right. He can stay up a little longer.

3.

Tom:	*Jenny's mother:*
Can/may I talk to Jenny, please?	Sorry, Tom, you can't/may not.
Can Jenny come tomorrow?	No, she can't. She can't/may not/mustn't get up.
Must she stay in bed all day?	Yes, she must.
Must she take medicine?	No, she needn't.
Can/may I see her this afternoon?	No, you can't/may not see her today.
Can/may I see her tomorrow?	... you can/may ring her up again in the evening.

4.

1. I mustn't go to school.
2. I must stay in bed for three days.
3. I must take my medicine.
4. I mustn't play with my friends.
5. I mustn't watch too much TV.
6. I must tell my mum to take my temperature every morning.
7. I must come to his surgery again on Monday at 4 o'clock.

5.

She must take her medicine.
She mustn't ride on her bike.
She mustn't go to school.
She needn't do her homework.
She can ring up her friends.
She can write letters.
She needn't kiss her doctor.
She can watch TV.
She can read a book.
She needn't/mustn't clean her room.
She needn't/mustn't help her mother.
She can listen to music.
She mustn't play football.
She needn't wash her clothes.

6.

1. No, you needn't.
2. Yes, you must.
3. No, you needn't.
4. Yes, you must.
5. No, you can't.
6. Yes, you can.
7. Yes, you must.
8. Yes, they may …
9. Yes, you can/may.
10. Yes, you must.

7.

– Are you very ill?	Yes, I am.
– Must you stay in bed?	Yes, I must.
– Must you stay indoors all day?	Yes, I must.
– May you get up for an hour or two?	Yes, I may.
– Have you got a temperature?	Yes, I have.
– Can you go to school on Thursday?	No, I can't.
– Are you happy that you needn't go to school?	Yes, I am.
– Are your teachers happy, too?	No, they aren't.

8.

1. He needn't go to school.
2. He can go to kindergarten.
3. He can play with other children there.
4. Must he go there every day?
5. No, he needn't.
6. Can/may he go there alone?
7. No, he can't/may not/mustn't.
8. Can/may he take his bike? No, he can't/may not/mustn't.
9. Must Tom fetch him in the afternoon?
10. Yes, he must fetch him on Thursdays and Fridays.

9.

Shall I do the shopping for you?
Shall I clean the rooms?
Shall I go to the chemist's?
Shall I get your medicine?
Shall I cook the meals?
Shall I make an appointment?
Shall I do the washing up?
Shall I make your bed?
Shall I buy you some lemonade?
Shall I open the window?
Shall I ring up the doctor?
Shall I look after my sister/brother?

Test

1.

a) A doctor must examine his patients.
b) He must take their temperature.
c) He must listen to what they tell him.
d) He must give them a prescription.
e) He must go and see his patients.
f) He must ask them how they feel.
g) He must send his patients to hospital when they are seriously ill.

2.

a) A good patient must do what the doctor tells him/her.
b) A good patient must take his/her medicine.
c) A good patient must stay in bed when he/she is ill.
d) Correct.
e) Correct.
f) A good patient must listen to his/her doctor.

3.

Mögliche Antworten:

- Shall I carry it for you?
- Shall I make you a sandwich?
- Shall I look for it?
- Shall I do it for you?
- Shall I clean them for you?
- Shall I help you?
- Shall I shut the windows?
- Shall I buy her a present?

Das *simple present* von Vollverben 9

1.

1. He gets up …
2. Then he washes and puts on his clothes.
3. Then he goes down …
4. There he has breakfast.
5. Then he looks for his school bag.
6. After that he leaves the house.
7. Then he goes to the bus stop.
8. He usually takes the bus …
9. He arrives …
10. He says hello …

2.

After school

- Tom goes home. He does his homework with Jenny; then they play games or watch TV.
- Kate goes to her room. She listens to music or she rings up her friends or plays.
- Mike sits in front of his computer. He plays computer games. He often forgets his homework.
- Ann and Barabara send SMS messages. Then they listen to music or read magazines.
- John has tea. He eats a lot of sandwiches. Then he lies down on his bed and has a nap.

3.

1. They don't get up in the morning.
2. They don't have an early breakfast.
3. Mr Brown doesn't wash his car.
4. Mrs Brown doesn't do the cooking.
5. Often, their children don't go to school.
6. They don't like school.
7. Helen doesn't like her teachers.
8. She doesn't do her homework.

4.

Tom likes bananas, but he doesn't like oranges.
He likes Jenny, but he doesn't like Ben.
Jenny and Kate like volleyball, but they don't like tennis.
They like sports, but they don't like all sports.
Timmy likes cornflakes, but he doesn't like tea.
He likes dogs, but he doesn't like cats.
Mike likes photos, but he doesn't like comics.
He likes music, but he doesn't like singing.
The Browns don't like work, but they like sleeping.
They don't like books, but they like TV.

5.

Lösungsvorschläge:

I like tennis, but my mother doesn't.

I don't like maths, but my neighbour does.

My friends like pop music, but my parents don't.

My parents don't like Kate, but I do.

6.

1.	Do you like your new school?	Yes, I do.
2.	Do you play football?	Yes, I do.
3.	Does your sister go to our school, too?	Yes, she does.
4.	Does she play tennis?	No, she doesn't.
5.	Do you and your sister go to school by bike?	Yes, we do.
6.	Do you play an instrument?	No, I don't.
7.	Does your father work in York?	Yes, he does.
8.	Does your mother like York?	Yes, she does.
9.	Do your parents like it here?	Yes, they do.

7.

1.	Where do you live?	I live in …
2.	When do you get up in the morning?	I get up at …
3.	When does your mother get up?	She gets up at …
4.	What do you have for breakfast?	I have … for breakfast.
5.	Why don't you like cornflakes?	I don't like them because …
6.	When do your parents leave the house?	They leave the house at …
7.	When do they come home again?	They come home again at …
8.	How do you get to school?	I get to school by …
9.	Why don't you take the bus?	I don't take it because …
10.	What do you do in the afternoon?	In the afternoon, I …
11.	What games do you like?	I like …
12.	What do you do in the evening?	In the evening, I …
13.	When do you go to bed?	I go to bed at …
14.	When do you switch off the light?	I switch off the light at …
15.	When do your parents go to bed?	They go to bed at …

8.

Where does Mike live now?

What doesn't he like?

How does he go to school?

When does his mother drive him to school?

What does his mother do?

When does he leave the house?

Where does he usually arrive at 8.30?

Where does he have lunch?

Why does he have lunch at school?

When does he often go to see Tom?

When does the first lesson begin?
When does he get up?
What does he leave at a quarter to eight?
What do they play together until 6 or 7 o'clock?
What do they do?
Where does Mike go then?

9.

1. When do you get up?
2. When do you start work?
3. When do you leave the house?
4. What do you drive?
5. Who do you collect from the villages?
6. Where do you take them?
7. When does school start?
8. When do you fetch them?
9. Where do you take them?
10. What do you clean then?
11. What do you often find in the bus?

Test

1.

He goes …
She writes …
He uses …
He teaches …
She does …
She sees …
He closes …
He carries …
He loses …
This sounds …
He throws …
He loves …
She brushes …
He empties …
She wears …
He wants …
He takes …
He ties …
He misses …
He chooses …
She flies …

2.

have – listen – does – make – talks – shows –find – talk – knows – have – listens – tries

3.

When do you usually get home?
What do you usually do after school?
Do you like going to the cinema?
What kind of films do you like?
Do you often go to the cinema?
When do you do your homework?
How much time do you need for it?

10 *Simple present* und *present progressive*

1.

This is Dad. He is sitting in the bus.
This is Dad again. He is cleaning the bus.
This is our house. We live there.
This is Mum. She is leaving the house. She always leaves at 8.
This is our garden. Look! Mum is working in it. She likes her garden.
This is our corner shop. Mum works there. She is selling something.

2.

1. Mike usually gets up at 7, but today he is still in bed. He is still sleeping.
2. He usually has breakfast at 7.30, but today he is still lying in bed.
3. He often has no time to wash, but this morning he is taking a bath.
4. He usually puts on his school uniform, but today he is wearing different clothes.
5. He usually has lunch at school, but today he is having lunch at home.
6. Mike usually helps his mother, … His father is washing the dishes.
7. His parents usually leave the house … They are going for a walk.
   Do you know why? Well, it's Sunday.

3.

Mögliche Antworten:
On Sundays I usually get up late/go for a walk/do my homework.
On Sundays I often watch TV/ring up my friends/play football/write letters.
On Sundays I sometimes help/Mum and Dad/brush my shoes.
On Sundays I never clean my room/clean my bike/go to school/learn English.
On Sundays I always play computer games/listen to CDs/go to Church.

4.

Mr Mason usually gets up at seven o'clock. Then he washes and has breakfast. After that he gets in his car. He opens his surgery at 8.30. He examines sick animals between 9 and 12. Then he has lunch at a restaurant. At 5 p.m. he usually has a cup of tea. He closes the door of his surgery at 5.30. He usually comes home at 6.

5.

Mögliche Antworten:
I get up at …, then I wash and have breakfast. Then I go to school. I usually come home at … In the afternoon I first …, then I … After that I … In the evenings I usually … I go to bed at …

6.

First they break the eggs and put them in a bowl.
Then they add some milk, salt and pepper.
Then they stir the eggs.
Next they put fat in the frying pan.
Then they put everything in the frying pan.
After that they cook the eggs in the frying pan.
Then they put the scrambled eggs on a plate and eat them.

7.

1. is shining – are still sitting
2. always have – is still missing – is sleeping
3. goes – opens – sees – tries – doesn't listen – goes back – tells – is still sleeping
4. says – doesn't want
5. fetches – goes – is shouting

Test

1.

a) Mike is taking a picture of his new school. He likes taking pictures. He often takes pictures.
b) He doesn't only take pictures of schools, he takes pictures of everything. Here he is taking a picture of Tom and Jenny.
c) He always puts his pictures in an album. Look! He is putting a picture in his album now.
d) He has already got a lot of albums. He keeps them in his room.
e) He often shows his pictures to his friends. Here he is showing an album to Tom.

2.

likes – learns – likes – wakes up – sits up – listens – is playing – jumps – rushes – switches – turns – goes – is sleeping – hears

11 Verneinung, Fragen und Kurzantworten

1.

Lösungsvorschläge:

I think Jenny doesn't begin to cry.

I think she must laugh.

I think she writes a letter, too, and shows it to her neighbours.

I think Jenny is very unhappy.

I think she begins to cry and must leave the classroom.

I think she is very angry with him.

2.

Mögliche Antworten:

1. That's wrong. Good pupils aren't silly.
2. That's wrong, too. Some of them do, but others don't.
3. That's wrong again. Some of them are bad at sports, but not all of them.
4. This is right. Good pupils usually don't forget their homework.
5. That's wrong. Sometimes they forget things, too.
6. That's wrong. Some of them make their teachers angry, too.
7. That's wrong again. Good pupils talk in lessons, too.
8. That's wrong. Some of them have a lot of friends, others don't.
9. That's wrong. There are good pupils who don't talk to their teachers.
10. That's wrong. Good pupils aren't unhappy, but sometimes bad pupils are.
11. That's wrong again. Good pupils are interested in other things, too.
12. That's wrong. There are good pupils who go out with their friends, too.
13. That's wrong again. Some of them do, but others don't.
14. That's wrong again. Also good pupils don't know everything.

3.

- Are you often alone?
- Do you like your parents?
- Have you got any friends?
- Have you got any hobbies?
- Do your parents often play with you?
- Have you got anybody to talk to?
- Do you watch a lot of TV?
- Are most of your teachers nice?
- Are you often afraid when you are alone?
- Are your parents often out in the evening?

4.

- Can you sit still?
- Do you talk all the time?
- Can you listen?
- Do you listen only when your teacher gets angry?
- Do you often forget things?
- Do you do your homework?
- Do you find everything boring?
- Do you often sleep during lessons?
- Are you often late?
- Are you often ill for tests?
- Do you only like sports?

5.

1. Do you like school?
2. Do you often forget your homework?
3. Are you doing your homework now?
4. Is your mum helping you now?
5. Do your parents often help you?
6. Have you got nice teachers?
7. Do they like you?
8. Do they give you a lot of homework?
9. Can you talk during lessons?
10. May you eat chewing gum in the English lessons?
11. Have you got a school magazine at your school?
12. Do you read it?
13. Do you find it interesting?

6.

1. No, it isn't.
2. No, it isn't.
3. No, he isn't.
4. No, they aren't.
5. Yes, they are.
6. Yes, he is.
7. Yes, he does.
8. Yes, they are.
9. Yes, he is.
10. Yes, they do.
11. Yes, they do.
12. No, it isn't. It's a motorbike.

7.

1. What building ...?
2. How high ...?
3. What is ...?
4. Who are ...?
8. Who is running away ... ?
9. Why are they ... ?
10. Who are the two men?
11. Where is ....?

5. What is leaning ...?
6. How many people ...?
7. What are they ... ?
12. Who is ...?
13. What is ... ?

8.

1. Who doesn't know the building?
2. What is very high?
3. What is leaning against the wall?
4. Who is running away?
5. Who is running to a bike?
6. Who is running after them?
7. Who wants to catch them?
8. Who hasn't got a uniform on?
9. Who is afraid of him?

9.

1. Who is Tom's girlfriend?
2. Who is from Leeds?
3. What have they got?
4. Who is sometimes strict?
5. Who can't always see Tom? – Who can't she always see?
6. Who must she tell where she is going? – What must she tell her parents?
7. Who must be back early? – When must she be back?
8. When mustn't she be out?
9. What is ringing?
10. Who is at home? – Where is Tom?
11. Who is Jenny ringing up?
12. Who is very excited? – What is she?

10.

What have you got?
What is it?
What do you like?
What must you buy for it?
Where must I come?
What must I lend you?
What do you want to buy?
What is very bad?
Who can't you understand?

11.

1. How old is he?
2. Where does he sleep?
3. When do you usually get up?
4. What do you do then?
5. What does he usually have for breakfast?
6. When do you take him for a walk?
7. When do you go for work?
8. Where do you take him then?
9. How long does he stay there?
10. Where do you play?
11. What do you try to teach him?
12. What do you do in the evening?
13. What films does he like?
14. Why does he like westerns?
15. What does he do when he sees them?
16. Why is he barking now?

Test

1.

a) Jenny hasn't got a cat, she's got a hamster.
b) She doesn't keep it in her bedroom, she keeps it in a cage downstairs.
c) It doesn't sleep in her bed, it sleeps in its cage.
d) Jenny needn't talk to it a lot because it's not a budgie.
e) Tom needn't catch mice for it because it's not a cat.
f) She doesn't take it to school because her teachers don't like that.

2.

a) Yes, I have/No, I haven't.
b) Yes, I do. No, I don't.
c) Yes, … has/No, nobody has.
d) Yes, they do/No, they don't.
e) Yes, you must.
f) No, I needn't.
g) No, it needn't.

3.

a) Who has got a boyfriend? What has Jenny got?
b) Whose photo is on the wall? Where is his photo?
c) Who likes her? Who does he like?
d) Who likes him? Who does she like?
e) Who likes him, too? Who do they like?
f) Who is in the same class? Where are they?
g) Who often goes home together? Where do they often go together?
h) Who often rings her up? Who does Tom often ring up?
i) Who is sometimes happy? What are they sometimes?

12 Zeitformen zur Wiedergabe der Zukunft

1.

1. I think the weather will be nice.
2. I don't think it will rain.
3. I hope we'll spend a nice day together there.
4. I hope the water won't be too cold.
5. If the water isn't too cold, we'll go for a swim.
6. I hope you'll have a good time.

2.

Mögliche Antworten:

If the coach is late, they won't leave at 8 o'clock.
If it rains all day, they won't go to the beach.
If the sun doesn't shine, they won't go for a swim.
If some of the children are late, their teacher will be angry.
If their teacher is ill, there will be no excursion.
If there is too much traffic, they will be late.

3.

	Mögliche Antworten:
When will we be there?	We'll be there at …
Will we need a warm pullover?	Yes, you will/No, you won't.
Will you buy us an ice cream?	Yes, I will/No, I won't.
Will we have lunch on the beach?	Yes, we will/No, we won't.
Will we play games on the beach?	Yes, we will.
Will we go back by bus or by train?	We'll go back by bus.
What games will we play?	We'll play …
Will we be allowed to walk around on our own?	No, you won't.
Will we have time enough to go shopping?	Yes, you will.
When will we be back?	We'll be back at …
Will our maths teacher come with us?	Yes, he will/No, he won't.

4.

She hopes that the weather will be nice.
She hopes that it won't rain.

She hopes that she won't get a cold and fall ill.
She is sure that they will have lots of fun.
She hopes that her friends will go, too.
She is sure that they will see a lot of interesting things.
She thinks that her pocket money will be enough.
She hopes that there won't be too many teachers.
She hopes that there won't be any homework for the next day.

I hope the bus won't have a breakdown.
I hope our teachers will leave us alone.
I hope we won't have to visit that terrible museum.
Perhaps I'll find a nice present for my friend.

5.

Lösungsvorschläge:

When they are on the beach, they will take off their clothes/they will play games/they will go for a swim/they will look for shells/they will splash their teacher with water/they will have a picnic on the beach/they will be very noisy/they will run around/they will rush into the water

6.

Catherine: I'll buy something to drink, too.
Helen: I'll buy some, too.
Jim: Then I'll talk to her, too.
Ronny: Well, then I'll have a sandwich, too.

7.

1. work
2. she is going to help her
3. going to invite him
4. is going to write him
5. are going to buy her a new bike.
6. What is she going to do? Well, she is going to clean it.
7. is going to go
8. is going to spend

8.

1. What are you going to do about your tests, Kate? Are you going to work harder?
2. What are you going to do, Jenny? Are you going to help Kate?
3. What are you going to do, Kate? Are you going to invite Ben?
4. What are you going to do, Helen? Are you going to write Ben?
5. What are your parents going to do, Linda? Are they going to buy you a new bike?
6. What are you going to do with your room, Betty? Are you going to clean it?
7. What are you going to do in your holidays, Mary? Are you going to go to the seaside?
8. What are you going to do there? Are you going to spend your holidays there?

9.

1. If the weather is fine, we'll play in the garden.
2. I think everybody will like that.
3. But I hope Ben won't come. I'm not going to invite him.
4. Perhaps Jenny will help me.
5. I hope Tom will help me with the lemonade. I will ask him when I see him.
6. Who is going to buy/will buy all the rest?
7. Well, I'll ask Mum ... Perhaps he will be tired when he gets back.

10.

1. We won't write it before next Monday. I think I'll start next Sunday.
2. I'll ask my father.
3. What will it be about? I think I'll have to ask John.
4. I don't think it will be very difficult. And I'm quite sure he will help me this time, too.
5. I'll be terribly nervous on Monday.
6. I'm not going to miss it. I won't go to school.

Test

1.

Mögliche Antworten:

a) Then I'll do it for you.
b) I'll clean it for you.
c) I'll carry it for you.
d) I'll give/lend you some.
e) I'll look for it.
f) I'll try to find them/I'll look for them.
g) Oh, I'll kiss her for you.

2.

a) Tomorrow we will write an English test.
b) I hope it won't be too difficult.
c) I hope my neighbour will help me.
d) Perhaps I'll get a good mark then.
e) I'm going to ask her tonight if she wants to help me.
f) If she helps me, I'll give her a bar of chocolate.
g) But I'll only give it to her if I my mark is good.
h) If my mark is bad, I'll eat the bar of chocolate myself.

3.

Mögliche Antworten:

I'm going to play football/help Mum/play computer games/go for a walk ...

I'm not going to go to school/play with my teddy/work for school/see my teacher ...

Das *present perfect* 13

1.

lived, carried, said, showed/shown, caught, brought, left, spent, written, kept, spoken, read, heard, given, played, lain, felt, thought, told, bought, stood, taken, found, known, made, begun

2.

pay, choose, lose, throw, feed, sleep, wear, teach, fall, drop, try, buy, meet, run

3.

- They have booked a place for July.
- They have written to the local tourist office.
- They have had a look at the road map.
- They have tried to find out the best route.
- They have begun to check their caravan.
- They have bought a new bottle of gas.
- They have checked the tyres.
- They have repaired the rear window.

4.

We have washed the caravan, but we haven't cleaned the floor yet.
We have cleaned the windows, but we haven't made the beds yet.
We have put in some food, but we haven't bought a new frying pan yet.
We have put in Timmy's toys, but we haven't bought a new picture book yet.
We have taken Tom's tennis racket, but we haven't bought new tennis balls yet.
We have told the neighbours to look after the flowers, but we haven't given them a key yet.

5.

Have you bought a new picture book for me?
Have you put it in the caravan?
Have you packed my swimming things?
Have you taken away my pencils?
Have you found my red toy car?
Have you put my telephone in the caravan?
Have you seen my teddy?
Have you bought some chocolate?

6.

Mrs Mason: Yes, I have.
Mrs Mason: Yes, I have.
Kate: No, I haven't.
All: Yes, we have.
Timmy: No, I haven't.
All: No, we haven't.
Timmy: No, we can't.

7.

Mögliche Fragen:

Have you ever been to a caravan site?	No, I haven't. I have never been to a caravan site.
Have you ever cleaned a caravan?	No, I haven't. I haven't cleaned a caravan yet.
Has your father ever had an accident?	No, he hasn't. He hasn't had an accident yet.
Has your sister ever been to England?	No, she hasn't. She hasn't been to England yet.
Have your friends ever slept in a caravan?	No, they haven't. They have never slept there.

8.

1. The Masons have already packed everything.
2. They have given the key of their house to their neighbours.
3. They have put all their things in the caravan.
4. They have left York today.
5. They have already done 100 kilometres.
6. But they have not arrived at their camping site yet.
7. They have all enjoyed their trip so far.
8. They are sure they have never had such a nice trip.
9. Timmy has not been sick again yet.
10. He has not had anything for lunch.
11. But he has already been on his potty four times.

9.

Jenny has kissed him goodbye.

He has found them again.

They have packed everything.

Somebody has forgotten to shut it.

Test

1.

I have woken up.

I have got out of bed.

I haven't washed.

I have had breakfast.

I have taken my dog for a walk.

I have hurried to school.

I haven't been late.

I have tried to listen.

I haven't made much noise.

I have come here.

2.

Mögliche Fragen:

What has happened?

Have you had an accident?

Have you lost your money?

Have you written a bad test?

Have you seen your English teacher?

Have you got up on the wrong side of the bed?

Has your girlfriend left you?
Have you not had/haven't you had breakfast?
Has Sandra tried to kiss you?

3.

a) Mike has never been a good worker.
b) He has never liked working.
c) He has always had two left hands.
d) He has nearly never cleaned his room himself.
e) Has he already cleaned his room today?

14 Das *simple past*

1.

Regular verbs: visited, tried, laughed, tried, sounded, stopped, laughed
Irregular verbs: did, went, found, had, wasn't

2.

Irregular verbs: say, lead, read, buy, write, sit, feel, catch, set, ride, swim, think, feed, leave, fall, meet, fly, let, break, bring, lose, get, teach, pay

3.

said, played, carried, flew, bought, caught, fell, stopped, left, thought, let, taught, paid, led, sat, lost, wrote, set, fed, met, read, felt, rode, made, heard, broke

4.

Before they left, they checked their car.
They put a good map in it.
They packed their things.
They locked the doors.
They shut the windows.
They switched off all lights.
They said goodbye to their neighbours.
They looked up the route they wanted to take.

5.

wanted – was – got – was – wanted – was – knew – was – were –saw – was – got – went – shut – came – wanted – got – carried – were – heard – got – ran – was – arrived – was – were

6.

They finally left at 10 o'clock. Their first stop was at 11.30 because Timmy was sick. At 1 o'clock they had lunch, but when they left, they forgot Timmy's teddy. At 2 o'clock they got into their car again and drove on. They arrived at 6 o'clock at the camping site. There they tried to put up a tent for Tom, but it collapsed. They had supper at 8. At 9 they all went to bed because they were very tired.

7.

The first night Timmy did not sleep very well. He didn't have his teddy and it was not quiet enough at the camping site. At home he didn't sleep in the same bed with Kate. She didn't leave him enough room and she didn't want him in "her" bed. So Timmy wasn't warm enough. He didn't have nice dreams and was not happy that night.

8.

Did you sleep well tonight?	No, I didn't.
Did you miss your teddy?'	Yes, I did.
Was it quiet enough?	No, it wasn't.
Did you sleep with all that noise?	No, I didn't.
Did Kate leave you enough room?	No, she didn't.
Were you warm enough?	No, I wasn't.
Did you have nice dreams?	No, I didn't.
Did you like your first night here?	No, I didn't.

9.

Lösungsvorschläge:

The first day, they didn't get up early. They had a late breakfast.
Timmy was not sick any more. He felt better.
Tom wrote a letter to Jenny.
Kate looked for new friends.
Mrs Mason didn't do any work.
They didn't stay in the caravan that day.
They didn't lie on the beach, but went for a walk.
They didn't cook in the caravan, but had lunch in a restaurant.

10.

Mögliche Fragen:

What's the matter, Kate?
What happened?
How did it happen?
Did anything happen to Timmy?
Did he break anything?
Did he cry?
What did Tom do?
Where is Timmy now?

11.

Why didn't Timmy see the stone?
Where did the accident happen?
Did Timmy break his arm?
Did he cry a lot?
How did he look?
Was he sick?
Did they call a doctor?
When did the doctor come?
What did she tell them?
Did Timmy have to go to hospital?

12.

- Did it hurt, Timmy?
- How did the accident happen?
- Why didn't you see the stone?
- Did you fall on your arm?
- Did you cry?
- When did you come here?
- Was your teddy all right?
- Who helped you?
- Was anybody with you?

13.

1. couldn't
2. had to
3. didn't have to
4. were allowed to
5. couldn't
6. wasn't allowed to
7. was allowed to

14.

- He didn't have to make his bed.
- He was allowed to play with his teddy.
- He was allowed to draw pictures with his right arm.
- He didn't have to cook his meals.
- He didn't have to clean the room.
- He didn't have to stay in bed all day.
- He wasn't allowed to play in the corridor.
- He was allowed to look at his picture book.
- He had to be careful with his arm.
- He was allowed to talk to the nurses./He could talk to the nurses.
- He wasn't allowed to run around in the room.
- He wasn't allowed to stand on his right arm.
- He had to eat his meals.
- He had to keep his arm still.

15.

Lösungsvorschläge:

- Did you have to make your bed? No, I didn't.
- Were you allowed to draw pictures with your right arm? Yes, I was.
- Did you have to cook your meals? No, I didn't.
- Did you have to stay in bed all day? No, I didn't.
- Did you have to keep your arm still? Yes, I did.
- Were you allowed to look at your picture book? Yes, I was.
- Were you allowed to play with your teddy? Yes, I was.
- Could you talk to the nurses? Yes, I could.
- Were you allowed to run around in the room? No, I wasn't.
- Were you allowed to stand on your right arm? No, I wasn't.
- Did you have to eat your meals? Yes, I did.
- Were you allowed to play in the corridor? No, I wasn't.
- Did you have to be careful with your arm? Yes, I did.

16.

were allowed – didn't have to – wasn't allowed – didn't have to stay – had to be – wasn't allowed – wasn't allowed – had to take – didn't have to worry – had to look

17.

Lösungsvorschläge:

The last time I was ill, I wasn't allowed to go to school. I had to stay in bed all the time. My friends were not allowed to see me …

18.

Did you have to go there with your parents?

Did you stay at a hotel?

Did you have to sleep in a tent?

Did you have to take your German books with you?

Were you allowed to stay up late?

When did you have to go to bed?

Did you have to help your parents?

What did you have to do?

Did you make any friends there?

Were there other girls?

Why didn't you kiss them?

Were they nicer than Jenny?

What was the weather like?

Were you happy that you were back?

Test

1.

a) I didn't sleep very well.
b) My sister always took my blanket away.
c) She always kicked me.
d) I was very tired, but I couldn't sleep.
e) And it was very cold.
f) Some people were very loud outside.
g) They shouted and played games.
h) I missed my teddy.
i) And I had a bad dream.
j) It was about my teddy.

2.

My teddy was all alone in the house. Everybody was gone. He felt very lonely and there were big tears in his eyes. Why had they all left him? … It was dark and dusty there and he couldn't see a thing. And there were noises in the room, noises he didn't know. And they came nearer and nearer. He felt that there was somebody or something watching him. What was it? Suddenly he saw two green eyes and felt something touching him, something that was cold and slimy. He tried to run away, but something kept him back …

3.

Where did they go?
What did they enjoy?
Who played a lot of games?
What did Timmy read?
When did they go for long walks?
Where did they go for long walks?
Who did they watch?
What did Mr Mason and Tom do?
What did they tell everybody?

Simple past oder *past progressive?* 15

1.

1. First Tom sent Kate back to their parents.
2. So Kate ran back to the caravan and told her parents all about Timmy's accident.
3. Then Mrs Mason phoned a doctor.
4. When the doctor arrived, she examined Timmy. After that she called an amulance.
5. When the ambulance arrived, the ambulance men put Timmy on a stretcher. Then they carried him inside. After that they drove him to the hospital.

2.

Tom and Kate wanted to go to the beach, so I asked Mum if I could go there, too. First she did not want, but then she said yes. So I told Tom to wait for me. I went into the caravan and fetched my teddy. They walked very fast, so I had to run. There was a big stone in my way, but I didn't see it. So I fell over it and broke my arm. I didn't let go my teddy, but held it in my hand. I felt a pain in my leg. Then Tom and Kate came, but I don't know what happened then …

3.

Lösungsvorschläge:

When poor Timmy broke his arm,

- his father was smoking and talking,
- his mother was lying in the sun,
- his parents were just having breakfast,
- his parents were just getting up,
- his mother was writing a letter,
- nobody was looking after him.

4.

When Timmy had his accident,

- a woman was reading a magazine,
- a man was lying in a deckchair,
- some people were swimming,
- two children were playing with a ball,
- a boy was listening to the radio,
- a girl was putting on her clothes,
- a family was having a picnic.

5.

I was playing football when I fell to the ground and broke my arm.

I was climbing a rock when I slipped.

I slipped when I was having a shower. I broke three ribs.

I was cleaning the windows, when the ladder broke. I fell onto the floor.

I was lying in my deckchair when it collapsed.

While I was doing my homework, I fell asleep. I fell off the chair.

6.

had to be – couldn't go for a swim – had to keep him busy – often read ghost stories – was – wanted – came – was not shining – was raining – sounded – entered – filled – was – came – saw – heard – opened – saw – fell – were

7.

Timmy was lying in his bed. His teddy was sleeping beside him. Suddenly the door opened and somebody came into his room. When he opened his eyes, he saw that a dark figure was standing in front of his bed. It was looking at him. Then it sat down on his bed. A cold hand touched his face. He woke up with a loud cry. The lights went on. His mother was standing in front of him. "Are you dreaming, Timmy?" she said.

Test

1.

- The sun was shining. It wasn't raining.
- Some people were playing games.
- Other people were talking to each other.
- People were eating or having something to drink.
- Children were laughing and shouting.
- Some people were swimming in the sea.
- Others were lying in the sun.
- People were putting on their clothes or taking them off.
- Some people were going home.

2.

a) When Timmy came home, a big surprise was waiting for him.
b) A new picture book was lying on the table.
c) When Timmy saw it, he immediately opened it and began to "read".
d) While he was reading, his parents unpacked his things.
e) When they came back, Timmy was sleeping.
f) Mr Mason took him in his arms and carried him upstairs into his room.
g) There he put him in his bed.
h) Timmy did not wake up; he was dreaming of doctors, ghosts and other things.

Simple past und present perfect

1.

1. We came back yesterday.
2. I often went swimming.
3. I met Mike in the holidays.
4. I got to know a German boy.
5. I talked a lot of German.
6. We had an accident.
7. I didn't do any homework in the holidays.
8. I ate too much in the holidays.
9. I have become really fat.
10. We visited a lot of castles in the holidays.

2.

In the holidays we visited Carisbrooke Castle. Carisbrooke Castle is an old castle. It is famous, too, because Charles I was a prisoner there … People say that he hasn't found peace yet and that his ghost is still walking there.

When we came there, the sky was very dark. When we walked through the entrance, it began to rain. So we went into the castle, but it was very dark in there, too. There were lots of strange noises. Suddenly a door opened. When I looked there, I saw something green. It was coming towards me. I ran out of the building and told everything to my parents. They didn't believe me. They just laughed at me.

After the holidays were over, we had to go home again. The first night I went to bed early, but woke up at midnight. There was a strange noise again. I saw something green. It was sitting at my desk and was writing something in an exercise book. I was very afraid and did not move. Five minutes later it was gone. I got up and went to the desk. There I saw my German exercise book. It was open and there was a note in the book. It ran: … This is what the ghost told me and that's why I did not do any homework last Tuesday.

3.

This was our hotel. We stayed there for two weeks.
We always went swimming there.
We had an accident. We haven't repaired our car yet.
We visited the castle. Did you know that Charles I was a prisoner here?
I played with him a lot. We often went to the beach and had a swim together.
And that girl over there is his sister. We played with her sometimes.

4.

1. When did you come back?
2. Where did you go?
3. Did you like your stay there?
4. Have you ever been to Italy?

5. Did you do anything for school as our teacher told you?
6. Did you play tennis in the holidays?
7. How many postcards did you write?
8. Where did you buy these shoes?
9. What was the weather like? Did it rain a lot?
10. Have you already seen Mike?

5.

Mögliche Antworten:

I couldn't do my homework because
- my neighbour was ill.
- I left my book at school.
- my mother/father/sister was ill yesterday.
- I felt so ill in the afternoon.
- my pen did not work.
- I forgot my school bag.
- my exercise book was full.
- I had to repair my bike.
- my mother had no time to help me.
- I couldn't open my school bag.
- my printer didn't work.
- my computer broke down.

I can't show you my homework because
- I have left it on the bus/at home.
- I have forgotten my school bag.
- my baby brother/sister has ruined it.
- my baby brother made a plane out of it.
- somebody has stolen it.

Test

1.

a) I put the luggage in the car.
b) Then we all got into the car.
c) We had to stop at a traffic light.
d) Somebody crashed/bumped into our car.
e) We all got out of the car.
f) Nobody was injured.
g) But our car was damaged.
h) Then we had to wait for the police and couldn't drive on.

2.

Tom:

Did you get my letters?/Have you got my letters? I wrote the last one two days ago. But tell me, when did you come back? How did you like London?

Jenny:

I got your other letters, but I haven't got the last one yet. How many letters did you write? I came back two days ago.
Well, I liked it, but my aunt was terrible sometimes. She just thought that I was a small baby. She always said that I was too young to look after myself. And she didn't like your letters, Tom.

Tom:

Didn't she like my handwriting?

Adjektive

17

1.

Mögliche Antworten:

My friend? He is tall and thin, but he is very strong, too.
My friend? She is fat and small, but she is exciting, too.
My sister? She is nice and funny, but she can be difficult, too.
My brother? He noisy and fat, but he but he can be nice, too.
...

2.

Mögliche Antworten:

The boy/girl I'd like to meet should be clever/intelligent/interesting/funny ...
He/she shouldn't be boring/difficult/stupid ...
My dream boy/dream girl should be intelligent/funny/nice ...

3.

Mögliche Antworten:

Comics are boring/interesting/wonderful/exciting/fantastic ...
Films are boring/funny/interesting/exciting/wonderful ...
Books are interesting/exciting/wonderful/fantastic/funny...
Football is exciting/boring/fantastic/dangerous/interesting/difficult ...
TV is boring/bad/exciting/fantastic/dangerous/interesting ...
English tests are wonderful/fantastic/exciting/funny/interesting ...
Boys are exciting/dangerous/wonderful/clever/intelligent ...
Teachers are loud/boring/dangerous/strange/crazy ...
Baby brothers/sisters are loud/fat/noisy/boring ...
Pop music is beautiful/fantastic/wonderful/loud ...

4.

a funny girl	–	a boring girl
an old town	–	a new/modern town
a small boy	–	a tall boy
a good mark	–	a bad mark
a boring film	–	an interesting/an exciting film
a fast runner	–	a slow runner
a bad driver	–	a good driver
a slow worker	–	a fast worker

a clever pupil	–	a silly pupil
a quiet boy	–	a noisy boy
a happy child	–	an unhappy child
a difficult test	–	an easy test
a silly person	–	a clever/an intelligent person
a terrible story	–	a nice story
a rich man	–	a poor man
a dirty room	–	a clean room

5.

bad, worse, the worst; beautiful, more beautiful, the most beautiful; good, better, the best; boring, more boring, the most boring; busy, busier, the busiest; careful, more careful, the most careful; crazy, crazier, the craziest; exciting, more exciting, the most exciting; fantastic, more fantastic, the most fantastic; noisy, noisier, the noisiest; fat, fatter, the fattest; loud, louder, the loudest; modern, more modern, the most modern; poor, poorer, the poorest; powerful, more powerful, the most powerful; quick, quicker, the quickest; slow, slower, the slowest; strange, stranger, the strangest; tall, taller, the tallest; small, smaller, the smallest; thin, thinner, the thinnest; strong, stronger, the strongest; worried, more worried, the most worried; nice, nicer, the nicest; clever, cleverer, the cleverest; intelligent, more intelligent, the most intelligent; funny, funnier, the funniest; heavy, heavier, the heaviest; dangerous, more dangerous, the most dangerous, interesting, more interesting, the most interesting; wonderful, more wonderful, the most wonderful; difficult, more difficult, the most difficult

6.

Mögliche Antworten:

Tom's dad is the tallest in the family. He is taller than Grandpa and he is taller than Mum/his wife. Tom is the tallest of the children. Kate and Timmy are smaller than Tom. Timmy is the smallest of them all.

7.

Susan: I think tennis is more difficult than swimming.
Betty: No, it isn't, but it's more expensive.
Susan: More expensive? I think swimming is as expensive as tennis.

Susan: I think English is nicer than German.
Betty: No, it isn't, but it's more useful.
Susan: More useful? I think it's as useful as English.

Susan: I think comics are funnier than books.
Betty: No, they aren't, but books are more interesting than comics.
Susan: More interesting? I think comics are as interesting as books.

8.

... I think he's the tallest boy in our class.
... No, I think David is taller than him.
... He must be the strongest boy ...
... He is even nicer than Tom.
... It has got the same colour as your hair.
... or you'll get a prize for the silliest question.
... I need somebody who is cleverer than Tom. You know, at maths Tom is even worse than me.
... He looks a bit silly, but perhaps he is better at maths than he looks.
... Anne told me his photos are the best photos she has ever seen.
... Then they must be good. She always thinks she's the nicest girl in our class.

9.

1. Has your English become better?
2. Let's hope it hasn't become worse.
3. Is the number of mistakes in your English tests smaller or bigger than before?
4. Were the exercises very boring?
5. Were they more interesting than in your textbook?
6. Were they as boring as in your textbook?
7. Or were they worse?
8. Was the grammar clear enough?
9. Or was the grammar in your textbook easier?
10. We hope that you didn't find things too difficult.

Test

1.

a) York is one of the oldest cities in England.
b) It was, together with London, the most important town in Roman times.
c) York has many monuments. It has ... the largest medieval Cathedral in Northern Europe.
d) The Jorvic Viking Centre is one of the most interesting museums ...
e) It is the biggest railway museum in the world.
f) It offers one of the most beautiful sights in Northern England.

2.

a) New York is much bigger than York.
b) York's population isn't as mixed as New York's population.
c) York is much older than New York.
d) New York's history isn't as old as York's, but it's certainly as interesting.
e) New York's climate is different. It's much hotter in summer and much colder in winter.
f) There is more money in New York today than in York. Most people are richer, but there are also many people who are poorer.

18 Adverbien

1.

1. She dances well.
2. He runs fast.
3. She sings beautifully.
4. She does everything quietly.
5. He always runs around noisily.
6. She works hard.
7. She always answers cleverly.
8. He always laughs happily.
9. She dances terribly.
10. He speaks German very well.

2.

Lösungsvorschläge:

a) I can speak English very well. I also play football very well. I am a good worker and do my homework very carefully. My teachers think that I'm very intelligent; I always answer cleverly and do things intelligently. I understand things easily, too.

b) My friend is a bit slow. He does everything very slowly, but he does things carefully. He doesn't speak English very well, but he is very good at maths. He often writes very badly, so I can't read it very easily. Sometimes he is a bit boring, but he sings wonderfully.

3.

quietly – silly – thick – red – excited – quiet – angrily – afraid – quickly – slowly – good – carefully – quickly – ready – slowly – sure

4.

1. Lots of windows were still open.
2. Some pupils were running around excitedly …
3. Others were still quietly packing their things.
4. One pupil was busily copying his homework … He wasn't even writing very fast.
5. He didn't think it was dangerous to remain in the building.
6. Some were excitedly watching the smoke …
7. Others were happy that there was a fire at their school.
8. A good fire is less boring than an English lesson, one of them said excitedly.
9. And there will be no English tomorrow, somebody else added quickly.

5.

Lösungsvorschläge:

1. Four men jumped out of it quickly.
2. Two of them ran into the building quickly.
3. They busily raised a ladder.
4. One man carefully climbed up the ladder.
5. Another man quickly fetched the water hose.
6. "Where can we take the water from?" one man asked nervously/worriedly.
7. "Where do we begin?" one man asked nervously.

Test

1.

a) When there is a fire, don't be nervous, don't run around excitedly, but keep cool and pack your things quickly.
b) Shut all windows and doors carefully ... leave the room as fast as you can.
c) ... try hard not to get excited.
d) Follow the instructions of the firemen carefully.
e) Make a good job out of a bad thing.

2.

Mögliche Antworten:

a) I was quietly sitting in the classroom ... I quickly understood the danger we were in.
b) ... managed to put out the fire quickly.
c) Teachers and pupils were running around fast/excitedly/nervously.
d) There were quite a lot of pupils who behaved stupidly.
e) I quickly ran along the corridor with the other pupils of my class; we loudly shouted ...
f) My neighbour coughed badly when the smoke got into his lungs.

19 Die Wortstellung im Englischen

1.

On Monday, I am going to play table tennis with Tom at 4 p.m.

On Tuesday, I am going to watch a film on TV at 8.15 p.m.

On Wednesday, I am going to learn for a German test with Tom after school.

On Thursday, I am going to help Kate with her maths homework at 6 p.m.

On Friday, I am going to buy a birthday present for Sarah at 5 p.m.; then I am going to ring her up.

On Saturday, I am going to go to Sarah's birthday party at 2 p.m.

On Sunday, I am going to ring up Tom and go for a walk with him at 4 p.m.

2.

1. Today I am ill.
2. Today I needn't get up.
3. Today I can stay in bed.
4. Today I needn't go to school.
5. Today I needn't do any homework.
6. Today I have got no German.
7. Today I have got a temperature.
8. Today is a beautiful day.

3.

Did I give it to you, Christine?

Perhaps you gave it to Sandra.

Can any of you lend me some money?

I've already lent some to Tom.

You can have your chips and bring me your money tomorrow.

I won't forget to give it back to you.

4.

There are pupils

- who usually forget their homework.
- who have never forgotten their homework.
- who often do their homework at school.
- who have never copied it from their neighbours.
- who never know what they must do.
- who never write down what they must do.
- who always forget their homework at home.
- who usually do it on the way to school.
- who sometimes leave their exercise book at home.
- who sometimes forget it on the bus.

5.

Mögliche Antworten:

1. I usually do my homework/Yes, I do.
2. I usually/always do it in the afternoon/in the evening/in the morning.
3. I usually do it at home/on the bus/at school.
4. I don't usually forget it/No, I don't.
5. I sometimes forget it when I have got no time/when I don't think of it.
6. I never copy it from my neighbour/No, never. I only sometimes copy it from him/her.
7. No, I'm not. I usually play with my neighbour or talk to him/her.
8. No, they needn't. They needn't often help me/Yes, they must. They must often help me.
9. He/she must often help me in …
10. Yes, he/she has/No, he/she hasn't. He/she has never helped me.

6.

1. English pupils already go to school when they are five.
2. Most English pupils go to a comprehensive school when they are eleven.
3. They can leave school when they are 16.
4. In many schools they must wear school uniforms.
5. The school colours in Tom's school are blue and grey.
6. The pupils' parents can buy the school uniforms in special shops.
7. In most English schools lessons begin later than in Germany.
8. Most English pupils also have lessons in the afternoon.
9. There are lessons also in the afternoon, so many English schools have school cafeterias.
10. Pupils can have lunch in the school cafeteria during lunch break.
11. In many English schools pupils learn to cook.

7.

Mögliche Antworten:

Before I go to school, I usually do my homework.
When I don't want to go to school, I tell my mum that I am ill.
When it's too cold to get up, I stay in bed.
When I am late, I don't have breakfast.
When I must do my homework, I ask my friend to help me.
When I must go to bed, I still read an hour or two.
Before I get up, I often think that it is too early to get up.
Before I have breakfast, I usually wash.
When I go to bed, I switch off the lights.
When I can't find my homework, I get angry.

Test

1.

a) Today I'll play football. I usually play football on Fridays.
b) On Mondays, I sometimes go to the cinema.
c) After school, I often go to Tom.
d) What we do there? We usually play games or do our homework.
e) No, we seldom play with Kate.
f) When I'm at home, I often watch TV.
g) Yes, I usually do.
h) If my parents are often out? ... sometimes they are and sometimes they aren't.
i) I always go to bed at 10.
j) I usually get up at 7.
k) If I'm often late? I'm never late.

2.

a) As you know, German schools are different from English schools.
b) Pupils usually start school at the age of 6 or 7.
c) In Germany lessons start earlier than in England.
d) In most cases German schools are no all-day schools.
e) German pupils usually have lunch at home.
f) Most German schools have no school cafeterias.
g) So German pupils don't spend so much time at school.
h) They usually are at home in the early afternoon.

Philip Hewitt

Englisch

Grammatik

7./8. Schuljahr

Inhalt

Vorwort

Liebe Schülerin, lieber Schüler,

dieses Buch macht dich **fit in englischer Grammatik.** Es bietet dir einfache Erklärungen, vielfältige Übungen und Tests, um deine Leistungen in diesem Fach zu verbessern. Vor dir liegt das gebündelte Wissen zur englischen Grammatik vom 5. bis zum 8. Schuljahr – greif zu! Zunächst werden die **wichtigsten Themen** der Schuljahre 5 und 6 bearbeitet; dann folgen die Schuljahre 7 und 8.

Mit diesem Buch kannst du den aktuellen Unterrichtsstoff mitlernen oder Inhalte aus vorangegangenen Schuljahren nachschlagen und festigen. Nimm es einfach immer wieder zur Hand und bearbeite einen Abschnitt daraus. Die folgenden Zeichen helfen dir bei der Orientierung:

Lies zunächst die **Regeln** und **Tipps**.

In zahlreichen **Übungen** kannst du die Regeln und Tipps dann anwenden.

Zusammenfassungen bieten dir einen Überblick über dein Wissen.

Mithilfe der **Tests** am Ende eines Kapitels kannst du kontrollieren, ob du alles verstanden und behalten hast.

Bei vielen Aufgaben hast du die Möglichkeit, deine Lösungen sofort ins Buch einzutragen. Für die anderen lege dir ein **Trainingsheft** an. Die richtigen Lösungen aller Aufgaben findest du am Ende eines Buchteils. Ob du nun Stoff wiederholen oder dich auf eine Klassanarbeit vorbereiten möchtest – dieser Band wird dich Schritt für Schritt zum Ziel führen und bringt dir maximalen Durchblick, maximalen Erfolg und maximale Sicherheit.

Und jetzt kann's losgehen!

1 Simple present oder present progressive?

Progressive form (Verlaufsform):
He **is cycling** to school.

Simple form (einfache Form):
He **cycles** to school.

Warum heißt es einmal *is cycling* und das andere Mal *cycles*?
In diesem Kapitel erklären wir dir den Bedeutungsunterschied zwischen *present progressive* und *simple present* und üben die richtige Anwendung der beiden Formen.

Der Gebrauch des *simple present*

Wann benutze ich das *simple present* ?

Diese Form wird verwendet:

1. für Einzelhandlungen – besonders Gewohnheiten –, die bisher regelmäßig in der Vergangenheit ausgeübt wurden und vermutlich in der Zukunft ausgeübt werden – nur nicht gerade im Augenblick.
   Signalwörter (Häufigkeit): never, always, sometimes, often, seldom, rarely, every day/week/month/year usw.
   He **is often** late home. We **rarely go** to Brighton.
   He **always cycles** to school. She **visits** me **every week.**

   Achtung: Achte auf die Stellung der Häufigkeitsadverbien im Satz: vor einem Vollverb, aber nach dem Verb *to be.*

2. für Gewohnheiten längerer Dauer, Gefühle, Vorlieben, Abneigungen, Besitz usw., die keine Einzelhandlungen sind:
   She **lives** in Glasgow. They **own** a big house.
   I **love** ice-cream. He **hates** potatoes – he **prefers** rice.

Dear Pen-friend,
My name is Pat and I live in Carlisle. Carlisle is a town on the border between England and Scotland. It's near the sea.
My family – my parents, my little sister Cindy and I – live in a small house near the town centre.
My mother works at a supermarket. My father is a bus-driver.
He hasn't got a job at the moment. There is a lot of unemployment in our part of Britain and it is difficult to find work.
I go to the local comprehensive school and my sister goes to the junior school next door. My hobbies are skateboarding, swimming, football and playing computer games. What kind of sports do you like?
My full name is Patricia, but I hate it and everyone calls me Pat. I don't know your name because this is my first letter to you. Our teacher says she will send all our letters in one envelope.
I hope that your letter is a bit longer than mine! Tell me where you live, what you do in your free time and something about your family.

Yours,
Pat McLaren

1.
Mache zwei Spalten und ordne die Sätze des Briefes zu:

Simple Present *(einfache Form)*	Auxiliary Verbs *(Hilfsverben:* be, have, can *usw.)*
I **live** in Carlisle.	My name **is** Pat.
…	…

2.

Was kannst du über dich und deine Familie oder deine Freunde sagen? Bilde zehn Sätze aus folgender Schalttafel:

My Uncle .../Aunt ...	lives	
I	work	
My brother(s)/sister(s)	works	to ...
My mother/father	go	at ...
My best friend	goes	in ...
Some of my friends	live	

3.

Setze die in Klammern stehenden Wörter in die Sätze ein.

1.	(ever)	Do you go to London?
	(often)	We go to London Airport to see the planes.
		And what about you?
	(every week)	We go shopping there.
2.	(never)	We buy "The Sun".
	(always)	But "The Times" is very interesting.
3.	(rarely)	I have time to read a daily newspaper, but
	(sometimes)	I buy a weekly paper.
4.	(regularly)	Do you go to a disco at the weekend?
	(seldom)	I have time – especially at the weekend.
	(often)	At the weekend I go to the cinema.
5.	(every day)	Does she walk to school?
	(often)	No, I see her at the bus-stop.
	(always)	She takes a 49 bus to town.

4.

Ergänze die Sätze wie im Beispiel. Vergiss die *s*-Endung bei *he, she,* und *it* nicht!

Beispiel: "I go to Windsor Comprehensive School." – "What about your sister?"
"She goes to Windsor Comprehensive School, too."

1. "We live in Windsor." – "What about your Uncle Jeff?"

____

2. "Jenny goes swimming every Friday." – "And Paul?"

____

3. "I like ice-cream." – "What about your brothers?"

____

4. "They play football on Saturdays." – "And you?"

____

5. "My teacher speaks French." – "What about his wife?"

____

6. "I often do the washing-up at home." – "And the cooking?"

____

7. "Jean plays the piano well." – "What about her friend Sheila?"

8. "Melanie and Jason fly to Spain for their holidays every year." –

   "And their mother?"

____

9. "Patrick cleans his room every week." – "And his bike?"

____

10. "The cats often sit beside the fire." – "What about the dog?"

____

Der Gebrauch des *present progressive*

Diese Zeitform wird verwendet:

1. für Handlungen, die gerade im Augenblick passieren.
   Signalwörter: now, at the moment usw.
   She **is watching** TV at the moment.
   John isn't here. He**'s cycling** to school.
   Look, the bus **is coming.**

   Beachte die Schreibweise: sit – sitting; come – coming

2. für Handlungen, die in einem längeren gegenwärtigen Zeitraum ablaufen und als vorübergehend empfunden werden.
   Signalwörter: this year/season/week, at present
   Michael **is working** in London this year.
   This week my sister **is speaking** English all the time with our guest from England.

   (Das *present progressive* kann auch verwendet werden, um zukünftige Handlungen auszudrücken. Näheres dazu findest du auf S. 50).

The new boy

"Who's that new boy in your class?"
"You mean Christian? His name's Christian Meier. He comes from Germany but his father is working over here in England for a year. He's a teacher at our school."
"So where is the family living now?"
"In the house where the Jenkins normally live. Mr Jenkins, our German teacher, is working in Germany for a year. He and his family are living in the Meiers' flat in Dresden."
"I see. Does Christian speak good English?"
"His English is quite good. He only speaks German at home, of course, because hardly anyone at our school learns German, worst luck!"
"Why? – Don't you like French?"
"French is OK, but French grammar is difficult."
"German grammar isn't easy, either. We're learning German at our school. All those endings! It's terrible!"

"Well, Christian says that English is easier for him than Russian was."
"Did he have Russian at school?"
"Only for one year. Then they changed to English. Why don't you come to the youth club this evening. You can talk to Christian there."
"Good idea."

5.

a) Trage alle Sätze, die im *simple present* bzw. im *present progressive* stehen, in die jeweilige Spalte ein. Sätze mit Hilfsverben (*to be, to have* usw.) lässt du bitte aus. Kürze die Sätze ab (z.B. "*Does he learn English?*" statt "*Does Christian Meier learn English at school?*").

Simple Present	Present Progressive
…	…
…	…

b) Schreibe kurz auf, warum die einfache Form oder die Verlaufsform benutzt wurde. Du kannst bei den Regeln auf den Seiten 8 und 12 nachschauen.

6.

Schau dir die Bilder an und schreibe auf, was im Augenblick gerade passiert:

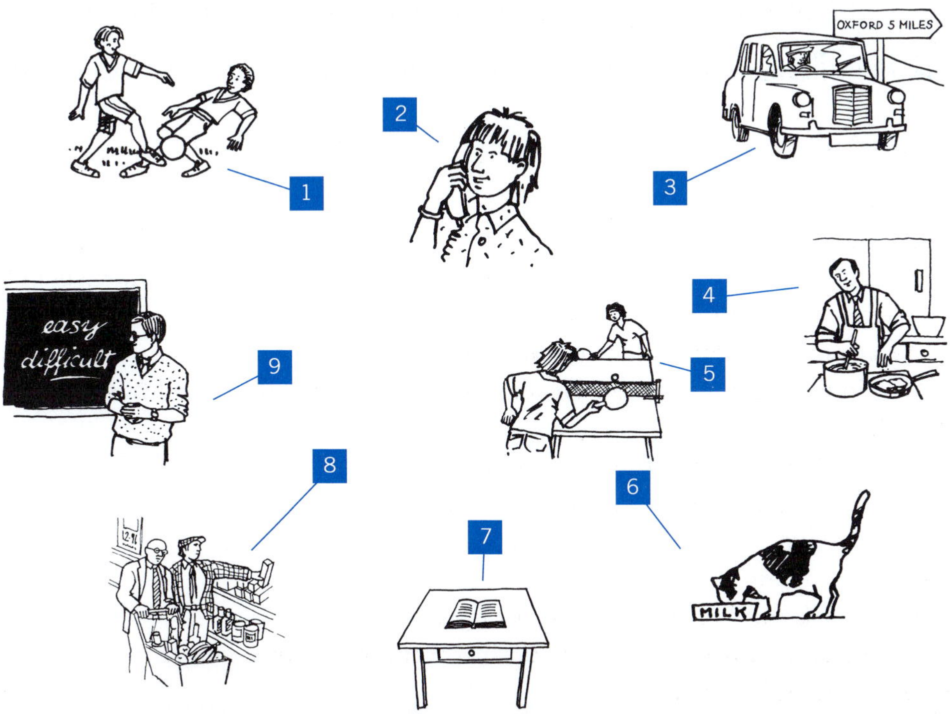

7.

Jetzt sollst du zeigen, dass du die beiden Formen richtig anwenden kannst. Wir fangen ganz einfach an. Bei dieser Übung musst du nur die (notwendigen) Satzteile zusammenfügen, damit zwei richtige Sätze entstehen. Die Signalwörter helfen dir dabei.

1.	Now Sometimes	Sylvia	is doing her homework. does her homework in the garden.		
2.	We	never	are smoking smoke	now. cigarettes.	
3.	Do you Are you	speaking speak	English	often? now?	
4.	He	doesn't isn't	sitting sit	there	every day. now.
5.	They	cycle are cycling	to school	this week. every morning.	

Merke

Fragen und Verneinungen

Bei der Zeitform *simple present* brauchen wir bei Fragen und Verneinungen die entsprechenden Formen von *to do.*

Aussage	**Verneinung**	**Frage**
I live in Bristol.	I don't live in London.	Do you live here?
She lives near me.	She doesn't live there.	Where does he live?

Bei Sätzen mit Hilfsverben brauchen wir *to do* bei Fragen und Verneinungen nicht:

Aussage	**Verneinung**	**Frage**
I'm waiting for the bus.	He's not waiting for the bus.	Is he waiting for the bus?
I've got my ticket.	I haven't got my ticket.	Have you got yours?

Auch bei Sätzen mit *to be* als Vollverb wird *to do* in Fragen und Verneinungen nicht benötigt:

Aussage	**Verneinung**	**Frage**
He's here.	He isn't here.	Is he here?

8.

Kannst du Fragen (?) bzw. Verneinungen (X) nach folgendem Muster bilden?

Beispiel:

He speaks French.	(you ?)	→ Do you speak French?
We live in London.	(they X)	→ They don't live in London.
She likes ice-cream.	(What – you ?)	→ What do you like?

1.	They are English.	(X German)
2.	I live in Berlin.	(Where – you ?)
3.	We like ice-cream.	(they X)
4.	John reads comics.	(his sister Sheila X)
5.	Peter is writing a letter.	(Who ... to ?)
6.	He often writes letters.	(X postcards)
7.	I've got a bike.	(she ?)
8.	We can speak German.	(X Welsh)
9.	My brother works in London.	(Where – your sister ?)
10.	These books cost £6.	(How much – those CDs ?)
11.	They are waiting for a bus.	(Which bus ?)
12.	He's upstairs in his room.	(What – do – there ?)

9.

Eine letzte Übung! Hier musst du nicht nur die richtige Verbform (*simple present* oder *present progressive*), sondern auch ein zur Situation passendes Verb einsetzen. *Good luck!*

1. "Hi, Paul. Is your sister Alex at home?"
   "No. She's in town. She _________ some new shoes.
2. She always _________ to town on Wednesday afternoons.
3. Can I _________ her a message?"
4. "Yes. Would you and Alex _________ to come to my party on Saturday?"
5. "Thank you, Jim. I'd love to come, and I'll ask Alex when she _________ back.
6. Can we _________ you at home this evening?"
7. "Well, we often _________ swimming on Tuesday evenings."
8. "What time _________ you usually _________ back home after your swimming?" – "About eight." – "OK, I'll ring you after eight."

Zusammenfassung

The present tense: simple and progressive forms

Simple

Formen:
I/we/you/they **live** here.
He/she/it/Phil/Tania **lives** here.

I/we/you/they **don't live** in London.
He/she/it/Phil/Tania **doesn't live** in London.

Do I/we/you/they **come** from London?
Does he/she/Phil/Tania **come** from London?

Verwendung:
Gewohnheiten, Zustände, Tatsachen

Signalwörter:
always, never, sometimes, often, usually, every week/month/day/year usw.

Progressive

Formen:
I **am** stay**ing** here for a week.
He/she/it/Phil/Tania **is** stay**ing** here for a week.
We/you/they **are** learn**ing** French.

I**'m/am not** learn**ing** Spanish.
He/she/it/Phil/Tania **isn't** learn**ing** French.
We/you/they **aren't** wait**ing** for anyone.

Am I interrupt**ing** you?
Is he/she/it disturb**ing** you?
Are you/we/they wait**ing** for someone?

Verwendung:
Handlungen, die
- im Augenblick des Sprechens ablaufen.
- in einem länger andauernden gegenwärtigen Zeitraum ablaufen und als vorübergehend betrachtet werden.

Signalwörter:
now, at the moment, at present

Test

Note 6!! Sabine hat überall Fehler gemacht! Kannst du ihre Sätze korrigieren?

1. I learn English at the moment.

   ____

2. She are rarely going swimming.

   ____

3. My father is owning a big car now.

   ____

4. Lives John in Stuttgart?

   ____

5. My friend Peter is come to my house every week.

   ____

6. He do not know the answer.

   ____

7. Where do you going now?

   ____

8. I like not ice-cream.

   ____

9. On Mondays I am always arrived late at school.

   ____

10. Are liking you potatoes with your meat?

    ____

2 Simple past oder past progressive?

... very fast I guess!

Wie im *present tense* gibt es auch im *past tense* eine einfache Form (z. B. *jumped*) und eine Verlaufsform (z. B. *were driving*). Da es im Deutschen diese Unterscheidung nicht gibt, werden bei der Verwendung von *simple past* und *past progressive* häufig Fehler gemacht.

Simple past und *past progressive* im Vergleich

Wann verwende ich *simple past*?

Bei Situationen in der Vergangenheit, wo

1. eine Tatsache festgestellt wird:
   It **was** the first day of the summer holidays.
   Tania **didn't live** in the country.
2. eine Einzelhandlung von kurzer Dauer ausgedrückt wird:
   Tania **woke** early.
3. eine Reihe von aufeinander folgenden Handlungen in der Reihenfolge des Geschehens aufgelistet werden:
   Tania **jumped** out of bed, **ran** to the window, **pulled back** the curtains, **opened** the window and **looked** out across the garden.

Wann verwende ich *past progressive*?

Bei Situationen in der Vergangenheit, wo eine oder mehrere Handlungen über längere Zeit stattfinden:
The sun **was** already **shining** brightly through the window of her bedroom, and the birds **were singing**.

Beide Formen können miteinander kombiniert werden. Die Handlung in der Verlaufsform bildet den „Hintergrund" zu dem Ereignis im *simple past.*
Tania suddenly **realized** that she **was** not **lying** in her own bed at home in London.

Diese Unterscheidung gibt es im Deutschen nicht. Deshalb ist es wichtig, die richtige Zeitform im Englischen zu wählen.

Verben, die nur kurze Handlungen ausdrücken und solche, die keine Handlungen, sondern Zustände, Besitzverhältnisse, Meinungen usw. ausdrücken, können nicht in der Verlaufsform verwendet werden.

Beispiele: to see, to hear, to break; to be, to become, to like, to hate, to have, to owe, to own

While wird oft zusammen mit der Verlaufsform, *when* dagegen mit der einfachen Form benutzt.
While I **was waiting** for the bus, I **heard** an explosion.
I **was waiting** for the bus when I **heard** an explosion.

1.
Beschreibe deinen Tag. Mach's ganz einfach am Anfang. Bilde drei oder vier Sätze in einer Handlungskette: "I got up at 7.45, washed, got dressed ..."

In einem zweiten Durchgang kannst du dann einige Hintergrundhandlungen in den Tagesverlauf einbauen: "While I was walking to school I saw ..."

Hier solltest du mindestens fünf Sätze bilden können. Auf die Plätze, fertig, los!

a) get up – have a shower – get dressed – have breakfast;
leave house – walk – arrive – talk to friends;
have English/PE/German – play in playground – write test;
go home – have lunch – do homework – watch TV/a video – listen to CD/music – go to bed
b) While I was ...-ing ... I saw/spoke to/listened to ...

2.

Setze die in Klammern stehenden Verben in die jeweils richtige Form. In dieser Übung kommt jede Verbform in jedem Satz einmal vor.

Beispiel: (talk – ring) While we … to John the phone … .
While we were talking to John the phone rang.

1. (see – wait) I … an accident while I … for my train.
2. (get – fall) A young man … off the train when suddenly he … onto the platform.
3. (run – lie) Several people … over to help him because he … still … there when the train left.
4. (be – examine) A woman who said she … a doctor … him when my train arrived.
5. (leave – sit) I looked out of the window and just as my train … the young man … up.
6. (bake – go) I … a cake when the light … out.
7. (look – come) While I … for some candles the light … on again.
8. (have to – wait) I … finish the cake quickly because my friends … for it.
9. (be – give) It … a birthday cake, and one of my friends … a birthday party at his house.
10. (put – ring) I … the cake into a bag when the doorbell … .
11. (go – stand) I … to the door and opened it. Two of my friends … at the front door.

Alles richtig gehabt? Wunderbar! Fehlerquote über 25%? Schau dir in diesem Fall die Regeln nochmals an, bevor du weitermachst.

3.

Diese Übung ist etwas schwieriger. Es gibt nämlich keine Gewähr, dass jede Verbform einmal vorkommen muss. Je nach Zusammenhang kann zweimal die *simple form* oder die *progressive form* notwendig sein.

1. (be – arrive) It … a stormy night when Jenny … at Norwich Station.
2. (rain – blow) It … hard and a strong wind … .
3. (remember – not have) As she got off the train she … that she … an umbrella.
4. (go – phone) So she … into the station and … her friend Paul.
5. (get – ring) Paul … into the bath when the phone … .
6. (hear – get) As soon as he … the phone, Paul … out of the bath.
7. (take – wrap) He … a towel and … it round his waist.
8. (want – ring) Just as Paul … to pick up the phone, the doorbell … .

9. (drop – walk) He … the phone on a chair and … to the door of his flat.
10. (go – hear) He … just … into the hall when he … the sound of water on the bathroom floor.
11. (run – turn) He … into the bathroom and … the water off.
12. (open – stand) Then he … the front door. His friend Stan … in the rain.
13. (tell – come) "Hi, Paul," said Stan. "Is Jenny here yet? She … me she … to visit you."
14. (be – ring) "Perhaps that … her on the phone," said Paul. "I wanted to answer the phone when you … the doorbell. Come in."
15. (walk – pick) He … back into the living-room, but when he … up the phone, there was no one there.
16. (be) Jenny … already on her way to the flat in a taxi.

4.

Was macht Tania auf dem Bauernhof ihres Onkels? Kannst du die Geschichte erzählen – natürlich unter Verwendung der richtigen Verben und Zeitformen? Jedes Verb darf nur einmal benutzt werden.

say, see, want, give, talk, answer, come, work, have, drink, arrive, sit

While Tania and her Uncle Jonathan … breakfast, Jethro … . Jethro … on Uncle Jonathan's farm. Jethro … down at the table and Uncle Jonathan … him a cup of tea. Aunt Helen … into the kitchen while they … their tea. "Good morning, Jethro," she … . "I … you in the village yesterday. You … to Joe Smith the policeman. What … he … to talk to you about?" "I'm afraid I can't tell you, Mrs Brown," Jethro … "It's a secret."

Merke

while und *during*

Das wichtigste Signalwort für die *past progressive*-Form ist *while* (während).
While Tania was staying with her uncle and aunt, she met Jethro.

During heißt ebenfalls „während". Es wird aber nicht mit einem Verb, sondern mit einem Substantiv verwendet.
During her holiday/stay with her uncle and aunt, Tania met Jethro.

Weil es für beide englischen Wörter im Deutschen nur ein Wort gibt, kommt es oft zu Verwechslungen.

5.
Setze das richtige Wort – *while* oder *during* – in die Sätze ein.

1. ... my holidays I learnt to windsurf.
2. ... Jean was having breakfast, the telephone rang.
3. I met Mr Jones ... he was staying with our neighbours.
4. In Britain, they usually play football ... the winter.
5. ... we were playing basketball, the other pupils were doing a class test.
6. I read an interesting book ... the flight to London.
7. ... the first week of his stay in Britain he visited a lot of interesting places.
8. ... my brother was asleep, I went into his room and borrowed his walkman.

6.
Schreibe die Sätze um, indem du das jeweils andere Wort (*while* statt *during* und umgekehrt) einsetzt.

Beispiel: While I was staying at Brighton ...
During my stay at Brighton ...

1. While we were driving through the forest, we saw several bears.
2. During his walk in the park he got very wet.
3. I went to Bristol while I was staying in England last summer.
4. She phoned her boyfriend during her lunch break.
5. While we were performing "Hamlet", there was a fire in the school hall.
6. During our flight to New York the weather got worse.
7. The fans screamed all the time during the Rolling Stones' concert.
8. We stopped five times during our drive to Scotland.
9. While he was taking his exams, he lost about two kilos.

7.

Schau dir jetzt die Bilder an, und schreibe zu jedem Bild einen Satz, der meist – aber nicht immer – eine einfache und eine Verlaufsform enthalten wird.

1

while – play football – rain

2

when – have a bath – telephone ring

3

while – wait for the bus – read newspaper

4

when – girl wash hair – friend arrive

5

while – boys play cards – teacher enter

6

when – arrive at the hotel – sun set

7

while – watch TV – boy wash up

8

when – bus arrive – girl get on

9

while – postman deliver letters – dog attack/bite

Zusammenfassung

The past tense: simple and progressive forms

Simple	Progressive
Formen:	**Formen:**
I/we/you/he/she/they **saw** him.	I/he/she **was** sitt**ing** in the garden. We/you/they **were** watch**ing** TV.
I/we/you/he/she/they **didn't talk** much.	I/he/she/it **wasn't** listen**ing.** We/you/they **weren't** wait**ing** for anyone.
Did I/we/he/she/it/you/they see the rainbow?	**Was** I/he/she/it wait**ing**? **Were** you/we/they listen**ing**?
Verwendung: Gewohnheiten, Zustände, Tatsachen, Einzelhandlungen und Handlungsketten in der Vergangenheit	**Verwendung:** Handlungen in der Vergangenheit von längerer Dauer
Signalwörter: yesterday, last week/month/year, when usw.	**Signalwörter:** while, during, at that time usw.

Meist bildet die Verlaufsform eine „Hintergrundhandlung“:

I **saw** my English teacher while I **was standing** at the bus stop.

Achtung!
Folgende Verben können nicht in der *progressive form* stehen
- Verben, die nur kurze Handlungen ausdrücken: *to see, to hear, to break* etc.
- Verben, die Zustände, Besitzverhältnisse, Meinungen usw. ausdrücken: *to be, to become, to like, to hate, to have, to own* etc.

Test

Erinnerst du dich an Jethros Geheimnis (Übung 4)? Was war es? Du bekommst es heraus, wenn du die richtigen Ausdrücke aus dem Kästchen in die Geschichte einsetzen kannst! Pass aber auf! Das Kästchen enthält mehr Wörter, als du brauchst, und du darfst jeden Ausdruck nur einmal benutzen!

while	during	were visiting		was seeing	when
were deciding	was ringing	watched		looked	saw
has been	was	visited	rang	decided	noticed

Sunday __________ Aunt Helen's birthday. On Saturday evenings, Aunt Helen and Uncle Jonathan usually __________ friends. Tania stayed at home that Saturday evening and watched TV. She was hungry, so she made herself a couple of sandwiches __________ one of the breaks. __________ she was watching a film, the doorbell __________. She was alone in the farmhouse, so she __________ out of the window before she opened the door. Joe Smith the policeman was standing outside! When she __________ that Jethro and five or six other people were with him, she thought that something must be wrong! She opened the door. "Don't worry," said Jethro __________ he saw her anxious face. "This is our surprise for your Aunt Helen. Your aunt told me that she and your uncle __________ Mr and Mrs Jenkins down in the village tonight. So we __________ to have a little party with a few more friends. After all, they won't be back until nearly midnight – and your aunt's birthday starts then!"

3 Simple past oder present perfect?

Warum schaut der Kleine wohl so verblüfft? Tja, verständlicherweise kann er sich nicht vorstellen, dass seine Oma **seit** 7 Jahren in diese Schule **geht** – das hat sie nämlich behauptet, als sie *present perfect (I've been)* als Zeitform wählte! Wir empfehlen dir, dieses Kapitel genau anzusehen, um derartigen Missverständnissen vorzubeugen ...

Der Gebrauch des *simple past*

Wann verwende ich das *simple past*?

Das *simple past* ist immer die richtige Form, wenn der Satz eine Zeitangabe in der abgeschlossenen Vergangenheit enthält.

Wichtige Signalwörter: yesterday, last Monday, last night, in 1994, two minutes ago, in December usw.

Zeitbestimmungen wie: when I was young; as soon as she arrived; when we lived in Birmingham

I **saw** Tina at school yesterday. (einmalige Kurzhandlung)
She **got** up, **washed, had** breakfast ... (Handlungsfolge)
We **lived** in London for ten years when I was a boy. (längerer Zustand)

1.

Wie wär's zunächst einmal mit einem Kreuzworträtsel? Setze die richtigen *simple past*-Formen in die Sätze ein. Wenn du Probleme hast, schlag einfach in einer Liste der unregelmäßigen Verben nach.

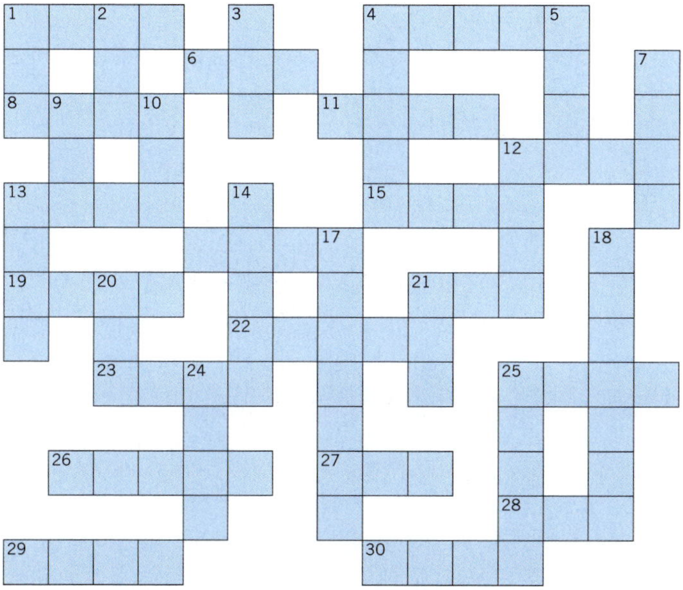

Across:

1. We ... late for school.
4. He said "Hello" and I ... his hand.
6. Her dog ... me in the leg.
8. The choir ... a folk song.
11. She slipped on a banana skin and ... heavily.
12. We ... across the river.
13. They ... to bed at midnight.
15. She ... her jeans on a sharp nail.
16. The hunters ... the fox.
19. The sun ... at 5.40 a.m.
21. He ... at the table reading a book.
22. The car-thief ... a brand-new Jaguar.
23. Tania ... early that morning.
25. He walked out and ... the door behind him.
26. Mr Smith cleaned the kitchen table and ... the floor.
27. The dog ... the bone in a hole in the ground.
28. She ... on her best clothes and went to the party.
29. After six whiskies he ... ill.
30. I ... my passport last week. I couldn't find it anywhere.

Down:

1. What ... his name?
2. The boys ... home quickly.
3. She ... the fire at 6.30 p.m.
4. He ... his name "Greene" with an "e" at the end.
5. The teacher ... the answers to our questions.
7. He knocked at the door and ... into the room.
9. He never ... fish and chips.
10. They ... married last year.
12. I ... her a ticket for the concert last week.
13. She never ... dresses – always jeans and T-shirts.
14. We had a choice of colours, so we ... a green one.
17. I ... about getting a job, but I finally decided to stay at school.
18. She ... me some flowers from her garden.
20. They ... the film last month.
21. His mother took out some plates and ... the table for tea.
24. Our teacher ... our exercise books for over a week. He said he had been too busy to mark our homework!
25. I was so tired that I ... until midday.

2.

Ergänze mit der Vergangenheitsform des Verbs aus dem ersten Satzteil.

Beispiel: Sally White lives in London now, but when she was a girl she lived in Bristol.

1. Usually Sally gets up early, but yesterday morning she … up late.
2. She sometimes takes an hour to get ready for work, but yesterday she only … twenty minutes.
3. She seldom goes to work by car, and yesterday she … to work by bus, as usual.
4. Normally Sally does not run to the bus stop, but on that day she … as fast as she could.
5. There are always a lot of people on the bus to work, but this morning there … only about ten.
6. The bus-driver usually drives quite fast, but yesterday he … slowly.
7. Sally often sees friends on the bus, but on that day she … no one she knew.
8. Sometimes people speak to her on the bus. Yesterday nobody … to her.
9. "I don't know what's wrong with everybody this morning," she thought. But when she arrived at work she … she had made a mistake.
10. The bank where Sally works stands on the corner of a street. Sally … in front of the locked door for a minute or two before she realized what was wrong. Yesterday was Sunday.

3.

a) Schreibe die *present perfect-* und *simple past-*Formen in zwei Spalten auf. Prüfe die Richtigkeit deiner Lösungen, bevor du weitermachst.

Joe: "Did you see Andy Wilson at the pub last night?"
Jethro: "No, I haven't seen him for days. Was he at the pub last night?"
Joe: "He hasn't been at the pub since last Saturday. He's been away all week."
Jethro: "What did you want to see him about, Joe?"
Joe: "Someone stole three or four sheep from Farmer Hunt's field one night last week."
Jethro: "What makes you think that Andy stole them?"
Joe: "Well, he's the only person in the village who has suddenly disappeared."
Jethro: "But I've known Andy for thirty years! He's never stolen anything!"
Joe: "Well, we found two of the sheep in his barn yesterday."
Jethro: "That doesn't mean he stole them! Have you phoned his sister in London yet?"

Joe: "I didn't know he had a sister in London."

Jethro: "Maybe he's gone to visit her. He was always talking about going to London. I'll ring her tonight. And I wouldn't talk to anyone about sheep-stealing if I were you, Joe. Let's keep it a secret until we can find out more."

b) Hast du alles verstanden? Das wollen wir gleich prüfen!
Setze die Satzteile richtig zusammen.

	has never stolen	some sheep last week.
	hasn't been to the pub	about Andy's sister.
Andy Wilson	wasn't at the pub	since Saturday.
Jethro	hasn't seen Andy	last night.
Joe Smith	has known	for some days.
Someone	didn't know	Andy for years.
	hasn't phoned	Andy's sister yet.
	stole	anything in his life.

Der Gebrauch des *present perfect*

Wann verwende ich das *present perfect*?

Das *present perfect* ist auf jeden Fall richtig,

1. wenn der Satz keine Zeitangabe in der Vergangenheit enthält.
   Hier ist die Tatsache, nicht der Zeitpunkt wichtig. Vergleiche:

Present perfect	**Simple past**
– Tatsache wichtig	– Zeitpunkt/-spanne wichtig
A: **Have** you **seen** Andy?	A: **Didn't** you **see** him yesterday?
B: No, I **haven't**.	B: No, I **didn't**.
A: **Have** you **done** your homework?	A: When **did** you **do** it?
B: Yes, I **have**.	B: I **did** it before I came home.

   Eine vergangenheitsbezogene Frage mit *when?* wird immer im *simple past* gestellt, weil ja eine Zeitangabe erfragt wird.
   "**When did** you do your homework?"

2. wenn eine ausgedehnte Handlung zwar in der Vergangenheit anfängt, aber bis in die Gegenwart hinein dauert. Vergleiche:

I **have lived** here for 10 years.	I **lived** here for 10 years.
(Ich lebe hier seit 10 Jahren.)	(Ich wohnte mal 10 Jahre lang hier.)

   Im ersten Satz weiß man, dass die Person immer noch (und vermutlich bis auf weiteres) dort wohnt, während sie im zweiten Satz auf jeden Fall nicht mehr dort wohnt, sondern mal dort gewohnt hat.

3. wenn eine Handlung (egal, ob kurz oder lang) in der Gegenwart zu Ende geht. Dieser Bezug zur Gegenwart gibt der Zeitform auch ihren Namen ***present** perfect.*

Present perfect	**Simple past**
– Vollendung in der Gegenwart	– Vollendung in der Vergangenheit
She **has** just **finished** the book.	She **finished** the book last week.
They **have arrived** at last!	They **arrived** late last time, too.
Signalwörter:	**Signalwörter:**
just, at last, now, since, not ... yet, ever? *(in Fragen)*	last week, yesterday, etc.

4.

Zunächst einmal eine leichte Übung. Wähle das passende Verb und setze es in der richtigen Form des *present perfect* ein. Jedes Verb darf nur einmal benutzt werden.

look	write	see	promise	fly
go	be	get	arrive	have

a) In the school playground at 8.45 a.m.

1. " ... you ... John this morning?"
2. "No, but I ... just ... ."
3. Perhaps he ... already ... to his classroom."
4. "No. I ... already ... in his classroom. There's nobody there."

b) At the youth club one Friday evening.

5. "How's your sister Stella? She ... n't ... to the youth club for a few weeks."
6. "Didn't you know? She ... to the USA for a year.
7. She ... a job as an au-pair girl."
8. "Lucky Stella! ... she ... a letter home yet?"
9. "No, she ... n't ... time. She only left yesterday.
10. But she ... to phone as soon as she can."

Merke

just

Die Bedeutung des englischen Wortes *just* hängt davon ab, mit welcher Zeitform es benutzt wird.
Mit der *progressive form* oder mit dem *present perfect* heißt es „gerade“, „soeben“:

We were just waiting for the bus when John arrived.
You're not late. The others have only just arrived.

Mit dem *simple present* oder *simple past* heißt es „einfach“, „nur“:

I just want to know where he lives.	Ich will nur wissen ...
She just stared at me.	Sie starrte mich einfach an.

5.

Bilde Sätze, in denen das Wort *just* die richtige Bedeutung erhält.

We have just	hope you know what you're doing!
I just	shouted at me. He wouldn't listen.
She has just	gone. If you run, you'll catch her up.
He just	didn't listen to their friends' advice.
They have just	thought you might want to come with us.
We just	seen a ghost.
I have just	sold their house.
They just	received a letter from Stella.

6.

Jetzt etwas Anspruchsvolleres: Setze das vorgegebene Verb in der richtigen Zeitform ein.

1. (do?)	"What ... you ... last night?"
2. (watch)	"I ... TV until midnight.
3. (be)	There ... a good programme on BBC2 about whales."
4. (see)	"I ... many good programmes on BBC2 recently."
5. (watch?)	"... you ... the same programme?"
6. (not have)	"I ... time to watch TV last night.
7. (be)	We ... very busy lately.
8. (see)	But we ... a film about Wales last Friday. Perhaps it was the same film.
9. (show)	It ... all the tourist attractions.
10. (see?)	"... you ever ... whales?"
11. (go)	"Wales? We ... there last year.
12. (misunderstand)	"But you ... me.
13. (not mean/mean)	I ... Wales – I ... whales: w – h – a – l – e – s !"
14. (see)	"Oh! Yes, we ... several whales during our summer holidays.
15. (see?)	... you ever ... a whale in the sea?"
	"No, only on TV."

7.

Der Polizist Joe Smith möchte einige Fragen an Andy Wilson stellen, der inzwischen von seinem Besuch in London zurückgekehrt ist. Joe möchte die Fragen vorher aufschreiben, damit er nichts vergisst. Kannst du ihm dabei helfen?

Beispiel: Last Friday night – Where?
Where were you last Friday night?

1. Ever keep sheep in your barn *(Scheune)?*
2. See sheep in Farmer Hunt's field last week?
3. Ever be to London?
4. First visit to London – When?
5. Stay with sister?
6. Sister in London – How long?
7. Back to your farm – When?
8. Find sheep in barn?
9. Phone police?
10. Why not?

Ob es Andy gewesen ist? Was glaubst du?

8.

Hier bist du als Journalist gefragt. Kannst du die Informationen über den berühmten Popsänger Johnny Purple für einen Zeitschriftenartikel in komplette Sätze umformulieren? In der richtigen Zeitform, versteht sich.

★ Born 1970
☆ 1970 – 1987: London
★ 1976 – 1986: Croydon Comprehensive School
☆ 1986 – 1987: work as assistant in music shop; guitar lessons for two years
★ 1988 – now: singer in pop group "Johnny's Purple Hearts"
☆ Six singles and one CD so far
★ Three tours in Europe and America
☆ Tour to South Africa last year
★ Married Sally Johnson in 1994
☆ Divorce one year later

Zusammenfassung

Ganz wichtig für die Wahl des *simple past* ist das Vorhandensein eines abgeschlossenen Zeitraums in der Vergangenheit.

Am Nachmittag fragt man:
"**Did** you **see** John this morning?"
Der Vormittag („this morning") gilt hier als **abgeschlossener Zeitraum**.

Ist der Vormittag noch nicht vorbei, muss dieselbe Frage so lauten:
"**Have** you **seen** John this morning?"

Ein weiteres Beispiel:
"I **have been** to London."
"I **was** in London last week."

Beide Sätze können sich auf denselben Besuch beziehen. Der Unterschied liegt darin, dass im ersten Satz nur eine Feststellung (ohne Zeitangabe) gemacht wird, während im zweiten Satz der abgeschlossene Zeitraum angegeben wird.

Test

Setze die richtige Zeitform des in Klammern stehenden Verbs in folgende Sätze ein. Klammern im Satz bedeuten, dass möglicherweise – aber nicht unbedingt – ein Hilfsverb zur Zeitenbildung benötigt wird:

1. (do) "___________ you ___________ your homework yet?"
2. (do) "Yes, Mum. I ___________ it when I got home from school."
3. (tell) "That's what you ___________ me yesterday!"
4. (believe) "It was true! You just _________n't ___________ me!"
5. (finish) "Are you sure you ___________ everything before you put the TV on?"
6. (come) "Yes, Mum. ___________ Dad ___________ home from work?"
7. (arrive) "Yes. He (___________) just ___________. Why?"
8. (say) "Well, a few days ago he ___________ he would test my French vocabulary with me.
9. (have) We _________n't ___________ a French vocabulary test for about a month, but we've got one tomorrow."
10. (have) "_________n't your class ___________ a vocabulary test on Monday?"

    "Yes, Mum. But that was for German. French is tomorrow."

4 Simple present perfect oder present perfect progressive?

He has been waiting for her for 2 hours – now she has come …

Simple present perfect und *present perfect progressive* im Vergleich

Wann brauche ich die Verlaufsform des *present perfect*?

simple present perfect ⟷	present perfect progressive
I **have read** the book. You can have it back.	I **have been reading** all afternoon.
= Fertige Handlung, die zu einem unwichtigen Zeitpunkt in der Vergangenheit zu Ende ging = *present perfect* ***simple***	= Beschreibung eines Verlaufs, der bis in die Gegenwart hineinragt und auch fortgesetzt werden kann – keine abgeschlossene Handlung = *present perfect* ***progressive***

Das Unterscheidungsmerkmal zwischen einfacher und Verlaufsform ist „Tatsache" ↔ „Beschreibung".

He **lived** here all his life.	Tatsache – jetzt ist er aber tot
I **have lived** here all my life.	Tatsache – „Handlung" geht weiter
I **have been living** here **for** three weeks/**since** August 1st.	Beschreibung einer ausgedehnten Handlung, besonders mit *for/since*

Bei Verben wie z.B. *live, work, learn, wait, play, watch, listen* usw. sowie mit *for/since* wird meist die Verlaufsform verwendet.

1.

Hier eine leichte Übung nur mit dem *present perfect progressive*. Jedes Verb darf nur einmal benutzt werden.

live	stand	do	eat	learn	lie
wait	play	listen	drink	watch	work

1. "How long … you … English?" – "For two years."
2. My cousin … here since 1986.
3. We … n't … here long – only about ten minutes.
4. "Since when … your brother … at the supermarket?" – "Since last month."
5. " … Julie … tennis all afternoon?" – "Yes – since lunchtime."
6. Radio announcer: "You … to a live pop concert from the Royal Albert Hall in London."
7. "Have you seen my English vocab notebook?" – "Yes. It … on the table in the hall all week."
8. "What … you … all evening?" –
9. "We … an interesting programme about Britain on TV."
10. "How long … we … for the bus?" – "About an hour."
11. The children aren't hungry. They … crisps all evening.
12. "Someone … my juice! The carton is nearly empty!"

2.

Jetzt geht's um die richtige Form – *simple* oder *progressive*?

1. (do – work)	"What … you … all afternoon?" – "I … in the garden."
2. (do – finish)	"… you … your homework yet?" – "Yes, I … just … ."
3. (write – not post)	"… you … to your uncle?" – "Yes, but I …. the letter yet."
4. (use – not see)	"Who … my pen? I can't find it." – "I … it anywhere."
5. (be – look)	"Where … you …? I … for you all morning!"
6. (go – do)	"All the lights … just … out. What … you …?" –
7. (not do – sit)	"I … anything. John and I … in the kitchen all evening."
8. (eat – eat)	"You've got chocolate around your mouth. … you … my chocolates again?" – "Me? No – I … anything since lunch."
9. (stand – watch)	"Look at these cigarette ends on the ground under the window! Someone … here for a long time in the dark and … us through the window!"
10. (stand – think)	"I … often … here waiting for a bus." – "… you ever … of taking a taxi?"

Der Gebrauch von *for* und *since*

since ⟵⟶	for
We **have lived** here **since** 1992 (and we are still living here).	We **have lived** here **for** three years.
since = seit + Ausgangszeitpunkt: 1992 = bis heute – und bis auf weiteres	*for* = seit + Zeitspanne: X Tage/Monate/Jahre bis heute – und bis auf weiteres

Vergleiche dazu die deutsche Ausdrucksweise mit der einfachen Gegenwart: „Wir **leben** hier **seit** 1992."

for kann auch für abgeschlossene Zeiträume in der Vergangenheit benutzt werden. Dann steht es mit dem *simple past*.
He **lived** here **for** three years. (Er wohnte hier drei Jahre **lang**.)
Bei „seit" = *for/since* heißt es eben: Gut aufpassen! Und auf keinen Fall *for* mit dem deutschen „vor" verwechseln!
Er wohnte hier **vor** drei Jahren. (He lived here three years **ago**.)

3.
Schau dir das Diagramm an und vergleiche die Angaben mit den Aussagen der fünf Personen. Wer sagt was?

1. "I have lived in London for six years."
2. "I lived in London for four years."
3. "I lived in London five years ago."
4. "I have lived in London since 1998."
5. "I have lived in London since two years ago."

4.

Die englische Abkürzung *„CV“* heißt *„curriculum vitae“* (Lebenslauf). Wenn du eine Stelle suchst, musst du in der Regel einen Lebenslauf einreichen. In Vincents Lebenslauf aber fehlen die Wörter *for, since* und *ago*. Setze sie richtig ein!

I was born in London 16 years ________ but I have lived in Birmingham ________ my parents moved there in 1986. My father worked as a clerk ________ 15 years but he had to give up his office job five years ________ and has been a postman ________ 2001. My mother has worked in a kindergarten ________ I started grammar school five years ________. I have one brother aged 18 and a younger sister aged 12. I am looking for a job now. ________ May I have written to several firms. I wrote to your firm some weeks ________ but have not received any answer yet, so I am writing again. Please let me know if you have any holiday jobs left.

5.

Wie wär's mit einem *Wordsearch-Puzzle*? Die Verbformen zur Ergänzung der folgenden Sätze findest du im „Buchstabensalat“ (ein Partizip haben wir für dich umkringelt). Die anderen liegen waagerecht, senkrecht oder quer (von oben links nach unten rechts) im ganzen Block verteilt. Viel Spaß!

A	L	O	S	T	Z	B	F	B	S
S	W	P	P	Q	S	E	E	N	P
K	U	W	O	N	A	G	A	E	E
G	T	A	K	E	N	U	T	R	N
N	I	K	E	T	D	N	E	T	T
G	O	V	N	W	G	O	N	E	N
D	R	I	E	E	N	N	N	S	Y
G	A	S	P	N	N	T	S	E	M

1. John has … his English book. — 2. Have you … to your teacher yet? — 3. Who has … my umbrella? — 4. My friends have … the film twice already. — 5. Who has … all the bananas? — 6. They have all … to the open-air concert. — 7. Where have you … ? I've been looking for you everywhere! — 8. Be quiet when you go into the cinema, please. The film has already … . 9. Have you … your homework yet? — 10. They have never … a prize in the lottery yet. — 11. I've just … my mother some flowers. It's her birthday. — 12. They have … all their money.

Zusammenfassung

Present perfect: simple and progressive forms

Simple

Formen:
I/we/you/they **have seen** her.

He/she/Phil/Tania **has seen** the new film.
I/we/you/they **haven't been** there.

He/she/it/Phil/Tania **hasn't been** there.

Have I/we/you/they ever **been** there?
Has he/she/Phil/Tania ever **been** there?

Verwendung:
1. Einzelhandlungen in der Vergangenheit ohne Zeitangabe;
2. Öfter wiederholte Handlungen, die in der Vergangenheit und bis heute wiederholt wurden;
3. Einzelhandlungen, die in der Vergangenheit anfangen und bis in die Gegenwart andauern.

Signalwörter:
always, never, sometimes, often, since, for

Progressive

Formen:
I/you/we/they **have been** wait**ing** for ages.
He/she/it/Phil/Tania **has been** wait**ing** for ages.
I/we/you/they **haven't been** wait**ing** long.

He/she/it/Phil/Tania **hasn't been** wait**ing** long.

Have I/we/you/they **been** wait**ing** long?
Has he/she/it/Tania **been** wait**ing** long?

Verwendung:
Bei Handlungen und Zuständen von längerer Dauer, die sich meist bis in die Gegenwart und vermutlich auch darüber hinaus erstrecken.

Signalwörter:
for, since

Test

Setze die richtigen Ausdrücke aus dem Kästchen in die Sätze ein. Pass aber auf! Das Kästchen enthält mehr Wörter, als du brauchst, und du darfst jeden Ausdruck nur einmal benutzen.

for	since	have deserved	waited	have been walking		
been	have been arriving	walked	have been deserving			
have been waiting	have	arrived	have been sending			
send	did	didn't	arrive	sent	has	hasn't

Late for the disco

"Where ___________ you ___________? I ___________ for you ___________ half an hour!"

"Sorry I'm late. I ___________ over twenty minutes for a bus. But in the end I ___________ here. Let me sit down. I'm so tired! I feel as if I ___________ all afternoon!"

"Never mind. Sit down. If you walked all the way you ___________ a rest!"

"Where's Geoff? ___________he ___________ yet?"

"He ___________ just ___________ me an SMS. He's standing outside the wrong disco! He's been there ___________ seven o'clock. I sent him an SMS back. He'll be here in a few minutes."

5 Das past perfect

Englisch:
After he **had finished** his computer game, he **went** to bed.

Deutsch:
Nachdem er sein Computerspiel **beendet hatte**, **ging** er ins Bett.

Eigentlich wird die Vorvergangenheit – das *past perfect* – im Englischen genauso verwendet wie im Deutschen. Wenn da nicht wieder die verflixte *progressive form* wäre ... Zum Glück gelten, wie du in diesem Kapitel sehen wirst, viele Regeln für die Verwendung der Verlaufsform auch für diese Zeitstufe.

Der Gebrauch des *simple past perfect*

Die Zeitform **past perfect** (Vorvergangenheit) wird im Englischen genauso verwendet wie im Deutschen. Sie zeigt an, dass eine Handlung **vor einer anderen Handlung abgeschlossen** (= „perfekt") war.

Vergleiche: I ate my breakfast in bed and then got up.
1 2

I ate my breakfast after I had got up.
2 1

Beim zweiten Satz zeigt die Zeitform *(past perfect)* an, welche der beiden Handlungen vor der anderen passierte, und zwar ganz unabhängig von der Reihenfolge im Satz. Die Vorvergangenheit wird meist im selben Satz mit einer Handlung in der einfachen Vergangenheit (niemals im *present perfect!*) kontrastiert.

In der Reihenfolge der Handlungen kann es keine Verwechslung geben. Die *past perfect*-Form wird immer für Handlung 1 verwendet.
Oft reicht zur Kontrastierung auch ein Vergangenheitsbezug (ohne eine *simple past*-Form im Satz):
He had never been there before. – Er war nie vorher dort gewesen.

Past perfect, simple form

Die wichtigsten Signalwörter:

1. After — **After** they **had gone**, we did the washing up.
   She phoned her boyfriend **after** she **had finished** her homework.
2. Before — Besonders wenn die erste Handlung nur „theoretisch" war bzw. durch die zweite unterbrochen wurde:
   Before I **had started** breakfast the doorbell rang.
   They arrived **before** I **had finished**.
3. Because — Begründungen mit *because* stehen oft im *past perfect*:
   I moved away from Birmingham **because** I had never liked the place.

1.
Lies nun den folgenden Text durch und schreibe (in verkürzter Form) die Sätze auf, die *past perfect*-Formen enthalten.

The computer exhibition

Last week some friends and I wanted to go to the National Computer Exhibition in Birmingham. My boyfriend Geoff had read about it in a magazine and because we all had a Young Person's Railcard, we decided to take the train.
We arrived at the station early, bought our tickets, went to platform 1, got on the train that was standing there, and waited for it to start. After we had waited for about a quarter of an hour, Peter got out again and asked a porter if it was the right train to Birmingham Exhibition Centre.
The porter laughed and told us that the train to Birmingham had left ten minutes ago. The train we were sitting in was not leaving until an hour later. Geoff told the porter that the man at the ticket office had said "Platform 1", and the porter said the man had meant "the front end of Platform 1". We had got into the last coach. The train to Birmingham had been the first four coaches at the front end of the platform. They had already gone, and we had been in one of the last four coaches which had been left behind.
So we went and had a cup of coffee and waited for the next train to Birmingham Exhibition Centre.

Prüfe deine Lösung im Schlüssel, bevor du weitermachst. Hast du dir auch die eine Passivform im *past perfect* aufgeschrieben?

2.

Jetzt zur Abwechslung eine kleine Bildgeschichte zum Thema Zelten. Zu jedem Bild schreibst du einen Satz, der die vorhergehende Handlung nochmals aufgreift.

Beispiel:

Jean and Sheila decided to go camping. → After they had decided to go camping, they checked their camping equipment.

Dein erster Satz fängt also mit *„After they had checked their ...“* an. Das Verb für die nächste Handlung steht über jedem Bild.

3.

Aus zwei mach eins: Verbinde die beiden Sätze mit *after* oder *because.*
Vergiss nicht, dass die Reihenfolge der Handlungen nicht immer der Reihenfolge der Sätze entspricht. Bei Sätzen mit (x) dahinter gibt es 2 oder manchmal sogar 3 Lösungsmöglichkeiten. Schreibe sie alle auf.

1. We bought tickets. We went to the pop concert. (x)
2. They sold their house. They bought a bungalow. (x)
3. I phoned the police. My car was stolen.
4. She left school. She found a job. (x)
5. Did you go to Brighton? You visited London.

6. I phoned the number quickly and got the job.
7. The woman shouted at the girl. She burned the cakes.
8. We found out their address. We wrote them a letter.
9. He phoned his parents. He arrived in England
10. I passed my driving test. I bought a motor-bike. (x)
11. I went to the lost-property office. I lost my umbrella. (x)
12. They lost the rugby match. They drank a lot of beer. (x)
13. We came to London. We wanted to improve our English.
14. She went swimming. She bought a new bikini. (x)
15. The tourists visited the castle. They went back to their hotel.

4.

Jetzt sollst du die Sätze eigenständig zu Ende führen. Vervollständige die Sätze mit Hilfe der in Klammern stehenden Wörter. (Dies ist die Fortsetzung der Geschichte über die Computerausstellung).

Beispiele:

We (take) the next train to Birmingham after (drink – cup of coffee).
→ We took the next train to Birmingham after we had drunk a cup of coffee.
The train (stop) before we (arrive – station).
→ The train stopped before we had arrived at the station.

1. We (look) at the scenery after the train (leave – station).
2. After we (pass Rugby Station) the train (go) into a long tunnel.
3. Suddenly the train (stop) before we (reach – end – tunnel).
4. After the train (stop) the guard (come) into our coach.
5. He (want) to know if anyone (pull – emergency brake = Notbremse).
6. Nobody (said) anything because nobody (pull – brake).
7. Some passengers (be) frightened because (train – stop – tunnel).
8. After (guard – tell – passengers) that there was no need to worry, he (speak – driver – train telephone).
9. Before (guard – finish speaking) we (hear) the driver's voice over the coach loudspeakers.
10. He (tell) us that there (be) a small fault in the train's computer system but that everything (be) OK now.
11. Five minutes later the train (start to move again).

Bevor du weitermachst, prüfe nach, ob du alles richtig hast. Wenn nicht, mache zuerst deine Verbesserungen (eventuell lohnt es sich, vor der Korrektur die Regeln auf Seite 43 nochmals durchzusehen).

Der Gebrauch des *past perfect progressive*

Die Verlaufsform der Vorvergangenheit betont eine länger andauernde Handlung. Sie wird, wie alle Verlaufsformen, mit der *ing*-Form gebildet.

Vergleiche:
We went down to the beach after we **had had** breakfast.
We reached the beach after we **had been walking** for about ten minutes.

Da die Verlaufsform einen „Verlauf" ausdrückt, wird sie nicht bei Tätigkeiten verwendet, die von kurzer Dauer sind.

Vergleiche:
After we **had moved** to London, we lost contact with our friends in Leeds. (Der Umzug dauerte nicht lange.)
After we **had been living** in London for a while, we lost contact with our friends in Leeds.

Verben, die oft in der Verlaufsform stehen, sind z.B.:
to live, to work, to study, to learn, to watch **(aber nicht *to see*)**,
to listen **(aber nicht *to hear*)**, to stay, to travel, to talk

Verben, die Zustände *(to be, to become)* oder sehr kurze Handlungen beschreiben, können nicht in der Verlaufsform benutzt werden z.B.:
to start, to stop, to finish, to see, to hear, to arrive, to take, to be, to become

5.

Zuerst – wie immer – eine etwas leichtere Übung. In jedem Satz wird die *past perfect progressive*-Form des Verbs benutzt.

1. (live) "How long … you … here before you moved to London?" – "Three years."
2. (study) He started to learn French after he … English for two years.
3. (drink) People … 'Wonder-Cola' for years before scientists discovered that it was a serious danger to health.
4. (wait) The bus only arrived after the passengers … in the rain for almost an hour.

5. (work) She became the boss's assistant before she ... at the firm for six months.
6. (do) "You looked very dirty when I saw you yesterday! What ... you ... ?"
7. (dig) "I ... the garden."
8. (not play) The pop group ... long when the fire started.
9. (smoke) "How long ... she ... cigarettes before her doctor told her to stop?" – "Only about two years."

6.

Hier ist mal die einfache Form, mal die Verlaufsform des *past perfect* gefragt.

1. (write) In an interview last week, the pop star Johnny Purple said that he ... songs for many years but that he (not write) ... a really successful one since 1994.
2. (collect) My friend told me that he ... CDs since 1989 and that he ... now ... over 300.
3. (travel) He ... never ... by Underground before. After he ... for a quarter of an hour he realized he was going in the wrong direction.
4. (drive) "How long ... you ... before you had your first accident?" – "Three years – but I ... over 100,000 kilometres in that time, so it wasn't surprising!"

Prüfe deine Lösungen der ersten vier Sätze, bevor du mit den restlichen fünf weitermachst, denn hier musst du dir die Verben selbst einfallen lassen! Wenn du Probleme hattest, schau dir die Regeln nochmals gründlich an.

FOOTBALL IN THE PARK

5. We ... football in the park for half an hour when a park keeper came up and told us to stop. We told him we ... always ... football there.
6. The man said he ... as a park keeper for 25 years and that football had never been allowed in the park.
7. We just laughed. None of us knew him – none of us ... ever ... him before. He began to get angry and warned us that he would be back in five minutes. Then he began to walk away.
8. Just then an old man who ... us play came over and began to speak to the park keeper.
9. After they ... for about a minute the old man came over and spoke to us. "You can carry on playing," he said. "What about the park keeper?" I asked. "Don't worry about him!" said the old man. "He won't be back! When I was a keeper in this park 30 years ago, he and his friends played football here every day!"

Zusammenfassung

The past perfect: simple and progressive forms

Formen:
Wie beim *present perfect* wird zur Bildung des *past perfect* immer eine Form von *to have* gebraucht.

After I **had seen** the film ...	Nachdem ich den Film gesehen hatte ...
After we **had gone** ...	Nachdem wir weggegangen waren ...
After we **had been waiting** ...	Nachdem wir gewartet hatten ...

Signalwörter: after, before
Wichtigstes Signalwort für das *past perfect* ist *after.*
Before wird mit dem *past perfect* oft bei Handlungen benutzt, die nicht geschehen konnten oder noch nicht beendet waren, als sie unterbrochen wurden.

Before I had finished speaking, the people began to shout at me.

Kombinationen:
1. sehr häufig als Kontrast zu einer späteren Handlung im selben Satz, die dann im *simple past* steht.
2. seltener allein im Satz, aber auch dann nur zusammen mit Sätzen, die im *simple past* stehen.

John arrived late. The food **had been eaten** and the wine **had been drunk**. His friends **had** all **gone** home. Only a few strangers were standing around.

Indirekte Rede:
Das *past perfect* ist ziemlich oft in der indirekten Rede anzutreffen. Alle Verben, die in der direkten Rede im *simple past, present perfect* oder *past perfect* gesprochen werden, werden nach einem Einführungsverb in der Vergangenheit (*he told me, she said...* usw.) um eine Zeitstufe „nach hinten" verschoben und stehen dann in der *past perfect*-Form (siehe S. 112).

He told me that he **had had** an accident on the way to school.
She said that she **had finished** her homework.

Test

Schon wieder Note 6!! Diesmal ist es Claus, der alles falsch hat! Kannst du ihm helfen, die richtigen Zeitformen einzusetzen?

1. After I have finished my homework, I watched TV.

   ____

2. I had learnt English for two years before I had gone to Britain for the first time.

   ____

3. She finished her lunch long before I had arrived.

   ____

4. My father had driven for half an hour when he realized that he was on the wrong road.

   ____

5. He told me that he borrowed my book.

   ____

6. After he went home I saw that he forgot to take his CDs with him.

   ____

7. When he arrived I told him that he had been late.

   ____

8. I have gone out to play football with them after I had finished my homework.

   ____

9. Before I had been getting up I already had breakfast – in bed!

   ____

10. We had been walking to the station before the rain began, so we didn't get wet.

    ____

6 Zeitformen zur Wiedergabe der Zukunft

Im Deutschen spielt das Futur eine geringe Rolle. Vor allem in der gesprochenen Sprache wird es häufig durch das Präsens ersetzt: „Ich fliege nächste Woche nach Spanien“ ist geläufiger als „Ich werde nächste Woche nach Spanien fliegen“. Ganz anders im Englischen! Hier werden zukünftige Handlungen mit Verbformen wiedergegeben, die Zukunft ausdrücken. Und zwar nicht nur mit einer bestimmten Verbform, sondern mit mehreren – je nachdem, ob es sich um eine reine Absichtserklärung, eine Vermutung oder eine feste Vereinbarung handelt.

Will-future, going to-future und *present progressive*

Wie drücke ich eine Handlung in der Zukunft aus?

1. Hast du eine zukünftige Zeitangabe im Satz (z.B. *tonight, tomorrow, next week, on Monday, next month*) dann solltest du das ***present progressive*** benutzen:
   "Can you come to my party next week?"
   "I'm sorry. We**'re flying** to Spain for a week next Monday."
   („Wir fliegen nächsten Montag nach Spanien.“)

   Wie immer bei der Verlaufsform gilt auch hier: *present progressive* ist nur bei Verben möglich, die einen Verlauf ausdrücken (vgl. S. 46)

2. Handelt es sich um etwas, was man in der Zukunft zu tun beabsichtigt, ohne zu wissen, ob alles wirklich so abläuft, wie man sich das vorstellt, dann verwendest du am besten ***going to* mit dem Infinitiv**.
   Vergleiche:
   "**I'm going to stop** smoking right now!" (fester Vorsatz)
   "**I'll stop** smoking when you do!" (Versprechen bzw. Vorhersage)

3. Handelt es sich um eine Vorhersage bzw. um eine Situation, die noch nicht durch 1. und 2. abgedeckt wird, dann ist die Konstruktion mit ***will/won't*** **plus Infinitiv** richtig, z.B.:

Vorhersage:	"Snow **will fall** in many areas tonight."
Neutrale Frage:	"When **will** you **be** back?"
Spontane Entscheidung:	"I **won't** wait for Tom."
Im Hauptsatz bei Satzgefügen mit *if* und *when* im Nebensatz:	"When/If you go I'**ll go** with you."

Verwechsle das englische *will* nicht mit dem deutschen „will“:

Ich will hingehen.	I **want to** go there.
Willst du mitkommen?	**Do you want to** come with me?

1.

Lies den folgenden Dialog durch und schreibe dann die Sätze, die zukünftige Handlungen ausdrücken, in der jeweiligen Spalte auf:

Peter: What are you going to do this summer, Claire?
Claire: My parents haven't decided yet. But I expect we'll go to the seaside again.
Peter: John and I are going camping in Turkey this year.
Claire: That sounds great, but won't you need a lot of special equipment?
Peter: No. Last year we went camping in France and we had far too much in our rucksacks. We won't take more than we need this time! We're going to fly to Istanbul so 20 kilos of luggage will have to be enough.
Claire: Is John coming to the youth club tonight?
Peter: I'm not sure, but I'm seeing him after school, so I'll ask him. Why?
Claire: Well, I'm going to bring Barbara with me, and she wants to talk to John.
Peter: OK. I'll phone you when I've seen him. Will you be at home at about 6?
Claire: Yes. I'm not going to my jazz gymnastics tonight. But you needn't phone. We'll see each other at the youth club, and Barbara is going to come anyway. What about meeting at the café before we go to the club?
Peter: Good idea. I'll see you there at about half past six, then.

Neutrale Zukunft mit *will/won't*	Verlaufsform der Gegenwart mit Zeitangabe	Absicht mit *going to*
...	...	...

2.

Everything will be better in the future – so denken jedenfalls der Junge und das Mädchen in dieser Übung. Formuliere ihre Gedanken mit Hilfe der Wortvorgaben, und zwar in jeweils zwei oder drei Sätzen (positiv und negativ) nach diesem Muster:

run on batteries –
not need petrol
or diesel fuel

Cars will run on batteries.
We won't need petrol or
diesel fuel.

1

people use translation
telephones –
not learn foreign
languages

2

not go to school –
use home computers –
listen to lessons and
see them on computer
screen

3

people not
work – robots do
everything

4

have electric walkways –
not walk to school / not take
the bus – no pollution

5

secretaries not write letters
and faxes by hand – speak
into typing machines

3.

Stell dir vor, dass du eine Fahrradtour durch Nordengland geplant hast. Du erklärst einem Freund/einer Freundin, was du vorhast. Schau dir die Karte an, und beschreibe den geplanten Verlauf deiner Radtour. Benutze die folgenden Verben *take* und *cycle* zweimal, die anderen jeweils nur einmal!

Beispiel:

On the first day I'm going to take the train from London to Lancaster. Then … to Lancaster Youth Hostel.

TAKE (2 x)

VISIT   FOLLOW

WALK   CATCH

PAY

STAY   CYCLE (2 x)

NOT SPEND

CLIMB

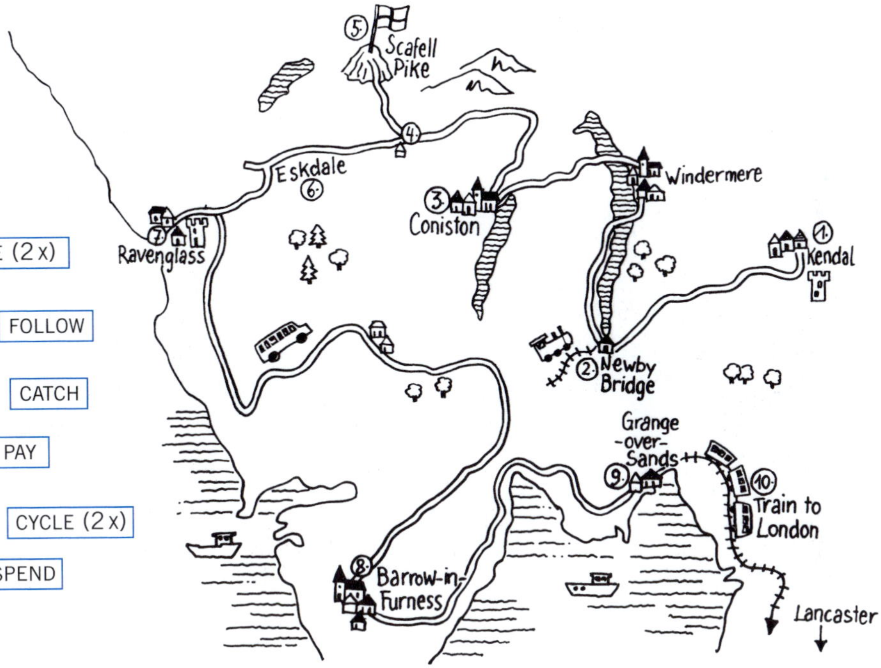

1. On the second day … to Kendal.
2. On the third day … the working railway museum.
3. On the fourth day … from Windermere to Coniston.
4. On the fifth day … at the Youth Hostel near Scafell.
5. On the sixth day … Scafell Pike (3,210 feet!).
6. On the seventh day … a visit to Eskdale and its Roman fort.
7. My friend Alan lives in Ravenglass, so … the night at a Youth Hostel.
8. On the eighth day Alan and I … the bus to Barrow-in-Furness and stay with some friends there.
9. On the ninth day we … the road along the coast to Grange-over-Sands.
10. On the tenth day I … the train back to London.

4.

Schau dir den Terminkalender von Frau Schmidt an! Kein Wunder, dass sie wenig Zeit für ein Gespräch mit ihrem englischen Geschäftskollegen Mr Wilson hat! Aber Mr Wilson hat auch wenig Zeit. Sein *appointments book* ist randvoll. Wie kommen die beiden wohl zusammen? Kannst du das Telefongespräch zwischen den beiden vervollständigen?

Mr Wilson:

Monday	**2**	
Tuesday	**3**	Computer exhibition - London
Wednesday	**4**	
Thursday	**5**	9 a.m.! Golf with Mr Makamoto
Friday	**6**	Drive to Manchester (a.m.) Meet Dr Müller in Leeds (p.m.)

W: Hello. Is that you, Mrs Schmidt? Wilson here. When can we have our meeting?

S: Oh hello, Mr Wilson. Just let me look at my calendar. On Monday I'm … . What about Tuesday?

W: Let me see – No, on Tuesday …, but I'll be free on Wednesday.

S: On Wednesday … our factory in Bremen. What about Thursday?

W: Just a minute – I'm not … anything on Thursday afternoon.

S: What about Thursday morning?

W: Sorry. … with a Japanese customer. Can't we make it the afternoon?

S: No. … a new project with my staff on Thursday afternoon. What about Friday?

W: Friday? Well … in the morning and … in the afternoon. What … on Monday next week?

S: Having a meeting with you – I hope!

Frau Schmidt:

2.	*Montag*	Flug nach Berlin
3.	*Dienstag*	
4.	*Mittwoch*	in Bremen
5.	*Donnerstag*	Nachmittag: Projektdiskussion
6.	*Freitag*	

5.

Sieh dir die Bilder an und bilde einen Satz mit der passenden Zukunftsform. Die Wörter über und in den Bildern werden dir dabei helfen.

1. The weather

2. They

3. The boy

4. Someone?

5. I

6. Flight BE 782

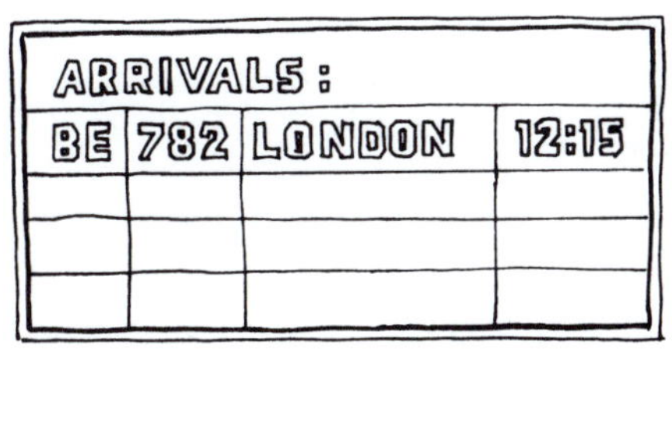

Zusammenfassung

Ways of expressing the future

Zum Ausdruck für Zukünftiges gibt es – unter anderem – folgende drei Möglichkeiten:

1. die neutrale Zukunft mit *will/won't* + Infinitiv	**I'll fly** to London. We **won't be** there.	Ich werde nach London fliegen. Wir werden nicht dort sein.
2. *ing*-Form mit Zeitangabe	**I'm flying** to London next week.	Ich fliege nächste Woche nach London.
3. Absicht mit *going to* + Infinitiv	**I'm going to** fly to London next year.	Ich habe vor, ... zu fliegen.

Test

Setze in folgende Sätze diejenige Form des in Klammern stehenden Verbs ein, die am besten in den Zusammenhang passt:

1. (see) "Bye, Paul! I ______________ you at the disco tomorrow!"
2. (be) "I ________n't ______________ at the disco, Jenny.
3. (go) I ______________ to the cinema tomorrow.
4. (come) ______________ you ______________ with me?"
5. (have) "I ______________ to ask my mother.
6. (cost) How much ____________ my ticket ______________?"
7. (buy) "Nothing. I ______________ your ticket. You paid last time."
8. (ask) "Fine! I ______________ Mum as soon as I get home.
9. (be) When _________ you ______________ at home this evening?"
10. (go) "I ______________ swimming this evening, but I should be back at about 9. You can ring me then."

7 Bedingungssätze

If I'd known then what I know now
– I thought I did, you know – somehow
if I could have my time again
I'd take the sunshine – leave the rain!

Roger Whittaker

Wie oft denkt man darüber nach, was wohl gewesen wäre, wenn ... ? Aber dann immer diese lästigen Bedingungen, die erfüllt werden müssen! Denn die meisten *if*-Sätze sind Bedingungssätze.
Manche Bedingungen sind relativ leicht erfüllbar, andere nur schwer, andere wiederum ganz und gar unerfüllbar. Warum? Das wirst du im Verlaufe unseres dreiteiligen Krimis erfahren.

If-Satz Typ I: Bedingung leicht erfüllbar

Bedingungssätze bestehen aus zwei Teilen: einem Nebensatz, in dem *if* die Bedingung aufstellt, und einem Hauptsatz, in dem das Ergebnis geschildert wird. Die Reihenfolge der Sätze ist beliebig.

Folgende Zeitformen werden für Sätze des Typs I benutzt:

if*-Satz – *present simple	**Hauptsatz – *will + infinitive***
If he wins the prize,	he will be very happy.
if they don't hurry up.	They'll miss the film
Unless you work hard, (unless = if ... not)	you won't pass your exams.

1.

Suche alle Bedingungssätze aus dem Text heraus. Schreibe sie in eine Tabelle mit den Spalten „Nebensatz mit *if*“ und „Hauptsatz“. Dann unterstreiche die Zeitformen. Woran siehst du, dass der jeweilige Sprecher die Bedingungen als leicht erfüllbar ansieht?

Sherlock McGnome, Master Detective – Part 1

Sherlock McGnome, the famous Scottish detective, was walking along a dark Edinburgh street. He was going to the empty house where he had hidden the diamonds which had been stolen from the Royal Museum. He had only found them a few hours before, and had just telephoned the King of Scotland to tell him the good news.
Suddenly he heard a voice behind him: “Stop! If you turn round, I'll shoot!” The detective could feel something hard in his back.
“What do you want?” asked McGnome. He thought he knew the voice.
“If you tell me where the King of Scotland's Diamonds are, I will let you go.”
“What will you do if I don't tell you where they are?” asked McGnome.
“Then,” said the voice, “I will kill you!”

2.

Bilde *if*-Sätze vom Typ I zu folgenden Situationen.

Beispiel: “If I pass my driving test, I'll buy a car.”

1

pass driving test / buy car

2

save enough money / buy dog

3

work hard at school / go to university

4

go to party / meet John

5

get a well-paid job soon / go to Spain for holidays

6

parents allow it / invite friends to party

3.

Wir wissen nicht, wie sich Thomas Alva Edison – Erfinder der Glühbirne und vieler anderer nützlicher Sachen – als kleiner Junge seine Zukunft ausmalte. Vielleicht wollte er schon immer ein berühmter Erfinder werden. Vielleicht dachte er sich aber in etwa Folgendes:

Beispiel: Work hard at school – Go to college
"If I work hard at school, I will go to college."

1. Learn a lot at grade school *(Grundschule)* – Go to high school
2. Go to high school – Learn a lot more
3. Work hard – Pass my exams
4. Get good marks in my exams – Get a place at college
5. Go to college – Study hard
6. Study very hard – Do well at college
7. Pass my college exams – Get a good job
8. Get a good job – Earn a lot of money
9. Save some of my money – Soon be rich
10. Be rich – Be able to enjoy life while I'm still young.

Mehr über Edison im zweiten Teil dieses Kapitels.

Merke

Im Deutschen wird das Wort „wenn“ für zwei Wörter im Englischen benutzt: *if* und *when*. Vergleiche:

„Ich rufe dich an, **wenn** ich zurückkomme.“

könnte auf Englisch heißen:

“I'll phone you **when** I return.” oder: “I'll phone you **if** I return.”

Der Satz mit *when I return* ist ein Versprechen. Es ist nur eine Frage der Zeit, bis der Anruf kommt. Im zweiten Satz zeigt das Wort *if*, dass die Rückkehr die Bedingung für den Anruf ist. Kehrt der Sprecher nicht zurück, kann sein(e) Gesprächspartner(in) lange auf den Anruf warten!

Es handelt sich um einen ***if*-Satz Typ I** (= leicht erfüllbare Bedingung).

Sätze mit *when* haben mit der Zeit zu tun – die Zeitformen, die benutzt werden, sind manchmal anders als bei Bedingungssätzen.

If und *when* also immer auseinander halten!

4.

if oder *when*? – Setze das richtige Wort in die Lücken ein.

1. I'm going to watch TV ... I have finished my homework.
2. My mother lets me watch TV ... I finish my homework before tea-time.
3. Please give me the book back soon – only ... you have read it, of course.
4. ... we have plenty of snow we sometimes go skiing.
5. ... we have some snow tomorrow, we'll go skiing.
6. I don't know ... I'll see him next. On Thursday perhaps.
7. Please come to my party ... you can.
8. ... you don't stop shouting, I'll tell your mother!
9. We can go to the disco tomorrow ... you like.
10. Do you remember ... the concert starts?

If-Satz Typ II: Bedingung schwer erfüllbar

Auch die Bedingungssätze Typ II bestehen aus einem Nebensatz mit *if* (für die Bedingung) und einem Hauptsatz (für das Ergebnis). Die Reihenfolge von Haupt- und Nebensatz ist auch hier beliebig. Folgende Zeitformen werden benutzt:

if*-Satz – *past simple	**Hauptsatz – *would* + *infinitive***
If he won the prize,	he would be very happy.
if they didn't like it.	They wouldn't listen to the music

Viele „Typ-II-Sätze" sind nicht erfüllbar, weil sie sich mit reinen Vermutungen oder gar mit Wunschdenken befassen. Dazu gehört auch der Ausdruck *If I were you …* (An deiner Stelle …).

If I were you,	I wouldn't eat that meat.
if he were here.	He would tell us the answer

Die Form *were* ist für alle Personen gleich: *If I were, if you were, if he/she were,* etc.

5.

Jetzt aber zum zweiten Teil unseres Krimis. Wie du dich sicher erinnern kannst, wurde der Detektiv Sherlock McGnome gerade von einem bewaffneten Verbrecher bedroht.

Schreibe alle Sätze mit *if* auf. Unterstreiche die Zeitformen im *if*-Nebensatz und im Hauptsatz. Sind es alles Bedingungssätze Typ II?

Sherlock McGnome, Master Detective – Part 2

"If I knew where the diamonds were," replied McGnome, "I wouldn't be here. I'd be on the Bahamas writing postcards to my friends. If I had the King of Scotland's Diamonds, I'd be a multi-millionaire!"

"So would I!" said the voice, with an unpleasant laugh. "I know that you have found the diamonds. Unless you tell me where they are, I will shoot you!"
"Don't be silly!" laughed McGnome. "I won't be able to tell you where I have hidden the diamonds if you shoot me."
The gunman was silent for a few moments.
"Well," said the gunman, not so sure of himself now. "If you take me to the diamonds, I'll share them with you!"
"I don't think you would. If you found the diamonds, you would keep them all for yourself! The game's up, Your Majesty!" cried McGnome, turning round to face the King of Scotland, who looked rather silly now with his walking stick in his right hand instead of a gun.
"How did you know it was me, McGnome?" the King asked in surprise.
"Elementary, my dear King. Only you knew that I had actually found the diamonds. I had told nobody else."

6.

Thomas Alva Edison ging nicht auf die höhere Schule, sondern verließ die *grade school* mit 12 Jahren, um als „fahrender Bonbon- und Zeitschriftenverkäufer" in den Zügen zwischen Port Huron und Detroit seinen Lebensunterhalt zu verdienen. Er war nicht so glücklich über die ihm bevorstehende Zukunft in der Zeitungs- und Süßwarenbranche.
Bilde Sätze des Typs II nach folgendem Muster:

Beispiel: More money – Buy a bicycle
"If I had more money, I would buy a bicycle."

1. Bicycle – Not have to walk to the station
2. Not have to walk to the station – Leave home later
3. Leave home later in the mornings – Have more time for breakfast
4. More time for breakfast – Think about new inventions
5. Think hard – Get good ideas
6. Get good ideas – Invent useful things
7. Invent useful things – Soon get rich
8. Get rich – Give up my job on the trains
9. Give up job – Have more time for experiments
10. More time for experiments – Invent even better things

If-Satz Typ III: Bedingung nicht erfüllbar

if-Sätze Typ I und II beziehen sich auf die Zukunft, während Sätze des Typs III ausschließlich in die Vergangenheit zurückblicken:

"If I had known you were coming, I would have baked a cake."

Da man nichts vom Besuch wusste, konnte man keinen Kuchen backen. Auch hier sind die zu verwendenden Zeitformen im Normalfall festgeschrieben: Im Hauptsatz steht die Zeitform *conditional II* (*would have come*, etc.); im Nebensatz mit *if* steht das *past perfect* (wobei im Englischen *had* sowohl für „hätte" als auch für „wäre" steht:
had known/had come = hätte gewusst/wäre gekommen usw.).

if* + *past perfect	**Hauptsatz: *would have* + *past participle***
If we had left earlier,	we would have arrived on time.
if I'd known the answer myself.	I wouldn't have asked you
if he hadn't promised to pay you for your help?	Would you have helped him

Sherlock McGnome, Master Detective – Part 3

"If only the King had hired a real killer instead of saving money and trying to do the job himself," said Sherlock McGnome, "I would probably have taken him to the jewels."
"But he would have killed you if you had done that!" cried McWatson in alarm.
"If you had been listening to me, you would have realized that there was never any danger for me."
"Perhaps you could explain that."
"I would never have taken such a risk if you hadn't been waiting at the hiding place, my dear friend."
McWatson looked at the master detective in surprise. But McGnome went on:
"If you hadn't received my note, how would you have known where to wait?"
"Note? – What note? I didn't receive any note!"

"You mean … ?"
"If I had received a note, I would have been there to help you!"

7.
Schreibe alle Sätze des Textes auf, die das Wort *if* enthalten, und unterstreiche die Zeitformen. Sind es alles *if*-Sätze des Typs III?

Merke

Vorsicht! „wäre / hätte" ist nicht gleich „wäre / hätte"

Viel Ärger kannst du dir bei einer Klassenarbeit mit *if*-Sätzen ersparen, wenn du daran denkst, dass das deutsche „wäre/hätte" nicht *had* entspricht. Im deutschen Hauptsatz handelt es sich um eine Zusammenziehung von „würde … haben/sein".
Vergleiche:

„Wenn ich das gewusst hätte, hätte ich ihn angerufen."
"If I **had known** that, I **would have phoned** him."

„Wenn er nicht gekommen wäre, wäre das Mädchen ertrunken."
"If he **hadn't come**, the girl **would have drowned**."

8.
Thomas Alva Edison starb 83-jährig im Jahre 1931. Kurz vor seinem Tod mag er auf sein langes Leben zurückgeblickt und sich gedacht haben, wie alles hätte anders verlaufen können, wenn … .

Beispiel: Live in Europe – Not have the same opportunities as in the USA
"If I had lived in Europe, I would not have had the same opportunities as in the USA."

1. Go to high school – Work hard
2. Work hard – Pass my exams
3. Go to college – Not have time to invent things
4. Do well at college – Become a teacher
5. Become a teacher – Never become an inventor
6. Not become an inventor – Not invent all those useful things
7. Become a teacher – Not have to work so hard
8. Not work so hard – Perhaps be happier
9. Move to Europe – Be more successful
10. Die when I was young – Never invent the electric light bulb

9.

Bilde aus folgender Schalttafel sinnvolle Sätze:

If ...

you hit me	I will help her with hers.
I knew her address	we wouldn't have lost the match.
he had waited	you would like her.
she helps me with my homework	we'll soon be home.
you knew her better	we would have had a nicer holiday.
they had asked me to help	we would have taken him with us.
we walk this way	the girls would bring theirs.
the sun had shone more often	I will tell Mum!
the boys brought their CDs	I would write to her.
we had played harder	I would have done my best.

10.

Jetzt aber zur Abrundung! Wir geben dir einen Satzteil vor, den anderen musst du mit Hilfe des in Klammern gesetzten Verbs ergänzen. Mal ist es der Hauptsatz, mal der *if*-Satz, der vorgegeben wird.

1. (tell)	He ... you the story if you asked him.
2. (have)	If I ... enough money I would buy that computer game.
3. (see)	If I ... him I'll give him your message.
4. (steal)	If he ... the car he wouldn't have left it here. He'd have sold it!
5. (call)	Unless you stop I ... the police.
6. (buy)	He ... the house if he had had enough money.
7. (not tell)	If he ... his friends he would never have been caught.
8. (not leave)	If her parents had understood her she ... home.
9. (not go)	We ... unless we have to.
10. (ask)	If you ... me no questions I'll tell you no lies.
11. (want)	Tell them I've gone to London if they ... to know where I am.
12. (say)	Don't shoot unless I ... shoot!
13. (not stop)	He'll never finish his homework if he ... watching TV!
14. (be)	If I ... rich I'd buy a fast car.
15. (know)	I'd have come to your party if I ... about it earlier.

Merke

Gibt es Kombinationen mit anderen Hilfsverben?

Ja. Das im Hauptsatz verwendete Hilfsverb ist nicht immer *will, would* oder *would have.* Wird *will* oder *would* verwendet, dann tritt das Ergebnis der Bedingung **immer** ein.

If we go to London, we **will** visit the Tower.	(Wir werden es tun!)

Andere Hilfsverben im Hauptsatz drücken – an Stelle von „werden" – folgende Bedeutungen aus:

If we go to London, we **can** visit the Tower.	(Vorschlag: können)
If we go to London, we **could** visit the Tower.	(könnten)
If we go to London, we **may** visit the Tower	(gut möglich)
If we go to London, we **might** visit the Tower.	(weniger wahrscheinlich)
If we go to London, we **should** visit the Tower.	(sollten)

Ähnliche Bedeutungen lassen sich mit Sätzen der Typen II und III ausdrücken, wobei die Wahrscheinlichkeit für die Erfüllung der Bedingung abgeschwächt wird. Die Hilfsverben sind auf *might (have)* und *could (have)* beschränkt:

If you listened to me, you **could/might** learn something.
(da du aber nicht hinhörst ...)
We **would/could** be in London in half an hour if we took a taxi.
We **might have** caught the train if we had run faster!

11.

Stell dir diese Situation vor: Zwei Minuten vor Abfahrt des Schulbusses rennen zwei Schülerinnen aus dem Klassenzimmer. Zur Haltestelle brauchen sie meist vier Minuten – aber wenn sie rennen würden? ...
Kannst du ihre Gedanken in Worte fassen?
Benutze nicht *would* sondern nur *could/might (have).*

Beispiel: Be quick! – Catch bus!
"If we were quick, we might/could catch the bus!"

1. Work hard! – Pass your exams!
2. Talk to Jenny! – Invite me to her party!
3. Borrow £ 20! – Buy those CDs!
4. Phone his friends in Germany! – Get help with German homework!
5. Help your sister! – She would help you!

Zusammenfassung

Bedingungssätze im Englischen verwenden im Allgemeinen feste Zeitformenpaare. Die Wahl des richtigen „Typs“ hängt von der Wahrscheinlichkeit ab, mit der die Bedingung erfüllt werden kann.

Die drei *if*-Satz-Typen sehen in etwa so aus:

	„Typ I“	„Typ II“	„Typ III“

Wahrscheinlichkeit:	50–99%	0–49%	0%

Typ I: Bedingung leicht erfüllbar – kein Problem!
(Wahrscheinlichkeit der Erfüllung 50–99%)

Zeitformen-Reihenfolge:
Hauptsatz: **will + Infinitiv** – **if**-Nebensatz: **present simple**

She won't come if you don't invite her.
Will you help me with my maths if I help you with your English?

Typ II: Bedingung schwerer zu erfüllen – bzw. im Bereich der Wunschträume. Erfüllbarkeit bis 49%.

Zeitformen-Reihenfolge:
Hauptsatz: **would + Infinitiv** – **if**-Nebensatz: **past simple**

She would come to your party if you invited her.
If I had enough money, I would buy a Jaguar.
If we knew where they lived, we'd give you the address.

Achtung: Bei *to be* wird in der 1. Person meist die Form *(I) were* anstelle von *(I) was* verwendet: I'd go by train if I were you.

Typ III: Bedingung nicht erfüllbar, da Situation in der Vergangenheit liegt.

Zeitformen-Reihenfolge:
Hauptsatz: **would have**-Form – **if**-Nebensatz: **past perfect**

I would have helped her, if she had asked me.
If they hadn't come, we would never have eaten all the food.

Test

Setze bei den unten stehenden Sätzen die Verben im Kästchen in die richtige Zeitform. Du darfst die vorgegebenen Verben beliebig oft verwenden. Füge außerdem bei den kurzen Strichen die richtige Konjunktion ein: *if*, *when* oder *unless*.

go	not lend	come	feel
promise	be	bring	give

1. "When will you see Pat?" – "This afternoon. I ______________ her your message _____ I see her."
2. "Will you lend me £20 _____ I ______________ to pay you back on Thursday?" – "I ______________ you any more money _____ you pay me back what you already owe me! _____ I ______________ you, I'd find a weekend job and earn some money instead of borrowing it!"
3. "______________ you ______________ to my party _____ I invited you?" – "Of course. I'd love to come. I love parties! _____ you hadn't invited me I ______________ angry with you!"
4. "I think she's OK. I saw her yesterday. She would have gone to the doctor's _____ she ______________ ill."
5. "We could be in New York tomorrow _____ we ______________ by plane." – "_____ I had known you wanted to fly to New York, I ______________ my passport with me and gone with you!"
6. "You must show your German test to your father _____ he ______________ home."

8 Aktiv oder Passiv?

Die einfachen Zeiten im Passiv

Ein Passivsatz bietet sich an, wenn der Täter
1. unbekannt ist
2. selbstverständlich bzw. relativ unwichtig ist oder – im Gegensatz dazu –
3. so wichtig ist, dass er verschwiegen werden muss.

Vergleiche:

1. *Active:* Someone has stolen **my bicycle**!
   Passive: **My bicycle** has been stolen!
2. *Active:* Car makers make **thousands of cars** a day.
   Passive: **Thousands of cars** are made every day.
3. *Active:* My boss made **a serious mistake** last week.
   Passive: Last week **a serious mistake** was made.

Das Objekt des Aktivsatzes wird zum Subjekt des Passivsatzes und so in den Vordergrund gerückt.

Das Passiv wird im Deutschen mit „werden“, im Englischen mit *to be* gebildet.

Aktiv- und Passivformen im Vergleich

Active ←→	Passive
Present	
These farmers grow potatoes. *Diese Bauern bauen Kartoffeln an.*	Many potatoes are grown here. *Viele Kartoffeln werden hier angebaut.*
Past	
I bought these videos yesterday. *Ich kaufte diese Videos gestern.*	These videos were bought cheaply. *Diese Videos wurden billig gekauft.*
Present perfect	
She has only seen him once *Sie hat ihn nur einmal gesehen,*	but he has been seen twice in York. *aber er ist zweimal in York gesehen worden.*
Past perfect	
After he had phoned her ... *Nachdem er sie angerufen hatte ...*	After she had been phoned ... *Nachdem sie angerufen worden war...*
Mit Hilfsverb (z.B. Future)	
They will phone him later. *Sie werden ihn später anrufen.*	He will be phoned later. *Er wird später angerufen werden.*
We must tidy up the playground. *Wir müssen den Schulhof aufräumen.*	The whole school must be tidied up. *Die ganze Schule muss aufgeräumt werden.*
I can't find the money. *Ich kann das Geld nicht finden.*	The money cannot be found. *Das Geld kann nicht gefunden werden.*

Bei Verben, die mit Präpositionen benutzt werden *(phrasal verbs)*, kommt die Präposition nach dem Partizip:

His niece will look after him.	He will be looked after by his niece.

1.

Lies diese kurze „Geistergeschichte“ durch und schreibe alle Sätze auf, die ein Verb im Passiv enthalten. Du darfst die Sätze auch verkürzen. Ordne sie bitte nach Zeitformen.

The old village inn where we spent the night was haunted – or so the local people said. All the other rooms had been booked, so the innkeeper asked us if we would mind sleeping in the "haunted bedroom". My wife did not mind, so I asked the landlord for the story.
"About fifty years ago," he said, "a woman was murdered in the room you have been given. She was found dead one morning, and all her money and jewels had been stolen. No trace of the murderer could be found. Sometimes strange noises are heard at night, so the room is not often used. I hope you are not disturbed. Sleep well!"
We were not disturbed during the night, although I secretly hoped that we would be woken by a scream or the sound of a gun. I began to disbelieve the landlord's story.
We were packing our suitcases the following morning when my wife's wedding ring rolled off the table and vanished underneath the bed.
The heavy bed had to be moved before we could find the ring. The floor had not been swept for a long time, and beside the ring was a bullet from an old-fashioned gun. Had the rich woman been killed by this bullet? We said nothing to the landlord when we paid our bill.
Later the bullet was put in a special glass box and placed on our mantlepiece. All our visitors are told the story of the rich woman who had been killed with it.

Present passive: …

Past passive: …

Present perfect passive: …

Past perfect passive: …

Auxiliary + passive infinitive: …

Auxiliary + passive infinitive: …

2.

Zuerst eine Schalttafel. Hier geht es vor allen Dingen darum, ein Gefühl für die richtige Zusammenstellung (Hilfsverb + Partizip) der Passivformen zu bekommen. Du musst natürlich auch die richtige Zeitform für die jeweilige Situation auswählen.

I		built so far this year.
Many tourists	am / are / is	announced, everyone was happy.
Mount Everest	was / were	made at the new factory.
This car	has / have been	phoned tomorrow morning.
When the news	had been	introduced, the concert began.
After the band	will be	stranded at airports last week.
Many new hotels		climbed in 1953.
She		woken every morning at 6.30.

3.

Jetzt geht's weiter – aber vorerst nur mit den beiden „einfachen" Zeitformen. Folgende Sätze wurden alle von *„Dr. Bean's Patent Text Machine"* erstellt und klingen etwas komisch. Wie kann man die Aussagen treffender machen?
Achte besonders darauf, dass du im Passivsatz dieselbe Zeitform verwendest wie im Aktivsatz! Eine Umschreibung mit *by* wird in keinem der Sätze benötigt.

Beispiel: People feed the ducks in winter. — The ducks are fed in winter.

1. Somebody often drops rubbish in the playground.
2. A thief stole some money from my jacket pocket.
3. No one likes the new English teacher.
4. My mother burned our supper.
5. A gardener cuts the grass every week.
6. The waiter serves lunch at 1 p.m.
7. An unknown burglar broke into their house.
8. Drivers often break the speed limit.
9. Someone wrote the song "Greensleeves" in the 12th century.
10. Builders build many new houses every year.
11. The police arrested the two young men at the airport.
12. People do not look at these old pictures much nowadays.
13. Does anyone speak English in this shop?
14. Did anything spoil your fun?
15. Nobody expects you to wait.
16. They didn't build Rome in a day.

4.

Jetzt geht's mit den zusammengesetzten Zeitformen in längeren Sätzen weiter. Einige Sätze sind in der Frageform, einige enthalten Präpositionen, um ganz sicherzustellen, dass du auch diese „Klimmzüge" bei der nächsten Klassenarbeit meistern wirst.

1. Nobody has seen him since January.
2. Someone will meet you at London Airport.
3. You can buy these souvenirs at any seaside town.
4. After the police had arrested him they took him to the police station.
5. Nobody has explored this part of the country before.
6. Will the judges choose the beauty queen on Saturday?
7. Don't touch that wire! The electricity would kill you if you did!
8. Has anyone ever seen the Yeti?
9. Haven't the police solved the murder yet?
10. They can't have sold all the tickets for the open-air concert yet!
11. You can order the magazine from England.
12. No runner has broken the world record yet.
13. People saw the missing boy in Edinburgh yesterday.
14. After an unknown person had called the police, they arrested the burglar.
15. Nobody will finish this work in time.

5.

Vor zehn Jahren wurde in diesem kleinen englischen Dorf der Umweltschutz ganz klein geschrieben! Jetzt aber ist – unter anderem dank der Initiative der örtlichen Schule – schon das Gröbste aus der Welt.
Eine Reporterin von der Schülerzeitung hat sich anhand der beiden Bilder Notizen gemacht. Kannst du die Notizen zu ganzen Sätzen ausformulieren?

a) Bilde zuerst Sätze nach folgendem Muster:
Ten years ago a lot of chemicals **were used** on the farms.
Now farming methods **have been changed**.

b) Bilde jetzt Sätze im *past perfect* mit *After …* nach dem Muster:
After the farming methods **had been changed**, the fields were/the river was cleaner/less polluted, etc.

Die Sätze kannst du selbst vervollständigen.

ten years ago

now

rubbish put in river: now cleared ✔
many cars parked in village: motor traffic now banned ✔
a lot of coal burned: houses converted to central heating ✔
pollution caused by factory: factory now closed ✔
litter dropped in streets: more litter bins provided ✔
houses made dirty by air pollution:now cleaned ✔

Verlaufsformen im Passiv

Gibt es auch Verlaufsformen im Passiv?

Ja, für länger andauernde Handlungen – aber nur zwei Formen: *present progressive* und *past progressive*.

Active ⟷	Passive
They are pulling down the old theatre. *Sie reißen das alte Theater ab.*	The police station is being pulled down, too. *Die Polizeiwache wird auch (gerade) abgerissen.*
Journalists were interviewing the victims *Journalisten waren dabei, die Opfer zu interviewen,*	while the bus driver was being interviewed by the police. *während der Busfahrer von der Polizei verhört wurde.*

Die Verlaufsform der Gegenwart wird besonders für Sätze gebraucht, in denen die *ing*-Form zum Ausdruck der Zukunft (auch im Passiven) benutzt wird. Vergleiche:

They are holding the meeting here *Das Treffen wird hier abgehalten,*	but the conference is being held in Edinburgh in two months. *aber die Konferenz wird in zwei Monaten in Edinburgh stattfinden.*

6.

Zuerst eine einfache Übung. Bilde aus folgenden Aktivsätzen die entsprechenden Passivsätze.

1. They are building a lot of new houses in our town.
2. Are they planting new trees in the woods?
3. People are not buying new cars at the moment.
4. Someone was playing a piano at the back of the house.
5. Young people are stealing a lot of bikes nowadays.
6. Was the waiter serving dinner when you arrived?

7. The young mechanic was not repairing my car.
8. Is anyone repairing the roof?
9. Were people photographing the Queen a lot?
10. Nobody is eating all the nice food I made!

7.

Nach der einfachen Übung 6 bist du jetzt doppelt gefordert. Manchmal musst du eine einfache Zeitform des Passivs in eine der Verlaufsformen umwandeln, manchmal gilt es, aus einem Aktivsatz einen Passivsatz zu bilden.

1. The famous pop singer John Jones is interviewed several times a week. In fact he ... now.
2. After the heavy snow the main roads were cleared quickly. They ... already when we woke up.
3. "They were still digging the Channel Tunnel when I was in Calais last." – "That's right it ... still ... when I was last in France."
4. While the guests at the birthday party were dancing, their cars (break into) ... one by one.
5. "Am I asking the questions or ... they ... by you?"
6. "They're opening a new supermarket in our village." – "Yes, lots of new supermarkets ... at the moment."
7. The king ... just (welcome) ... by the president when the bomb exploded.
8. "The new boss is making a lot of changes." – "Yes, but I think too many things (change) ... ."
9. "All these improvements (pay for) ... with public money. We're paying for everything nowadays!"
10. "Do you know where the next Olympic Games (hold) ...?" – "I've no idea. Manchester, I think."

"Mr Henderson, you're wanted on the phone."

Die Ergänzung mit *by*

Wann muss ich den „Täter“ erwähnen?

Eine Einbindung des Täters durch *by* am Satzende ist nur bei Autoren, Komponisten, Sängern usw. unbedingt nötig, denn Sätze wie: *"This book was written"* ergeben keinen Sinn. Alle Bücher werden geschrieben! Der Autor muss erwähnt werden.

Active ⟷	Passive
The Beatles wrote this song.	The other song was written by the Rolling Stones.
Beethoven composed this symphony.	That symphony was composed by Brahms.
Colin Dexter writes the best detective stories.	The best historical novels are written by Ellis Peters.

Ähnliches gilt für die Ergänzung durch *with* bei Sachen und *by* bei Verkehrsmitteln:
The woman was wounded with a knife.
The dog was run over by a bus.

Wenn mehr Nachdruck auf die von der Handlung betroffene Person gelegt werden soll, wird der Täter durch die Umschreibung mit *by* in den Hintergrund gerückt:

Terrorists killed the reporter.	The reporter was killed by terrorists.

8.

Wer hat was gemacht? Bilde einen Satz im Passiv mit entsprechender Ergänzung.

Beispiel: Mount Everest – climb – Sir Edmund Hillary – 1953
Mount Everest was climbed by Sir Edmund Hillary in 1953.

1. English Channel – swim – Captain Webb – 1875
2. The first car – build – Gottlieb Daimler – 1885
3. The song "Yesterday" – compose – John Lennon – 1964
4. The Football Association Cup – win – Manchester United – last year
5. Basketball – first – play – YMCA members – in America
6. The novel "1984" – write – George Orwell – 1948
7. The first steps on the moon – take – Neil Armstrong – 1969

9.

Hier sollst du selbst entscheiden, ob man eine Ergänzung durch *by* braucht. Natürlich handelt es sich auch um die „Verwandlung“ der Sätze aus dem Aktiv ins Passiv, aber du hast jetzt genügend Erfahrung, und die Wahl der richtigen Zeitform dürfte dir keine Probleme bereiten.

1. The boy found the purse in the school playground last week.
2. The girl has already posted the letter.
3. Demolition experts are demolishing the old school.
4. Someone had picked all the apples before I arrived.
5. Nobody can replace the clock he broke.
6. An idiot wrote this letter!
7. He took a taxi to the station because they were repairing his car.
8. Someone must report the accident to the police.
9. The woman who lives downstairs has asked us to turn the music down a bit.
10. Paul Simon wrote this fine song.

Zusammenfassung

Active or Passive?

Verwendung:

Das Passiv wird meist benutzt, wenn der Täter

1. unbekannt ist:
   My bicycle has been stolen!
2. selbstverständlich bzw. relativ unwichtig ist:
   Thousands of cars are made every day.
3. so wichtig ist, dass er verschwiegen werden muss:
   A serious mistake has been made.

Formen:

Das Passiv wird im Englischen mit der entsprechenden Form von *to be* + dritte Verbform *(past participle)* gebildet. Es gibt nur zwei Verlaufsformen des Passivs.

Simple present	He is seen.
Present progressive	It is being painted.
Simple past	I was/We were chosen.
Past progressive	The songs were being recorded.
Present perfect	The film hasn't been made yet.
Past perfect	John had been seen.
Auxiliary + infinitive	Will we be informed?

Verwendung von *by* zur Angabe des Täters:

1. Meist erforderlich bei Autoren, Komponisten, Sängern, Malern – Künstlern allgemein.
2. Wenn die von der Handlung betroffene Person wichtiger ist als der Täter.

Wortstellung:

Bei Verben, die mit Präpositionen benutzt werden *(phrasal verbs)*, steht die Präposition nach dem Partizip:
Last night our house was broken into.

Test

Setze folgende Sätze ins Passiv.

1. Someone has invited me to meet the Queen.

   ____

2. The police in Britain catch hundreds of criminals every day.

   ____

3. Nobody told the President the truth about the problem.

   ____

4. The boss will give you a new job when he opens the new factory.

   ____

5. Somebody must tidy up the garden.

   ____

6. They are arranging a Christmas concert at our school.

   ____

7. People had stolen hundreds of things from the shops before someone called the police.

   ____

8. Someone must have warned him that we were coming.

   ____

9. A reporter was interviewing survivors from the plane crash when I arrived.

   ____

10. Elton John has written dozens of good songs.

    ____

9 Der Infinitiv

Der Infinitiv ohne *to* nach Hilfsverben, *let* und *make*

Der Infinitiv ohne *to* steht nach den modalen Hilfsverben (*can, must, may* usw.) sowie nach den Hilfsverben *will/would* und *shall/should*:

She **can swim**.	Sie kann schwimmen.
I **must speak** to you.	Ich muss mit dir sprechen.
May we **go** to the party?	Dürfen wir auf die Party (gehen)?
We **will leave** at 8 o'clock.	Wir werden um 8 Uhr losfahren.
Shall we **call** the police?	Sollen/Wollen wir die Polizei anrufen?

Der Infinitiv ohne *to* steht außerdem nach *let* (lassen = erlauben) und *make* (lassen = zwingen).

They **let** him **go**.	Sie ließen ihn (dahin) gehen. (Erlaubnis)
They **let** him **go**.	Sie ließen ihn laufen. („Sie" = z.B. die Polizei)
She **made** me **wait** outside.	Sie ließ mich draußen warten. (= zwang mich, zu warten)
She **let** me **wait** outside.	Sie ließ mich draußen warten. (= erlaubte, dass ich wartete)

Die betroffene(n) Person(en) stehen dabei als direktes Objekt zwischen Verb und Infinitiv:

Our teacher made **us** stay five minutes longer.	... ließ uns/zwang uns ...

1.

Setze die richtigen Formen (auch die richtigen **Zeit**formen!) von *let* und *make* – je nach Zusammenhang – in folgende Sätze ein:

1. My mother always ... me finish my homework before she ... me watch TV.
2. It started to rain and we were still five kilometres from the youth hostel *(Jugendherberge)*. So our teacher ... us walk faster.
3. We live in the middle of a big town, so my parents have never ... me go to school by bike. They ... me walk or go by bus.
4. I was ill when we had our last English test. I hope our teacher will ... me take it separately. I think I'll get a good mark *(Note)* for it.
5. I don't like spinach *(Spinat)* much, but my mother always ... me eat it all up. She says it's good for me.
6. Big sister: "... me borrow your new CD. I want to listen to it!" – Little sister: "I haven't listened to it myself yet! You can't ... me lend it to you!"
7. "Last week our English teacher ... us learn twenty-five new English words! I hope she doesn't ... us learn fifty this week!"
8. "You're coat is very wet, Eric! Have you been standing out in the rain?" – "Yes, Mum. Our teachers didn't ... us stay in the classrooms during break. They ... us go out into the playground."

2.

Was ist erlaubt, und was musst du tun? Ergänze folgende Aussagen über deinen persönlichen Alltag:

1. When I get up, my mother makes me ______________________________.
2. Then she lets me ______________________________.
3. Then I go to school. If it's raining, I must ______________________________,

   but I needn't ______________________________.
4. Our English teacher lets us ______________________________,

   but he/she makes us ______________________________.
5. During the morning break, we can ______________________________.

   But we mustn't ______________________________.
6. When I/we get home from school my mum makes ______________________________,

   but then she lets ______________________________.
7. Before going to bed I may ______________________________.

Der Infinitiv ohne *to* nach Verben der Wahrnehmung

Der Infinitiv ohne *to* steht auch nach bestimmten Verben der Wahrnehmung. Die wichtigsten dieser Verben sind *to see, to hear, to watch, to notice, to feel.*

I **heard** him **come in**.	Ich hörte ihn hereinkommen.
We **saw** them **drive off**.	Wir sahen sie losfahren.
The citizens of San Francisco **felt** the earth **quake.**	Die Bürger San Franciscos fühlten, wie die Erde bebte.

Wie bei *let* und *make* (s. S. 82) wird die von der Handlung des Infinitivs betroffene Person als direktes Objekt zwischen Wahrnehmungsverb und Infinitiv eingesetzt.

He watched **a man** break into the house.	Er sah zu, wie **ein Mann** ins Haus einbrach.

Die Infinitivkonstruktion wird bei Handlungen verwendet, die kurz und bereits abgeschlossen sind.

3.
Zum Entspannen mal eine Übung, wo du nur das passende Objekt und die passende Handlung aus den Wörtern im Kästchen aussuchen musst.

Objekt: two cars, someone, the car's tyres, the Queen, the accident, a car bomb, three masked men, someone

Handlung: arrive, run, explode, put, scream, happen, crash, shout, jump

1. We stood outside Buckingham Palace and saw ____________ ____________.
2. I didn't actually see ____________ ____________. I was looking in the other direction. I only heard ____________ ____________ on the wet road. When I looked round, the car had stopped and the cyclist was already getting up from the ground.
3. The tourist in the crowded market felt ____________ quickly ____________ his hand into the back pocket of her jeans. He was probably trying to steal her money.
4. I heard ____________ ____________. I looked round and saw my friend Fred.
5. We were watching a motor race on TV. We saw ____________ ____________.
6. My friend actually saw the bank robbery. He saw ____________ ____________ out of a car and ____________ into the bank.
7. I was waiting for my bus when I suddenly heard ____________ ____________.

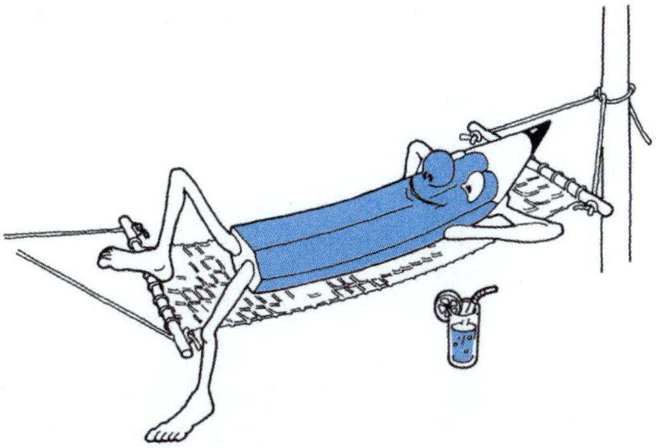

Der Infinitiv mit *to* nach Verben des Bittens und Wollens + Objekt

Nach vielen englischen Verben wird der Infinitiv mit *to* direkt angeschlossen.

I **hope to see** you soon.	Ich hoffe, dich bald zu sehen.
He **wants to talk** to you.	Er wünscht, dich zu sprechen.
They didn't **remember to write** to me.	Sie dachten nicht daran, mir zu schreiben.

Wie bei den Verben *let* und *make* (siehe S. 82) muss jedoch auch bei Verben des **Bittens, Befehlens und Wollens bzw. Nichtwollens** häufig zusätzlich die betroffene Person als Objekt zwischen Verb und Infinitiv eingeschaltet werden.

He **asked me to come**.	Er bat mich zu kommen.
The police **ordered people to stand back**.	Die Polizei befahl den Menschen, Abstand zu halten.
I **warned him not to touch** it.	Ich warnte ihn davor, es nicht anzufassen.
She **advised us not to wait**.	Sie riet uns, nicht zu warten.
They **recommended us to book** early.	Sie empfahlen uns, früh zu buchen.

Bei einigen Verben, die im Englischen ein Objekt + Infinitiv mit *to* anschließen, ist im Deutschen nur ein Nebensatz mit „dass" oder „wenn" möglich:

He **wanted** me to come.	Er wollte, **dass** ich komme(n sollte).
He **expected** me to come.	Er erwartete von mir, **dass** ich kam.
He **told** me not to come.	Er sagte mir, **dass** ich nicht kommen **soll**.
He **liked** us to be on time.	Er mochte es, **wenn** wir pünktlich erschienen.
He **hated** us to be late.	Er hasste es, **wenn** wir uns verspäteten.
He **preferred** us to be punctual.	Er hatte es lieber, **wenn** wir pünktlich kamen.

Dagegen ist im Englischen bei diesen Verben **kein** Nebensatz mit *that* möglich! Folglich **musst** du z.B. den Satz „Ich will, dass du kommst" mit *I want you to come* übersetzen – also mit Objekt + Infinitiv.

4.

Jetzt lasse deiner Fantasie freien Lauf und bilde neun oder zehn eigene Sätze aus folgender Schalttafel, die du nach Belieben ergänzen darfst! Auch Nonsens-Sätze sind ausnahmsweise erlaubt!

	prefers		
	doesn't want		
My teacher	hates	his/her pupils	
The soldier	likes	passengers	to …
The boss	requested	me	not to …
The postman	told	us	
The ticket inspector	ordered	them	
	didn't ask		
	warned		
	advised		

5.

Nun eine etwas schwierigere Übung: Verwende die Konstruktion Objekt + Infinitiv, um die beiden (Teil-)Sätze zu verbinden. Die Verben, denen sich die Infinitivkonstruktion anschließen soll, geben wir dir in Klammern vor. Achte aber auf die richtige Zeitform der Verben!

Beispiel: We're late. Our teacher doesn't like that. (like)
Our teacher doesn't like us to be late.

1. "Stand back!" the policeman said to us. (order)
2. "Don't be late again!" warned his boss. (warn)
3. "Please tell your parents about the school concert," said our music teacher. (ask)
4. "Listen carefully," the teacher said to the whole class. (tell)
5. The stewardess said it would be better if we sat on the other side of the plane. (ask)
6. "Work harder. That's what I expect," said the boss to his workers. (expect)
7. Mum: "Don't tell lies *(Lügen)*. You know I hate that!" (hate)
8. Father: "Put on a clean T-shirt every day. That's what I want." (want)
9. "Learn five new English words a day. That's what I would like," our English teacher told us. (tell)
10. "Don't come too close to the fire!" the fireman shouted to the people. (warn)

Der Infinitiv mit *to* anstelle von Nebensätzen

Der Infinitiv mit *to* kann Relativsätze mit modalem Hilfsverb ersetzen. In dieser Funktion drückt der Infinitiv oft ein „sollen" oder „können" aus.
Vergleiche:

She's the woman (whom) you should ask. = She's the woman **to ask.**	Sie ist die Frau, die du fragen solltest.
He's the best man (whom) you could take with you. = He's the best man **to take** with you.	Er ist der beste Mann, den du mitnehmen könntest.

Diese Konstruktion wird auch mit Superlativen (siehe letztes Beispiel) und Ausdrücken der Ausschließlichkeit *(the **first** woman **to climb** Mount Everest, the **last** man **to leave** the sinking Titanic, the **only** boy in the class **not to know** the answer)* verwendet.

Wichtig:

Relativpronomen wie *who/whom/which* und *that* verschwinden ganz, wenn diese Infinitivkonstruktion benutzt wird:

He was the last man **who** left the Titanic.	He was the last **man to leave** the Titanic.

Wörter wie *what* (= „das, was", „was"), *where, how* und *when* bleiben aber vor dem Infinitiv erhalten:

He told us **what** we should do.	= He told us **what to do.**
She asked me **when** she should phone.	= She asked me **when to phone.**
"**How** can I find the answer?"	= He asked me **how to find** the answer.

6.

Benutze einen Infinitiv, um folgende Sätze zu verkürzen:

1. "What's the best thing which we could do in this situation?"
2. "I know which (= the) way we should go."
3. "I can show you the best vegetables which you can grow in your garden."
4. There were no houses in which people could live.
5. "I've got nobody I can talk to," said the old man.
6. John was the only one who lost his way.
7. Our teacher told us what we should learn for the class test.
8. "How can I ring Germany from Britain?" he asked me. He asked me ...
9. Notice: Will the last person who leaves the office please turn the lights off.
10. "When should I meet you?" she asked. She asked me ...

7.

Zur Abwechslung mal ein kleines Quiz: Wer hat was zuerst – oder auch zuletzt – gemacht? Benutze die Infinitivkonstruktion in deinen Antworten.

Michael Schumacher Edmund Hillary Mikhail Gorbachev

Boris Becker Neil Armstrong Gertrude Ederle

1. Who was the first person who climbed Mount Everest?

____

2. Who was the first German who won the Men's Singles at Wimbledon?

____

3. Who was the last person who ruled the Soviet Union?

____

4. Who is the only racing driver who has been World Champion five times?

____

5. Who was the first woman who swam the English Channel?

____

6. Who was the first person who walked on the moon?

____

Zusammenfassung

Der englische Infinitiv wird **wie im Deutschen** benutzt:

ohne *to*:

1. nach modalen Hilfsverben, *let* und *make* (= zwingen):

I can **swim**.	Ich kann **schwimmen**.
Let me **explain**.	Lassen Sie mich das **erklären**.
She made me **stop** at the shop.	Sie ließ mich am Laden **anhalten**.

2. nach Verben der Wahrnehmung (*to see, to hear, to watch, to notice, to feel)*:

They saw me **fall**.	Sie sahen mich **fallen**.

mit *to*:

1. nach vielen Verben, wie im Deutschen:

We hope **to come** to your party.	Wir hoffen, auf deine Party **zu kommen**.

2. nach Verben des Bittens, Befehlens, Wollens und Nichtwollens + Objekt:

She asked **me not to tell** her.	Sie bat **mich**, (es) ihr **nicht zu sagen**.
He recommended **us to go**.	Er empfahl ***uns***, (dahin) **zu gehen**.

Der englische Infinitiv mit *to* wird **im Gegensatz zum Deutschen** benutzt

1. bei einigen Verben, die im Deutschen durch Nebensätze mit „dass“, „wenn“ usw. ergänzt werden, wenn das Verb mit einem Objekt benutzt wird.
   Die wichtigsten sind: *to want, to expect, to tell, to prefer, to like (= to want), to hate (= not to want)*:

We expected **her to win** the prize.	Wir erwarteten, dass sie den Preis gewinnen würde.
They wanted **us not to win**.	Sie wollten, dass wir nicht gewinnen.
She hated **people to arrive** late.	Sie hasste es, wenn die Leute zu spät kamen.

2. um einen Relativsatz mit modalem Hilfsverb (besonders *should* und *could*) zu ersetzen:

He's the man **to ask**.	Er ist der Mann, den du fragen soll(te)st.
She's a teacher **to respect**.	Sie ist eine Lehrerin, vor der man Respekt haben kann.

   Hier verschwinden Relativpronomen ganz. Fragewörter bleiben aber erhalten:
   "**How** can I get there?" She asked me **how to get** there.
   "**What** shall I do?" she asked, so I told her **what to do** and **what not to do**.

Test

Setze die richtigen Verben oder Infinitivformen aus dem Kästchen in folgenden Dialog ein. Vorsicht! Es gibt mehr Wörter im Kästchen, als du brauchst!

see / to see	let	to come / come
talk / to talk	sit / to sit	understands / to understand
must	need / needn't	treat / to treat *(behandeln)*

Mr Gifford is a rather nervous old gentleman. One morning he feels ill and phones a friend, who recommends a good doctor. But will Dr Everard see him immediately? He hurries to the surgery *(Praxis)* and talks to the receptionist *(Empfangsdame, Arzthelferin)*.

1. "Good morning. I'd like _________ to Dr Everard, please. I must see her at once!"
2. "_________ me see ...
3. I think I heard her ________ in a few minutes ago.
4. Do you have an appointment *(Termin)*, Mr ...?" – "Gifford, Clive Gifford. It's very important. I'm a new patient, but I'm sure Dr Everard will see me. I feel very ill..."
   "Mr Gifford, there are five doctors in the surgery this morning. Why do you want _________ one particular doctor?"
5. "A friend of mine recommended her to me. He said she was the only doctor _________ all about old people's problems!
6. I _________ to see her!"
7. "I must ask you _________ down for a minute. If you're so ill, you mustn't get so excited."
8. "You can't make me _______ down!"
9. "You _________ shout, Mr Gifford.
10. If you want Dr Everard _________ you, please sit down and wait a moment. I'm sure she'll see you in a minute."

10 Das gerund

Das Gerundium (hier *eating*) wird im Englischen sehr häufig verwendet. Ihm entspricht im Deutschen häufig ein (substantivierter) Infinitiv: „im Würstchenessen".

Das *gerund* als Subjekt und Objekt

	Englische Konstruktion	Deutsche Konstruktion
1. *Gerund* als Subjekt	Swimming is fun.	(Das) Schwimmen macht Spaß.
– mit Erweiterung	Swimming in the sea is fun.	Das Schwimmen im Meer/ Im Meer zu schwimmen macht Spaß.
– mit eigenem Objekt	Eating ice-cream is fun.	Eis essen macht Spaß. (Hier hört's im Deutschen mit dem *gerund* schon auf.)
2. *Gerund* als Objekt	I like swimming.	Ich schwimme gern.
– nach bestimmten Verben	I prefer skiing to swimming.	Ich ziehe das Skilaufen dem Schwimmen vor.

– mit Erweiterung	We like swimming in the sea.	Wir schwimmen gern im Meer. (Kein *gerund* möglich im Deutschen.)
– mit eigenem Objekt	She hates eating cabbage.	Sie hasst es, Kohl zu essen./Sie isst ungern Kohl.
	I prefer reading books to writing letters.	Ich lese lieber Bücher, als dass ich Briefe schreibe.

Besonders häufig wird das *gerund* im Englischen **nach folgenden Verben** benutzt: *to enjoy, to finish, to like, to love, to hate, to prefer, to not mind (I don't mind ...-ing), to go (shopping, swimming, etc.), to be keen on* (etwas sehr gerne machen), *to be mad about* (verrückt danach sein) etc.

1.

Lies den folgenden Text durch und unterstreiche erstens alle *ing*-Formen und zweitens – in einer anderen Farbe – die Wörter, welche das jeweilige *gerund* ergänzen, z.B. *skateboarding for young people, injuring other people* usw.

Fun on 4 wheels only?

Skateboarding is popular with young people all over the world. Skateboarding is not like skiing as it can be done in most places and at most times of the year. But if you do not like skateboarding, what about windsurfing or snowboarding? You need the right equipment, of course, and the right conditions – water and wind or snow – but there is less risk of hurting yourself and less danger of injuring other people, too.

Many young people have the chance of learning to windsurf when they go on their summer holidays. But you should not go windsurfing if you are not fond of swimming! Most beginners spend more time climbing out of the water than standing on their boards, but after mastering the basic techniques you will usually become quite good at staying on your board and may enjoy windsurfing on the sea almost as much as skateboarding in the city.

2.

Bilde acht Sätze mit Hilfe der folgenden Schalttafel. Du kannst, wenn's dir Spaß macht, auch fünf Unsinnssätze bilden. Wir geben die lustigsten Varianten in den Lösungen mit an. Viel Spaß!

Swimming			
Walking	in bed		
Reading	in the sea		hobbies.
Eating	letters to friends	is one of my	bad habits.
Listening	in the garden	is not among my	interests.
Writing	the car		weekend activities.
Working	to good music		
Playing	...		

3.

Was meinst du? Schau dir die dargestellten Tätigkeiten an und sage, was du davon hältst.

Beispiel: "Dancing is fantastic/stupid/a waste of time."
oder: "Swimming in the sea is a hobby of mine."

Benutze folgende Wörter für Tätigkeiten, die du magst:
fun / fantastic / super / wonderful / a hobby of mine / terrific / easy
Benutze folgende Wörter für Tätigkeiten, die du nicht magst:
boring / terrible / stupid / a waste of time / dangerous / horrible / difficult

dancing

swimming

hang-gliding

playing football

learning English

cooking

making models

writing letters

cycling

camping

4.

Benutze die hier vorgegebenen Wörter, um deine eigenen Vorlieben und Abneigungen auszudrücken.

1. I like …-ing (…)
2. I don't mind …-ing (…)
3. I hate …-ing (…)
4. I prefer …-ing to …-ing
5. I'm keen on …-ing (…)
6. I'm not so keen on …-ing (…)
7. I love …-ing (…)
8. I'm (not) mad about …-ing (…)

5.

a) Schau dir die Schilder an, und bilde Befehle mit dem *gerund* nach dem Muster *"No …-ing"*

b) Bilde ganze Sätze, welche die Bedeutung der Schilder erklären: *"No …-ing" means that you can't/it's forbidden to/you're not allowed to …*

Das *gerund* nach Präpositionen

Wie ein Substantiv kann auch ein *gerund* im Englischen nach einer Präposition stehen. Nach bestimmten Verben, Substantiven und Adjektiven, die fest mit einer Präposition verbunden sind, folgt meist das *gerund*: Im Deutschen wird eine andere Konstruktion (meist mit Infinitiv) benutzt.

	Englisch	**Deutsch**
Nur Präposition	I'm **for** going to the disco.	Ich bin dafür, dass wir in die Disco gehen.
	She's **against** smoking.	Sie ist gegen das Rauchen.
	Instead **of** waiting ...	Statt ... zu warten ...
Verb + Präposition	He **went on** speaking.	Er sprach weiter.
	She **kept on** asking for my address.	Sie hörte nicht auf, nach meiner Adresse zu fragen.
	They **succeeded in** reaching the bank.	Es gelang ihnen, das Ufer zu erreichen.
	I'm **looking forward to** going to England.	Ich freue mich auf meine Reise nach England.
Substantiv + Präposition	There's no **risk of** losing your way.	Du kannst dich unmöglich verlaufen.
	Is there any **chance of** borrowing that CD?	Gibt es eine Chance, dass ...
Substantiv ohne Präposition	It's no **use** asking him.	Es hat keinen Zweck, ...
	There's no **point** waiting.	Es hat keinen Sinn, zu ...
Adjektiv + Präposition	Are you **interested in** windsurfing?	Bist du an Windsurfen interessiert?
	I'm **fond of** eating rice.	Ich esse gern Reis.
Adjektiv + Ergänzung	He's not **used to** driving on the left.	Er ist es nicht gewohnt, links zu fahren.
Adjektiv + eigenes Objekt	Are they **good at** learning languages?	Sind sie im Fremdsprachenlernen gut?

6.

Setze die richtige Form der unten aufgeführten Wörter in den folgenden Text ein. Es wird nicht immer möglich sein, ein *gerund* zu verwenden. Bei Bedarf muss das *gerund* auch durch die entsprechende Präposition ergänzt werden (= „Doppellücke“).

lie	persuade	talk	take
stay	swim	let	go
spend	skateboard	swim	allow

It was June, and John was already looking forward ____ ______________ on holiday. His parents wanted ______________ three weeks at the seaside again, but John was not keen ____ ______________ on the beach in the sun. He preferred ______________ to ______________ in the sea. He was not very good ____ ______________ . There was no chance ____ ______________ at home while his parents were on holiday, so John asked his father if he could ______________ his skateboard with him.

At first his father was against ______________ John to take such a big thing in the car with them, but finally John succeeded ____ ______________ his mother ______________ to his father. At last John's dad agreed ______________ John take his skateboard.

When they put their luggage into the car, there was only just room for John's skateboard. "It's a good job you haven't got a surfboard, John," his dad said.

Zusammenfassung

Das *gerund* wird wie im Deutschen verwendet:

Als Subjekt:	Skiing is fun.	Das Skilaufen macht Spaß.
Als Objekt:	I like skiing.	Ich mag das Skilaufen.

Das *gerund* wird – zum Teil anders als im Deutschen – mit Erweiterungen verwendet:

Als Subjekt:	Skiing in the mountains is fun.	Das Skilaufen in den Bergen macht Spaß.
Als Objekt:	I like swimming in the sea.	Ich schwimme gern im Meer.

Das *gerund* wird – im Gegensatz zum Deutschen – nach Präpositionen (auch Verb, Substantiv und Adjektiv + Präposition) benutzt:

She's for waiting.	Sie ist dafür, dass wir warten.
He's looking forward to coming.	Er freut sich darauf, dass er kommt.
I'm afraid of losing my way.	Ich habe Angst davor, mich zu verlaufen.
We have no chance of winning.	Wir haben keine Chance zu gewinnen.

Test

Eigentlich war der letzte Englischtest gar nicht so schwierig, trotzdem hat Dorothee eine 5 geschrieben. Nur zwei ihrer zehn Sätze waren richtig. Verbessere die acht falschen Sätze und mache nur bei den zwei richtigen einen Haken im Kästchen! Also aufgepasst!

1. She prefers roller-skating to skateboard.

   ______________________________ ☐

2. Sing is one of my hobbies.

   ______________________________ ☐

3. I enjoy to learn English.

   ______________________________ ☐

4. She succeeded in passing her exam.

   ______________________________ ☐

5. We're not used to learn ten new English words a day.

   ______________________________ ☐

6. It's no use to ask him. He doesn't know the answer.

   ______________________________ ☐

7. Instead to wait we should leave right away.

   ______________________________ ☐

8. She's looking forward to get an e-mail from her pen-friend.

   ______________________________ ☐

9. "No, I'm not at all interested to meet you at the disco!"

   ______________________________ ☐

10. They love eating fish and chips.

   ______________________________ ☐

11 Die modalen Hilfsverben

Tja, schon wieder die alte Verwechslung zwischen *you mustn't* („du darfst nicht") und *you needn't* („du musst nicht"). Damit du bei den englischen Modalverben nicht ins Wanken kommst, empfehlen wir dir ein gründliches Studium dieses Kapitels.

Must und *needn't*

Die modalen Hilfsverben *(modal auxiliaries)* dienen zum Ausdruck von Fähigkeiten, Möglichkeiten, Verpflichtungen usw.

must

German	English auxiliary	substitute	
müssen	–	to have to	We will have to wait.
muss	I must	I have to	He must/has to go now.
muss nicht	I needn't	I don't have to	I don't have to wait.
musste	–	she had to	She had to go.
gemusst	–	I have had to	I've often had to wait.

Achtung:
mustn't = *darf nicht*: You mustn't drink whisky!

needn't und *to need*

needn't heißt „nicht müssen, nicht brauchen“, kommt aber **nur in dieser Präsensform** vor.
Was heißt dann „Ich brauchte nicht“? Hier bedienen wir uns des Vollverbs *to need* (= brauchen), das meist mit Gegenständen benutzt wird:

You need a new bike!
We needed money.
Did you need to ask permission?
She didn't need a book.
You didn't need to come.

1.
Setze die richtige Form – oder Ersatzform – von *must* ein.

1. "I must go to the dentist's soon." – "I … go last week."
2. " ... we do this exercise?" – "Yes, of course you … !"
3. "You … eat all the food. John hasn't had any yet."
4. "Do you … go to the meeting?" – "No, we … go if we don't want to."
5. "We'll … ask our teacher."
6. She has plenty of money. She does not … go to work.
7. She did not … take the job, but she wanted to.
8. We have never … work so hard before!
9. I cannot do it myself. You will … help me.
10. I can do it myself. You … help me.

2.
Setze das entsprechende Hilfsverb *mustn't* (nicht dürfen) oder *needn't* (nicht müssen) in die Lücken ein.

1. You can have one of these cakes, but those are for the party this evening. You … eat them.
2. There's a meeting of the football club after school this evening, but it isn't important, so we … go.
3. The match starts at 3 o'clock, so we … be late.
4. You … phone me if you're coming to the youth club tomorrow. We can talk there.
5. I've got a map, so you … buy one.
6. The traffic lights are red. You … cross the street.
7. We … wait for Sally. She can't come.
8. We … wait any longer for John or we'll be late.
9. You … shout. You'll wake the baby.
10. You … shout! I'm not deaf!

can/could und *may/might*

can/could

German	English auxiliary	substitute	
können	–	to be able to	He won't be able to go.
er kann	he can	he is able to	I can/am able to swim.
ich konnte	–	I was able to	We were able to leave.
sie konnte nicht	she couldn't	she wasn't able to	She wasn't able to/ couldn't come.
er könnte	he could	–	He could come with us.
gekonnt	–	we have been able to	She hasn't been able to write until now.

may/might

German	English auxiliary	substitute	
dürfen	–	to be allowed to	We will be allowed to go.
Darf ich?	May I?	Am I allowed to?	May we touch them?/ Are we allowed to touch them?
er darf nicht	he may not/ must not	he isn't allowed to	You may/must not park here. You aren't allowed to park here.
ich durfte	–	I was allowed to	We weren't allowed to wait.
sie dürfte	she might	–	She might be about 17.
(= sollte)	she should	–	She should be home by now.
Dürfte ich?	Might I?	–	Might I ask you a question?

3.

Hier sind drei kurze Dialoge: Junge Leute planen ihre Woche. Kannst du die Sätze richtig ergänzen?

1. "I can't see you tomorrow evening, but I'll ... see you in the afternoon."
2. "What a pity. I had hoped that we would ... meet tonight."
3. "Well – I suppose I ... see you tonight if it was really important."

4. "I'm sorry I haven't ... call you until now."
5. "Why ... n't you phone me at the weekend?" – "Because we were away."
6. "... you ... come to my party on Friday?" -"I ... n't ... tell you until tomorrow."

7. "If I promised to help you with your English homework tonight, ... you ... help me with my maths before the test on Thursday?
8. I ... only ... answer five questions in the last test."
9. "I don't think I'll ... help you before Wednesday. Is that OK?"
10. "I don't see why you ... help me tonight, when I have finished helping you with your English!"

4.

Jetzt eine kleine Dolmetschübung zu *may*. Du besuchst mit einem jungen Bekannten einen kleinen Privatzoo in England. Dein Bekannter fragt, was er alles machen darf. Du stellst die Fragen auf englisch an ein Mädchen, das dort arbeitet.

„Guck mal! Kleine Ziegen. Dürfen wir die Ziegen streicheln?"

1. You: "... we stroke the goats, please?"
2. Girl: "Yes of course. You ... to stroke all the animals in this part of the zoo."

„Ist es erlaubt, die Affen zu füttern?"

3. You: "My friend wants to know if it ... to feed the monkeys."
4. Girl: "Of course you may. But you are only ... to feed them with food you buy here."

„In Hamburg durften wir unsere eigenen Erdnüsse verfüttern!"

5. You: "My friend says that in Hamburg we ... to feed them our own peanuts."
6. Girl: "I'm afraid you ... not feed your own food to the animals here."
7. You: "OK, thank you. If the weather is good tomorrow, I ... come again with a few friends."

shall/should, ought to und *will/would*

shall/should und *ought to*

"Shall we call the police?"	„Sollen wir die Polizei holen?"
"Should we go?"	„Sollten wir hingehen?"
"No, we shouldn't. We should stay at home."	
"Ought we to go?"	„Sollten wir eigentlich da hingehen?"
"No, we oughtn't (to). We ought to stay here."	

will/would

Die Hilfsverben *will* und *would* werden in erster Linie zur Bildung der „neutralen" Zukunftsform (*will*, siehe S. 50) und des Konditionals (*would*, siehe S. 62) benutzt.
Darüber hinaus können *will* und *would* aber auch zum Ausdruck einer Bitte oder eines Wunsches verwendet werden:

"Will you help me?"	„Hilfst du mir?"
"Would you help me?"	„Würdest du mir bitte helfen?"
"Won't you sit down?"	„Wollen Sie sich nicht setzen?"
"Will you please be a little quieter!"	„Seien Sie doch etwas ruhiger!"
"Would you please be a little quieter!"	„Seien Sie doch bitte etwas ruhiger!"

Dabei wirkt *would* etwas höflicher als *will*.

5.

Setze *shall/should(n't)/ought(n't) to* in folgenden Sätzen ein:

1. "There's a nice café over there? … we go in for a cup of coffee?"
2. "OK, but we … stay too long. I really … to go home soon."
3. "Look – there's Carl and Elaine. … we ask them to join us?"
4. "Carl? Oh – he … to be here! He told me he was going to London today."
5. "Well, he hasn't gone to London. What … we do? They've seen us! They're coming over here."
6. "Hello, Carl! … n't you be in London?"
7. "London? You … to listen more carefully, Phil. I'm going to London tomorrow."
8. "Well, never mind that now. … we go into that café for a coffee?"
9. "OK, but Elaine and I … n't to stay long. We're going to the cinema.
10. The film starts at 3 o'clock and we … be there in good time."
11. "It's only 2 o'clock. You … n't to be late!"
12. "But we're not going to the local cinema. We're going to the new cinema in the city centre. There … be a bus in about half an hour. But there's always time for a coffee. Come on!"

6.

Shall oder *will*? Setze das richtige Hilfsverb in diese Sätze ein:

"What … we do at the weekend?"

"Let's have a barbecue in the garden. We can invite all our friends: Tania, Paul, Melissa, Jason, Liza."

"Good idea! … I phone them or … you?"

"I expect I… see most of them at the youth club tomorrow. … Maria be back from Spain by the weekend?"

"I'm not sure. … we write her a note?"

"… you do that? I …n't have time. But what … we do if it rains?"

"We … have the barbecue in Farmer Jones's old barn. He …n't mind."

"… we ask him if we can use the barn even if the weather is fine? It would be even better than a barbecue in the garden."

"Good idea. We … have a wonderful time!"

7.

Setze *will/won't* oder *would/wouldn't* oder die entsprechenden Kurzformen in folgende Sätze ein:

John is 16. He has just left school and this is his first interview for a job. Mr Sykes is a friendly man, but John is a bit nervous.

1.	Mr Sykes:	"Come in, John. ... you take your coat off?"
2.	John:	"... you mind if I kept it on, sir? I'm feeling a bit cold."
3.	Mr Sykes:	"No problem. ... you like something to drink? A cup of tea or coffee?
4.		Or ... you rather have a glass of water?"
5.	John:	"I ... mind a cup of coffee, sir. If it's no trouble."
6.	Mr Sykes:	"No trouble at all. (he picks up the phone) Jenny – ... you make us two cups of coffee, please?
7.		The coffee ... be long, John.
8.		While we're waiting, I ... ask you a few questions."
9.	John:	"I ... try to answer them, sir."
10.	Mr Sykes:	"I ... be too nervous if I were you! They ... be too difficult for you!"

8.

Was eignet sich zur Einübung von Möglichkeiten *(can/can't)*, Geboten *(must/should/ought to)* und Verboten *(mustn't/shouldn't/oughtn't to)* besser als ein Blick ins britische *„Highway Code“*? Auch als Radfahrer solltest du genug über folgende Verkehrszeichen wissen, um mindestens zwei Sätze zu jedem Verkehrsschild zu bilden. Die darunter stehenden Wörter sind als Hilfe gedacht.

1

Stop and give way at major road ahead

2

Wild animals

3

Level crossing

4

No right turn

5

No overtaking

6

Maximum speed limit 30 miles per hour

7

Aircraft noise

8

River bank, canal or quayside

	I may not …	I mustn't …
When I see this sign	I must …	I should/shouldn't … (because) …
At this sign	I can …	I needn't …
	there may/might be …	I can't … (if/unless) …

Zusammenfassung

Die modalen Hilfsverben „helfen", die Handlung eines Verbs einzuschränken, indem sie ihr die „Modalität" des Könnens, Müssens, Dürfens usw. hinzufügen:

Can you help me? You **must**!	Kannst du mir helfen? Du musst!
We **mustn't** be late but we **needn't** rush.	Wir dürfen nicht zu spät kommen, aber wir müssen uns nicht beeilen.
You **should** be careful. You **ought to** know that.	Du solltest vorsichtig sein. Das solltest du wissen.
May I open the window? – No. – Well **might** I take my pullover off, then? It's very hot in here!	Darf ich das Fenster öffnen? – Nein. – Dürfte ich dann meinen Pulli ausziehen? Es ist sehr heiß hier drinnen!

Wie obiges Beispiel zeigt, ist bei den modalen Hilfsverben die zweite Form nicht die Vergangenheitsform, sondern die höflichere, ungewissere Form.
Vergleiche:

Can you come? **Could** your bring Bob?	Kannst du kommen? Könntest du Bob mitbringen?

Will und *would* können auch als modale Hilfsverben verwendet werden, und zwar zum Ausdruck eines Wunsches oder einer Bitte:

Will / would you help me?	Würdest du mir (bitte) helfen?

Shall wird fast nur in Fragen in der ersten Person verwendet.

Shall I call the police?	Soll ich die Polizei rufen?
Shall we go to the zoo?	Sollen wir in den Zoo gehen?

Was muss ich sonst über diese Verben wissen?

1. Mit Ausnahme von *ought to* wird der Infinitiv **ohne *to*** benutzt.
2. Die modalen Hilfsverben haben keine Verlaufsformen.
3. Um die Vergangenheit oder andere Zeitformen auszudrücken, musst du die entsprechende Form des Ersatzverbs *(substitute)* benutzen, z.B.:

Simple past:	I **had to** come.	Ich musste kommen.
Present perfect:	We'**ve been able to** stop.	Wir haben anhalten können.
Future:	They **won't be allowed to** stay.	Sie werden nicht bleiben dürfen.

Nicht vergessen:
You **mustn't** park here. = Du **darfst** hier **nicht** parken.
You **needn't** wait for me. = Du **musst nicht** auf mich warten.

Test

Füge das richtige Hilfsverb in folgende Sätze ein. Jedes Verb darf nur einmal benutzt werden:

might	can't	ought	should	may
couldn't	shall	needn't	must	mustn't

In the street outside the school playground, a pupil is practising skateboarding. A teacher comes round a corner and nearly falls over the pupil.

1. "Be careful! Why _________ you watch where you're going? You nearly knocked me over!
2. Don't you know that you _________ use a skateboard in the playground?"
3. "I'm sorry. And you _________ shout at me. I'm outside the playground.
4. And this is a play street. You _________ to know that. You're a teacher!"
5. "All right. But you _________ keep your eyes open in future."
6. "Keep my eyes open? You came round a corner! I _________ see you!"

Sonja has lost her keys. She asks her brother if he has seen them.

7. "I've no idea where they are. They _________ be anywhere!
8. _________ I help you look for them?"
9. "Thanks. They _________ be somewhere here in my room."
10. "There they are! On your desk! Right in front of your nose. _________ I make a suggestion *(Vorschlag)*, Sis?" – "What?" – "Get yourself some new glasses." She throws a book at him. "Ouch!"

12 Die indirekte Rede

Bei der indirekten Rede *(reported speech)* im Englischen heißt es immer „eine Zeitstufe zurück, wenn die Einleitung der nichtwörtlichen Rede in der Vergangenheit steht" – z.B.: *he said, she told me, they asked us* usw.
Bei Befehlen gestaltet sich die ganze Sache etwas einfacher. Deshalb fangen wir damit an. Viel Spaß!

Indirekte Befehle

"Stop!"	The policeman ordered us to stop.
"Don't move!"	The man told us not to move.
"Never lie to me!"	She told/warned me never to lie to her.
"Please wait for us."	Our friends asked us to wait for them.

Bei richtigen Befehlen nimmst du am besten *order*, bei Aufforderungen mit *please* ein Einführungsverb wie *ask*. Beim „freundlichen" Ermahnen ist *tell* oder *warn* geeigneter als *command/order*, und beim „Bitten und Betteln" nimmst du am besten *invite* oder *beg*.

Aufforderungen nach dem Muster *„No talking, please."* werden auch mit *not* + Infinitiv wiedergegeben: *He asked us not to talk.*

1.
Lies den folgenden Text durch und unterstreiche die indirekten Befehle.

The Big Black Bag

I had only been in England for five minutes when I experienced my first bomb scare. Our teacher had told us to keep our hand baggage with us at all times and not to leave anything on the plane.
A voice over the loudspeakers requested us to report any unattended bags or suitcases and not to touch them.
It was while we were waiting for our suitcases that I saw the Big Black Bag. There was nobody standing near it, and after watching it for five minutes I decided that it was certainly "unattended". A policeman was walking by and I stopped him ...
Within minutes a calm voice over the loudspeakers was ordering us not to panic but to leave the baggage area quietly. The voice also asked us to take all our personal baggage with us. Our baggage had not arrived yet, so our teacher told us to leave the baggage hall without it.
We waited outside for two hours. The voice over the loudspeaker invited us to have a cup of tea and a cake at the airport's expense, but not many of us were hungry or thirsty. We were far more interested in the Big Black Bag. Again the loudspeakers warned us not to get too close to the building and to stay away from the windows and glass doors.
Finally we were requested to return to the baggage hall and collect our suitcases. "Ladies and Gentlemen," the voice went on, "the police tell us that there was no danger after all, but we would like to thank the young lady who reported this piece of unattended baggage." My whole class looked at me, and many other people did, too. I had made them all two hours late!

2.
Auf dem Flug nach London wurden verschiedene Anweisungen gegeben. Wie würdest du sie weiterberichten? Benutze passende Einführungsverben.

Beispiel: Teacher: "Stay together in a group!"
Our teacher told us to stay together in a group.

1. Teacher: "Don't wander about!"
2. At the check-in counter: "Please put your baggage on the scales (Waage)."
3. Passport officer: "Show me your passport."
4. Assistant in duty-free shop: "Show me your boarding pass, please."
5. Stewardess: "Passengers in seats 1 – 40 please board now."
6. Steward: "All passengers fasten your seat-belts for take-off."
7. Captain: "Please listen carefully to the safety instructions."
8. Stewardess: "No smoking in the toilets!"

Indirekte Aussagen

Indirekte Aussagen

1. Einführungsverb im *present tense* oder *present perfect:*

direkte Rede ←——→	indirekte Rede
"I live in Berlin."	He says (that) he lives in Berlin.
"I lived in Berlin ten years ago."	He says (that) he lived in Berlin ten years ago.
"I have never been there."	He has often told me (that) he has never been there.

Nach einem Einführungsverb im *present tense* oder im *present perfect (he says, he has often told me (that) ...)* gibt es keine Zeitverschiebung! Die Zeiten der direkten Rede werden beibehalten.
Man kann die Konjunktion *that* bei indirekten Aussagen weglassen.

2. Einführungsverb im *past tense:*

direkte Rede ←——→	indirekte Rede
"I live in Berlin."	He said he lived in Berlin.
"I lived in Berlin ten years ago."	He said he had lived in Berlin ten years ago.
"I have never been there."	He said he had never been there.

Berichtet man über eine Unterhaltung, die in der Vergangenheit stattfand und deshalb mit einem Einführungsverb im *past tense (he said, she told me usw.)* eingeleitet wird, werden die in der direkten Rede verwendeten Zeitformen um einen Schritt in die Vergangenheit zurückverschoben.

Personen, die in der direkten Rede erwähnt werden, müssen meist in der indirekten Rede geändert werden:

"**I** live in Berlin."	She says **she** lives in Berlin.

Vorvergangenheit ← **Vergangenheit** ← **Gegenwart**

I live in London, but I am working in Berlin for six months. I have been in Berlin for two months and can give you my address if you will lend me a pen. I haven't brought one with me.

She said she lived in London but was working in Berlin for six months. She told me she had been in Berlin for two months and could give me her address if I would lend her a pen, because she hadn't brought a pen with her.

I lived in New York for six years. While I was living there I met a lot of nice people.

She said she had lived in New York for six years and that while she had been living there she had met a lot of nice people.

After I had lived in New York for six years I moved back to London and my family and I have been living there ever since.

She went on to say that after she had left New York she had moved back to London and had been living there ever since.

Merke

Nach einem Einführungsverb im *past tense* kommen somit **nur zwei Zeitformen** vor:

1. *past tense* (auch bei zeitformbildenden Hilfsverben: *will* → would) und
2. *past perfect*

So kannst du die Richtigkeit deiner Hausaufgaben kontrollieren. Alle anderen Zeitformen sind falsch!

3.

Verwandle die Sätze in die indirekte Rede. Verändere nur das Nötigste!
Achtung! Eine Zeitverschiebung ist nicht immer erforderlich.

1. "I go to school in London now, but I went to school in Scotland for two years."
   The girl said (that) ...
2. "Your pronunciation is good and you can understand a lot of English."
   My teacher says (that) ...
3. "He phoned my hotel after I had left."
   The young woman said (that) ...
4. "I have no idea what you are talking about. I have never seen you before!"
   He says (that) ...
5. "We are staying at the hotel for a week and so far we've been enjoying our stay."
   The guests told him (that) ...
6. "I want to become an airline pilot so I have to do well at school."
   She tells me (that) ...
7. "We saw him yesterday. He was standing in the school playground."
   The girls said (that) ...
8. "My grandmother has never seen the sea."
   Our young African visitor told us (that) ...
9. "Helena knows the answer but she won't tell me!"
   He said (that) ...
10. "Jim and Vera speak French very well because they've been living in France since 1990."
    My French friend Jean says (that) ...
11. "I was having a bath when the phone rang."
    She told us (that) ...

4.

Stell dir vor, du bist gerade in London angekommen, als eine Mitreisende, die nicht so gut Englisch kann, dich um Hilfe bittet. Sie hat ihren Rucksack mit sämtlichen Reisedokumenten verloren. Du musst auf dem Polizeirevier den Dolmetscher spielen. Also keine Verschiebung der Zeitformen.
Im schriftlichen Bericht wird jedoch alles „nach hinten verschoben", weil solche Berichte immer mit Einführungsverben im *simple past* geschrieben werden. Schreibe den Bericht anhand des Gesprächs zu Ende.

Policeman: "Can I help you?"
You: "Yes. My friend here can't speak much English. She says she has lost her rucksack."
Policeman: "What's your friend's name?"
You: "... – we're from Germany."
Policeman: "I see. Where exactly did she lose the rucksack?"
You: "At Victoria Station. She says she wanted to change some money at the station and that she took it off before she went into the bank."
Policeman: "You mean she just left the rucksack there?"
You: "No. A friend was looking after it, but he was talking to some other people and doesn't remember if anyone took the rucksack by mistake."
Policeman: "What was in the rucksack?"
You: "Mainly clothes and a wallet with money, traveller's cheques, passport and so on."
Policeman: "What colour is it?"
You: "Red and grey."
Policeman: "OK, we'll do our best to find it. Where are you and your friend staying?"
You: "Probably at the same youth hostel. I'm not sure. We'll ring you as soon as we have an address."

REPORT OF LOST ITEM

Name and address: ______________________________

Item Lost – red and grey rucksack.

Contents: clothes and wallet with money, traveller's cheques, passport etc.

The owner said she __________ her rucksack at Victoria Station. She said she __________ it off outside the bank at the station before she __________ into the bank. The owner said that a friend __________ after the rucksack but that he __________ to some other people and __________ if anyone __________ the rucksack by mistake. The two young people from Germany said they __________ not sure where they __________ but that they __________ later.

Modale Hilfsverben in der indirekten Rede

1. Die modalen Hilfsverben *can, may, will, shall* werden nach einem Einführungsverb in der Vergangenheit auch „verschoben“:
   "I **may** miss the train but I **can** wait if you**'ll** tell me the whole story."
   He said he **might** miss his train but **could** wait if we **would** tell him the whole story.

2. Es gibt keine „zweite Form“ von *must* und *needn't.* Nach einem Einführungsverb in der Vergangenheit werden hier Ersatzverben benutzt:

"You **must** leave quickly!"	He said I **had to** leave quickly.
"She **needn't** wait."	The teacher told her she didn't **have to** wait.

   Manchmal werden *must* und *needn't* auch unverändert übernommen.

3. Modale Hilfsverben in der „zweiten Form“ *(would, could* = könnte, *should, ought to)* werden unverändert übernommen, ganz gleich, ob das Einführungsverb in der Gegenwart oder in der Vergangenheit steht – Ausnahme: *could not* = „konnte nicht“!

"We **would** love to go!"	They say/said they **would** love to go.
"She **should** call the police."	He says/said she **should** call the police.
"They **ought to** know better."	She says/said they **ought to** know better.
"I **couldn't** come."	He said he **had not been able to** come.

5.
Jetzt eine Übung mit Hilfsverben.

1. "We should take a bus. It'll be quicker."
   My friend said ... because ...
2. "She can sit in the front of the car. She needn't sit in the back."
   The driver told the girl ...
3. "My friends couldn't help me because they didn't have time."
   John said ...
4. "You must go or you'll miss your train."
   My friend's mother told me ...
5. "I'd like to talk to your brother if I may."
   The girl said ...
6. "I ought to ask my mother if I can come with you."
   My friend said she ...
7. "My sister can't come to your party on Saturday because she is going to London."
   John told me ...
8. "It's going to rain. You should take your raincoats."
   The guide said ...
9. "It might be too cold for a barbecue in the garden. We can have it on the balcony."
   Dad told us ... and suggested (that) ...

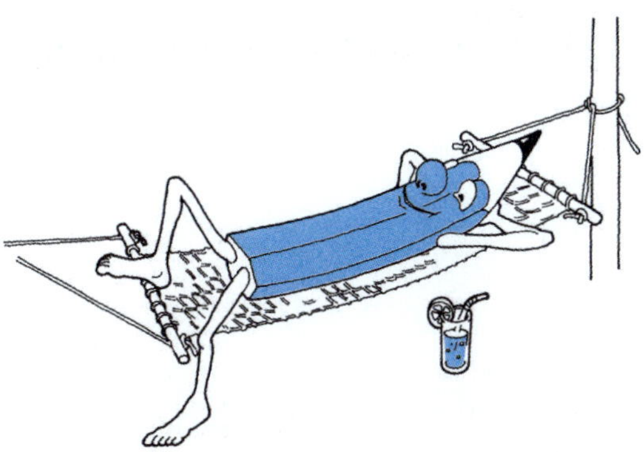

Fragen und Vorschläge in der indirekten Rede

Indirekte Fragen

1. Gibt es ein „*Wh*-Fragewort“ in der direkten Frage, so bleibt dieses in der indirekten Frage erhalten:

"Who is coming to the party?"
She wanted to know who was coming to the party.
"What is your name and where do you live?"
He asked me what my name was and where I lived.
Customs officer: "Where did you buy it and how much did it cost?"
The customs officer wanted to know where I had bought it and how much it had cost.

2. Gibt es kein „*Wh*-Fragewort“ in der direkten Frage, brauchst du *if* oder *whether* als Bindewort:

"Are you German?"
He asked me if I was German.
"Did you have a nice trip?"
Our teacher asked us if we had had a nice trip.

3. *Whether* wird statt *if* benutzt, wenn in der Frage die Worte „oder nicht?“ mitschwingen:

"Have you seen John (or not)?"
She wanted to know whether I had seen John (or not).

Man benutzt auch *whether* statt *if*, um unschöne Doppelungen von *if* zu vermeiden:

"Do you know if there's a bus to London soon?"
She asked me whether I knew if there was a bus to London soon.

6.

Setze die folgenden Fragen in die indirekte Rede.

Beispiel (Satz 1): "He/She asked me what time it was."

Bei den Fragen, die mehr Gedanken sind und an niemanden direkt gestellt werden (mit * gekennzeichnet) sollte *He/She wondered/wanted to know if/whether/what ...* usw. verwendet werden.

1. "What time is it?" (me)
2. "Are you English?" (her)
3. "Were you there?" (them)
4. "Have you phoned Phil?" (us)
5. "When does the film start?" (*)
6. "How much money have we got?" (me)
7. "Did you see Penny yesterday?" (him)
8. "Is the sun shining?" (*)
9. "Where were you born?" (me)
10. "Is there anybody there?" (*)
11. "How much do you earn?" (his friend)
12. "Has Paul phoned?" (*)
13. "Have you ever eaten lamb?" (her)
14. "Where did you go after you had left school?" (us)
15. "What would you like to drink?" (them)

7.

Die Polizei sucht eine junge Frau, die letzte Woche in einen Juwelierladen in Mannheim einbrach und Schmuck und Bargeld im Wert von € 125.000 erbeutete. Kommissar Habicht ist gerade dabei, eine junge Engländerin namens Jenny Jones, die kein Deutsch kann, zu verhören. Du musst dolmetschen. Da Verhör und Dolmetschen gleichzeitig erfolgen, werden die Zeitformen nicht verschoben. Nach einer Weile musst du aber auch Jennys Aussagen aus der indirekten Rede rekonstruieren.

	Habicht:	"Wo waren Sie letzten Donnerstag um Mitternacht, Frau Jones?"
1.	You:	"The inspector wants to know where ..."
	Jenny:	"I was at a friend's house. We were watching TV at midnight."
	You:	"Sie behauptet, um Mitternacht bei einer Freundin ferngesehen zu haben."
	Habicht:	"Wie heißt diese Freundin und wo wohnt sie?"
2.	You:	"He wants you to tell him ..."
	Jenny:	"Barbara Schäfer, 10, Goethestraße, Stuttgart-Rohr."

You: "Sie heißt …"
Habicht: "Ja ja! So viel Englisch kann ich schon! Frau Jones, Sie wurden um zehn Uhr abends hier in Mannheim gesehen. Wie kamen Sie so schnell nach Stuttgart?"
3. You: "He says you … and asks …"
4. Jenny: "I …"
You: "Sie sagt, sie habe den ICE um Viertel nach zehn genommen und sei um halb zwölf in Stuttgart angekommen."
Habicht: "Und wie ist sie so schnell zu ihrer Freundin gekommen?"
5. You: "The inspector is asking …"
6. Jenny: "…"
You: "Sie behauptet, ein Taxi genommen zu haben."
Habicht: "Wie viel haben Sie für das Taxi gezahlt?"
7. You: "He wants to know …"
8. Jenny: "…"
You: "Sie weiß es nicht. Sie hat es vergessen."
Habicht: "Warum sind Sie nach Stuttgart gefahren?"
9. You: "…"
10. Jenny: "…"
You: "Sie sagt, sie wollte einen anderen Einbruch *(burglary)* mit einigen Freunden planen."
Habicht: "So kommen wir nicht weiter! Fangen wir wieder von vorne an!"

Indirekte Vorschläge

Die Frage *"Why don't we go to the seaside?"* ist eigentlich keine Frage, sondern ein Vorschlag nach der Art: *"Let's …"*. Ein „indirekter Vorschlag" wird meist mit dem Verb *to suggest + ing*-Form eingeleitet.

Direkter Vorschlag	**Indirekter Vorschlag**
"Why don't we go/Let's go for a swim!"	Pat suggested going for a swim.
"Let's not wait for the bus."	John suggested not waiting for the bus.
"Shall we ring Jean up?"	Benny suggested ringing Jean up.

Schließt sich der Sprecher aus dem Vorschlag aus, wird das Verb *suggest(ed)* durch *that* + PERSON + *should* ergänzt:

"Why don't you start again?"	The teacher suggested that we should start again.

8.

Schau dir die sechs Bilder an und bilde Sätze mit indirekten Vorschlägen, die dazu passen.

Beispiel: The young man suggested …

Orts- und Zeitbestimmungen in der indirekten Rede

Wie die Zeitformen müssen auch Orts- und Zeitangaben „verschoben“ werden, wenn der Blickpunkt sich ändert. Wenn z.B. an einem anderen Ort bzw. zu einem anderen Zeitpunkt berichtet wird.
Übersetzt man als Dolmetscher sofort jeden Satz, so ändert sich nichts. Berichtet man später, so ist man unter Umständen nicht mehr am Ort des Geschehens. Dann ändert sich die Ortsangabe von „hier“ nach „dort“:
"I've lived here for years." → He says he has lived **here** for years.

Später (und an einem anderen Ort) berichtet, heißt es dann:
→ He said he had lived **there** for years.

Wenn man sich aber noch am „Ort des Geschehens“ befindet, heißt es:
→ He said he had lived **here** for years.

Ähnliches passiert mit Zeitangaben:

"I went there yesterday."	→ She says she went there yesterday.
Am selben Tag berichtet:	→ She said she had gone there yesterday.
Am nächsten Tag berichtet:	→ She said she had gone there the day before.

"We're going there tomorrow."	→ They say they are going there tomorrow.
Später am selben Tag:	→ They said they were going there tomorrow.
Am nächsten Tag berichtet:	→ They said they were going there today.(!)
Zwei Tage später:	→ They said they were going there **the next day**.

Direkte Rede:	**nach Zeitverschiebung*:**
"today"	→ that day
"yesterday"	→ the day before, the previous day
"tomorrow"	→ the next day, the following day
"next week/month/year/May"	→ the following week/month/year/May
"a few days/months ago"	→ a few days before etc.
"this summer/week/May/year"	→ that summer/week/May/year
"here"	→ there
"in this town"	→ in that town

* immer vorausgesetzt, dass Ort bzw. Zeit tatsächlich anders ist als in der direkten Rede.

9.

Jetzt machen wir eine kurze Übung gerade zu den Orts- und Zeitbestimmungen. Wir geben jeweils den Ort bzw. Zeitpunkt der Mitteilung in der indirekten Rede an, denn es könnte durchaus sein – wie unser Beispiel zeigt – dass keine Verschiebung nötig ist:

Beispiel: Have you seen John this morning?
(same day): She asked me if I had seen John this morning.
(reported next day): She asked me if I had seen John that/yesterday morning.

1. "How long have you been living here?" –
(reported at same place): They asked me …
2. "Is your sister going to the youth club tonight?"
(reported later the same day): John wanted to know …
3. "We went to the disco yesterday."
(reported two days later): Jim and Barbara said …
4. "We're going on holiday next month."
(reported later that month): They said …
5. "I'm going to London next month."
(reported two months later): He said …
6. "My mother's going to buy a new car this week."
(reported eight days later): …
7. "My class test is tomorrow."
(reported later the same day): …
8. "John told me he lives here."
(reported in front of the house): …
9. "John told me he lived in this street."
(reported at home): …
10. "We saw Paul and Jean a few days ago."
(reported the next day): …

Zusammenfassung

1. Direkte → indirekte Befehle:

"Stop talking!" → He asked/told/ordered us to stop talking.
"Don't wait for me." → She asked/told us not to wait for her.

2. Direkte → indirekte Aussagen:

Bei Einführungsverben im *present tense* bzw. *present perfect* wird die Zeitform der direkten Rede beibehalten:

"We live in London." → They say they live in London.
"We lived in London." → They say they lived in London.

Steht das Einführungsverb im *past tense*, werden alle Zeitformen der direkten Rede um eine Zeitstufe nach hinten verschoben:

"We live in London." → They said they lived in London.
"We lived in London." → They said they had lived in London.

Die Verschiebung bei Einführung in der Vergangenheit ergibt folgendes Bild:

Direkte Rede ⟷	Indirekte Rede
"live(s)" (simple present)	→ lived (simple past)
"am/is/are living" (present progressive)	→ was/were living (past progressive)
"lived" (simple past) "have/has lived" (present perfect) "had lived" (simple past perfect)	→ had lived (simple past perfect)
"was/were living" (past progressive) "has/have been living" (pres. perf. progr.) "had been living" (past perf. progr.)	→ had been living (past perfect progr.)

"can/could" → could | "will/would" → would | "must" → had to
"shall/should" → should | "may/might" → might | "needn't" → did not need to

3. Direkte → indirekte Fragen

"Where do you live?" → He asked me where I lived.
"Do you live in London?" → He asked me if/whether I lived in London.

4. Direkte → indirekte Vorschläge

"Let's go to the disco." → He suggested going to the disco.
"Why don't you home?" → He suggested that I/we/they should go home.

Test

Bevor du als Austauschschüler nach England gehen darfst, ringen dir deine Eltern zuerst mehrere Versprechen ab, geben dir einige Ratschläge und stellen einige Fragen. Als du endlich in England angekommen bist, erzählst du deinem Austauschpartner, wie nervig das alles war!
Setze die deutschen Sätze in die englische indirekte Rede. In einigen Sätzen geben wir dir eine Starthilfe:

1. *Mutter:* *Sei höflich* (polite) *zu deiner Gastfamilie!*
   Du: My mother told me ________________________ to my host family.
2. *Vater:* *Und gehe nicht zu oft in die Diskos!*
   Du: And my father warned me ________________________ too often.
3. *Mutter:* *Vergiss nicht, uns anzurufen, wenn du angekommen bist.*
   Du: They asked me ___________________________ when I arrived.
4. *Vater:* *Ich hoffe, du wirst eine schöne Zeit verleben* (have a good time).
   Du: My father said _______________________________________.
5. *Mutter:* *Ich habe an deine Gastfamilie geschrieben.*
   Du: My mother told me _________________________________.
   Did you get her letter? – Yes, we got it last week.
6. *Mutter:* *Ich hoffe, sie können mein Englisch verstehen.*
   Du: She said ____.
   – It was quite good, actually.
7. *Vater:* *Wir würden dich gerne in England besuchen.*
   Du: My parents said ___________________________________.
8. *Mutter:* *Wird das möglich sein?*
   Du: My mother wanted to know ____________________________.
9. *Vater:* *Gibt es ein interessantes Freizeitprogramm?*
   Du: My father asked ____________________________ leisure-time programme.
10. *Mutter:* *Wann werdet ihr in London ankommen? Hoffentlich nicht zu spät abends!*
    Du: And my mother never stops worrying about me! She wondered ______________________________ and said __________________ __________ too late in the evening! Aren't parents the absolute end!

13 Relativsätze

Tja, es ist so ein Kreuz mit den Relativpronomen: *who* bei Personen, *which* bei Sachen, *that* bei beiden – aber nur bei bestimmenden Relativsätzen ... Nun denn, dieses Kapitel wird versuchen, etwas Klarheit in die Sache einzubringen.

Relativpronomen als Subjekt des Relativsatzes

Für Personen und andere Lebewesen wird *who/that* verwendet, wobei *that* nur im bestimmenden Relativsatz verwendet werden kann:

Bestimmender Relativsatz
The woman **who/that** lives next door is 84.

Nicht bestimmender Relativsatz
Mrs Jones, **who** lives next door, is 84.

Für Sachen und andere Nicht-Lebewesen wird *which/that* verwendet, wobei *that* auch hier nur im bestimmenden Relativsatz möglich ist:

Bestimmender Relativsatz
The book **which / that** is lying on the floor is "Oliver Twist".

Im Englischen wird ein Komma nur benutzt, wenn im natürlichen Sprechrhythmus eine kurze Pause entsteht. Dies ist beim bestimmenden Relativsatz nicht der Fall.

Nicht bestimmender Relativsatz
"Oliver Twist", **which** is lying on the floor, is my favourite book.

Beim nicht bestimmenden Relativsatz wirken die „Pausenkommas" wie Klammern, welche die nicht notwendige Zusatzinformation von der Hauptaussage absetzen.

1.

a) Hier sollst du raten, was mit folgenden Definitionen gemeint ist. Da es sich um Definitionen handelt, sind alle Relativsätze „bestimmende Relativsätze“.

Beispiel: A fruit which grows on trees. = An apple is a fruit which grows on trees.

1. A device which tells the temperature.
2. A person who drives a bus.
3. A person who plays CDs and records at a disco.
4. A vehicle which has wings.
5. A man or woman who works in a school.
6. A sign that tells drivers what to do.
7. A boy or girl who goes to school.
8. A yellow fruit which is very sour.
9. A small, portable roof which keeps out the rain.

b) Jetzt musst du selbst versuchen, gute Definitionen zu geben – natürlich mit dem richtigen Relativpronomen.

Beispiel: A dictionary is a book which/that explains words.

1. A passport is a document
2. Chewing gun is something
3. A bus is a vehicle
4. A cat is an animal
5. An explorer is a person
6. A walkman is a device
7. Students are people
8. A snowboard is something
9. Rollerskates are things
10. A ghost is something

?
who
?
which
?
that
?

…
…
…
…

2.

Jetzt geht es darum, die „Zusatzinfos" den jeweils zutreffenden Personen bzw. Dingen zuzuordnen. Verbinde Haupt- und Relativsatz mit *who* bzw. *which* und füge die fehlenden Wörter bei Bedarf ein.

1. Prince Charles	works in a coal mine	red legs.
2. The blackbird	a city in Germany	a world language.
3. John Evans	lives in trees	could ride a horse.
4. The Mini	help sick people	speaks Welsh.
5. English	was a film star	still very popular.
6. Hamburg	was once a large port	is west of London.
7. Flying doctors	is a black mineral	is a large port.
8. Coal	a small two-door car	burns very well.
9. John Wayne	the son of the Queen	has two sons.
10. Bristol	spoken everywhere	work in Australia.

3.

Unterstreiche mit unterschiedlichen Farben die bestimmenden und die nicht bestimmenden Relativsätze in folgendem Artikel aus dem *„Croydon Advertiser"*. Du kannst sie natürlich auch in verkürzter Form *("A teenager who stole ...", "Thornton Heath, which is a suburb ...")* in zwei Spalten aufschreiben.

No 14, Thursday

Croydon Advertiser

Joyrider arrested

A teenager who stole a car in Croydon last week was arrested yesterday in Brighton after a 40-mile police chase. James Wilkinson, who lives at 69, High Street, Thornton Heath, is only 16 years old and has no driving licence. The car which he stole was a blue Morris 1100 that belong-ed to Ms Jane Campbell, who also lives in Thornton Heath. James broke into the car, which was parked outside Ms Campbell's house, and tried to steal the radio. He was unable to steal the radio, which was firmly fixed to the dashboard, but he found a spare set of keys and decided to steal the car instead.

The policemen who followed the stolen car are the same men who stopped two joyriders last month: PC John Laky of Croydon and his colleague, PC Alfred Frazer, who lives in Warlingham. The police car which they were driving was parked beside the A23, which is a busy road that is used by thousands of cars on their way from London to Brighton. PC Leaky recognized the number of the stolen car and began to follow it. The policemen, who could see that the driver was very young, did not wish to frighten the thief, who was driving at about 65 mph, so they followed the car slowly for a few miles.

When Wilkinson saw that the car that was following him was a police car, he tried to drive faster. Luckily the Morris 1100 which Wilkinson had stolen ran out of petrol just outside Brighton. Wilkinson tried to run away, but the crew of another police car from Brighton, which had been waiting near the end of the A23, caught him.

4.

Setze das richtige Relativpronomen *(who/which/that)* in die Lücken ein.

Come to Tenby for a seaside holiday ___________ is different!

People ___________ enjoy seaside holidays will love Tenby. This small seaside town in South Wales, ___________ has two wonderful sandy beaches, is also famous for the castle ___________ stands at the top of the town between the two bays. Tenby is an ideal place for young people ___________ want to do more than lie on the beach. There are many interesting paths ___________ follow the rocky coastline, and for those of you ___________ are not good walkers, there are plenty of places ___________ are worth visiting in the town itself. There are boat trips to the small island of Caldy, ___________ has a lighthouse and a Roman Catholic monastery. Jean Smith, ___________ has been coming to Tenby regularly for over 50 years, says: "Tenby is a place ___________ attracts all kinds of people, old (like me) and young (like my granddaughter), ___________ is here with me this year."

5.

Aus zwei mach eins. Füge die beiden Kurzsätze so zusammen, dass ein einziger Satz entsteht. Entscheide selbst, ob es sich um einen bestimmenden oder einen nicht bestimmenden Relativsatz handelt:

1. This is the man. He lives in the flat above ours.

   ____

2. Do you like the ice-cream? It tastes like toffee.

   ____

3. John Brown lives next door. He is a good friend of mine.

   ____

4. She is wearing a long skirt. It is very pretty.

   ____

5. The clothes are expensive. She buys them in Paris.

   ____

6. My girlfriend Alison is 19. She lives in Cleversulzbach.

   ____

7. This is the bus. It goes to Euston Station.

   ____

8. Here are the shoes. They cost me £60.

   ____

9. When did you see the man? He stole my car!

   ____

10. This coffee comes all the way from Kenya. It smells very fresh.

    ____

Relativpronomen als Objekt des Relativsatzes; *whose*

Relativpronomen als Objekt des Relativsatzes

Für Personen und andere Lebewesen wird *who(m)/that* verwendet, wobei *that* wiederum nur im bestimmenden Relativsatz verwendet werden kann. Im bestimmenden Relativsatz kann ein Relativpronomen, das als Objekt benutzt wird, auch weggelassen werden:

Bestimmender Relativsatz	Nicht bestimmender Relativsatz
The woman **who(m)/that** I saw lives next door. *oder:* The woman I saw lives next door.	Mrs Jones, **who(m)** I saw yesterday, lives next door.

Für Sachen und andere Nichtlebewesen wird *which/that* verwendet, wobei *that* nur im bestimmenden Relativsatz verwendet werden kann.
Im bestimmenden Relativsatz kann ein Relativpronomen, das als Objekt benutzt wird, auch weggelassen werden:

Bestimmender Relativsatz	Nicht bestimmender Relativsatz
The song **which/that** I was listening to was 'Yesterday'. The song I was listening to ...	'Yesterday', **which** was written by the Beatles, is a great song.

Vergleiche folgende Sätze mit Präpositionen:
„Der Mann, mit dem ich sprach ... “ =
“The man **to whom** I was speaking ... ” (sehr vornehm!)
“The man **who(m)** I was speaking **to** ... ” (sehr korrekt – aber eher in der Schriftsprache zuhause!)
“The man I was speaking **to** ... ” (korrektes gesprochenes Englisch)

„Der Tunnel, durch den wir fahren mussten, war sehr lang.“ =
“The tunnel **through which** we had to travel was very long.”
“The tunnel **which** we had to travel **through** was very long.”
“The tunnel we had to travel **through** was very long.”

6.
Setze das richtige Relativpronomen ein, aber nur wenn nötig!

The place ... I went to for my summer holidays last year was a little village ... is difficult to find on most maps of Scotland but a place ... you will easily find on a map of Canada: Calgary on the Island of Mull, ... is off the west coast of Scotland. The Canadian town ... is called Calgary was originally a small fort ... the Canadian Mounted Police founded in 1875 as Fort Brisebois, a French name ... few of the policemen could pronounce correctly. The fort was renamed Calgary, ... means "clear running water" in Gaelic, by Colonel James F. Macleod, ... came from the Island of Mull. The year in ... the fort was renamed was 1876. The small hotel ... we stayed at had a fine view of the bay, ..., with its blue sea and pure white sand, was ideal for bathing.

7.
Lies folgenden Text über die Geschichte der Londoner Untergrundbahn. Welche Sätze können gekürzt werden, welche nicht? Welche Relativsätze können anders formuliert werden?

1. The school project which we did was about London in the 19th century.
2. The teacher who helped us collect material was Mr Peters.
3. Some of the material which we collected was very interesting.
4. Anne Harrap, with whom I was working on the project, is a good friend of mine.
5. Our part of the project was something about which we didn't know much: the London Underground!
6. The first part of the London Underground, which is still the biggest underground network in the world, opened in 1863.
7. Even in those days the streets which connected the suburbs of West London with the banks and offices of the City were overcrowded.
8. This first underground railway, which many "commuters" used, was called the Metropolitan Railway.
9. The name which it was given was taken over by underground railways all over the world.
10. The Paris and Moscow "Metros", which are used by millions each day, are both named after it.
11. The first real "tube" railway on which electric trains were used was built in 1890.
12. At the end of the 19th century there were many miles of underground lines, which most people preferred to the horse buses above ground.

13. Londoners are proud of their Underground. But the man who did most to start up the system was an American.
14. Charles Tyson Yerkes, who had made a fortune in the USA, was the man to whom Londoners should be grateful for their Underground.
15. It was he who insisted on electric trains instead of steam engines in the early days.
16. The Glasgow Underground, which was for many years the only other "Metro" in Britain, had a very small, very dirty circular line with steam trains that lasted until the 1930s!

8.

Unser „rasender Reporter“ hat zu einigen Ereignissen des Tages nur stichwortartige Notizen machen können. Kannst du sie als ganze Sätze formulieren? Benutze nach Möglichkeit mindestens zwei Relativsätze pro Story.

Beispiel:

Football match – played last night – won by Huddersfield – town in Yorkshire

The football match which was played last night was won by Huddersfield, which is a town in Yorkshire.

1. The new Arrow sports car – made in Coventry – won rally – rally organized by the Automobile Club of Scotland.
2. Boy of 16 – built his own plane – flew 500 metres before crashing into car – parked in the middle of a field.
3. Melissa Ryman – lives in London – will swim for England – European championships – begin next week in Paris.
4. Open-air concert – cancelled last week – will take place next week at Folly Farm – near Oxford.
5. First British spacecraft "Britannia I" – launched next month – will carry four astronauts – chosen from over 1000 applicants.
6. Computer – developed by Irish company will be sold by Eurocomp – has headquarters in Dublin.

1. *whose*

Das Relativpronomen *whose* drückt Besitz oder Zugehörigkeit aus. Es wird meistens in Bezug auf Personen oder Tiere verwendet.

Bestimmender Relativsatz:
Darwin was a biologist. His ideas were revolutionary.
Darwin was a biologist whose ideas were revolutionary.

Nicht bestimmender Relativsatz:
This is Peter Piper. I'm sure you know his books.
This is Peter Piper, whose books I'm sure you know.

2. *of which*

Um Zugehörigkeit bei Dingen auszudrücken, wird statt *whose* meistens das nachgestellte *of which* gebraucht.

Bestimmender Relativsatz:
This is the house. Its roof was damaged.
This is the house the roof of which was damaged.

Nicht bestimmender Relativsatz:
23 High Street had to be demolished. Its roof was damaged.
23 High Street, the roof of which was damaged, had to be demolished.

9.
Aus zwei mach eins. Füge die beiden Sätze zu einem einzigen Satz zusammen.

1. James Watt was an inventor. His steam engine revolutionized industry.
2. Watt was born in Scotland. The capital of Scotland is Edinburgh.
3. This is the rare XL 320 sports car. Only 200 of them were built.
4. The man was very angry. His car had been stolen.
5. The Rolling Stones are still together. Their songs have been best sellers since the 60s.
6. The company is still doing well. Its collapse was forecast months ago.
7. Mr Smith was very happy. His son won the prize.
8. The car belonged to Mr Granger. Its door was damaged.
9. The man was very happy. His daughter won the prize.
10. The villages were cut off. Their streets were flooded.

Zusammenfassung

1. Ein **bestimmender Relativsatz** wird verwendet, um Personen bzw. Sachen genau zu bestimmen:
   I know the man. – Which man? – The man **who/that** lives next door.

   Relativpronomen im Objektfall können weggelassen werden:
   That book is boring. – Which book? –
   The book **(which/that)** you lent me.
   He was the winner. – Who was? – The man **to whom** I was talking.
   The man **(whom)** I was talking **to**.

   Das Relativpronomen für Personen und Lebewesen lautet: *who/that*.
   Das Relativpronomen für Nichtlebewesen lautet: *which/that*.
   That kann nicht nach einer Präposition verwendet werden.

2. Ein **nicht bestimmender Relativsatz** wird benutzt, um zusätzliche Informationen über Personen oder Sachen zu geben:
   John Williams, **who** lives in North Street, was at the party.
   I also saw Julie Wilson, **who** was in hospital last week.

   Das Relativpronomen für Personen und Lebewesen lautet: *who*.
   Das Relativpronomen für Nichtlebewesen lautet: *which*.

   Achtung:
   Im nicht bestimmenden Relativsatz können die Relativpronomen nicht weggelassen werden.

3. **whose**
   Um Besitz oder Zugehörigkeit auszudrücken, wird in Bezug auf Personen oder Tiere das Relativpronomen *whose* verwendet.
   The man **whose** wife was a painter was a friend of mine.
   John, **whose** wife works in London, is unemployed.

Test

Füge das richtige Relativpronomen in folgende Sätze ein. Denke dabei auch an die wichtige Unterscheidung bei der Komma-(= „Pause")Setzung. Füge nur Kommas ein, wenn sie unbedingt erforderlich sind. Als kleine Hilfe setzen wir immer dort ein Fragezeichen, wo du überlegen musst, ob ein Komma gesetzt werden soll oder nicht.

1. The house ? in __________ we live ? was built in 1906.
2. Mr Aloysius Prang ? __________ built it ? was a rather eccentric man.
3. The materials ? __________ he used ? were very modern at the time: concrete *(Beton)* and steel girders *(Stahlträger)*.
4. But the brickwork *(Mauerwerk)* on the front of the house ? __________ looks like most houses built in 1906 ? is only painted on the concrete!
5. Few people look twice at our house ? __________ my parents bought five years ago.
6. But a year ago an architect ? __________ had heard about the house ? visited us.
7. He told us he had heard about a house ? the front of __________ was painted to look like brick *(Backstein, Ziegelstein)*.
8. He was writing a book about architects ? __________ ideas had been ahead of their time.
9. He said that Aloysius Prang ? __________ house we were living in ? had been one of them.
10. So now our house is famous! There is a long article about our house in the book by the young architect ? __________ we talked to that day.

14 Die Pronomen

Ins Deutsche übersetzt würde die Bemerkung der alten Dame heißen: „Habt ihr euch wehgetan?“ und die Antwort der Kinder: „Nein! Wir haben uns (gegenseitig) wehgetan!“ – ein entscheidender Unterschied!

Die Formen der Personalpronomen

Ein Personalpronomen ersetzt in der Regel ein Substantiv (Nomen) oder einen Eigennamen – oft um unnötige Wiederholungen zu vermeiden:
“Have you seen **John** or **Mary**?” – “Yes. **He**’s in the living-room and **she**’s in the garden. Do you want to talk to **them**?”

Hier eine Zusammenstellung der Personalpronomen:

Subjekt-	*ich*	*du/Sie**	*er*	*sie**	*es*	*wir*	*ihr/Sie**	*sie**
form:	I	you	he	she	it	we	you	they
Objekt-	me	you	him	her	it	us	you	them
form:	*mich*	*dich/Sie**	*ihn*	*sie**	*es*	*uns*	*euch/Sie**	*sie**
	mir	*dir/Ihnen*	*ihm*	*ihr*	*ihm*	*uns*	*euch/Ihnen*	*ihnen*

* Zu Problemen, die aus der Mehrdeutigkeit von „sie/Sie“ entstehen können, siehe S. 140.

Im Gegensatz zum Deutschen gibt es keine Unterscheidung zwischen den Objektpronomen für Akkusativ und Dativ:
“I’m looking for John. Have you seen **him**? I want to give **him** a CD.”
*„Ich suche John. Hast du **ihn** gesehen? Ich möchte **ihm** eine CD geben.“*

1.

Lies diese kleine Geschichte durch. Sie enthält viele unnötige Wiederholungen, die wir in **Fettdruck** hervorgehoben haben. Schreibe die Geschichte in „Kurzform“ ab, indem du die fett gedruckten Stellen durch Pronomen ersetzt.

Yesterday **my friend Mary and I** went shopping by bus. The bus was late. When **the bus** arrived, we got on. The bus-driver asked **my friend and me** where we wanted to go. I said: "Tooting Station, please" and **Mary** said: "Tooting, too." **The bus-driver** smiled and said: "Two to Tooting!" The people in the bus heard **the driver. The people in the bus** laughed at his little joke. We thought **the people** were very silly. We didn't look at **the people.** We gave **the bus-driver** the money. He took the money and gave **Mary and me** our tickets and our change. He gave me 5p change and gave **Mary** 45p. My ticket said: 45p. Mary looked at **my ticket**, too. Then **Mary** looked at me and I looked at **Mary**. "Excuse me," I said to the driver. "You've given **my friend** the wrong change. She gave you a pound coin and **the fare's** only 45p to Tooting Station. You only gave **Mary** 45p change instead of 55p." **The bus driver** gave **my friend** another 10p. He was not smiling now. All the other people in the bus were looking at **the driver**. "He's given one of **those young people** the wrong change!" said an old man. **Mary and I** smiled at **the man**. "I'm going to Tooting, too!" **the man** said. This time everybody laughed – except the bus driver, of course!

2.

Fülle die Lücken in diesem Dialog mit den richtigen Personalpronomen aus:

"I've lost my keys, Dad. Can _____ help ____ to find ____?"

"Weren't _____ on the table in the hall this morning?"

"No, those were Mum's keys. I gave ____ to Mum. My keys were in my jacket pocket, but I can't find my jacket. Have ____ seen ____?"

"Your old jeans jacket? ____ think Mum gave ____ away this morning."

"Gave my jacket away? ____ was my favourite jeans jacket. ____ wore ____ almost every day – and ____ wasn't old. Only a year or two, anyway."

"There were some people at the door this morning. ____ were collecting old clothes for the Red Cross. I think Mum gave ____ your jacket – and a few of my old clothes, too."

"But surely Mum looked in the pockets before ____ gave the things away!"

"____'m not sure, Carol. By the way, have ____ seen my old black trousers? ____ were in the bedroom but now I can't find ____. There was a £20 note in the back pocket! Where's Mum, anyway. Just wait till I see ____! I'll give ____ a boot in the head if ____'s given my trousers away!"

Überprüfe deine Lösungen, bevor du weitermachst!

Merke

Die Entsprechungen für „sie / Sie" im Englischen

Bei Übersetzungen ist es oft schwierig, das richtige englische Pronomen für die deutschen Pronomen „sie" und „Sie" zu finden, zumal du die Großschreibung nicht hören kannst, sondern nur in der Schriftform erkennst! Die Verbform verrät oft, aber nicht immer, die Funktion von „sie/Sie" als Subjekt, nicht aber als Objekt! Vergleiche folgende Funktionen der deutschen Pronomen „sie/Sie" mit ihren englischen Entsprechungen:

Sie *kennt* ***sie*** *gut.*	**She** knows **her** well.
Sie *kennt* ***sie*** *gut.*	**She** knows **them** well.
Sie *kennt* ***Sie*** *gut.*	**She** knows **you** well.
Sie *kennen* ***sie*** *gut.*	**You** know **her** well.
Sie *kennen* ***sie*** *gut.*	**You** know **them** well.
Sie *kennen* ***sie*** *gut.*	**They** know **her** well.
Sie *kennen* ***sie*** *gut.*	**They** know **them** well.
Sie *kennen* ***Sie*** *gut.*	**They** know **you** well.

Die englische Sprache hat für jede Person ein separates Pronomen!

3.

Jetzt eine kleine Übung zu diesem Thema: Setze im englischen Satz das richtige Pronomen für das deutsche „sie/Sie" ein.

1. „**Sie** ist aus London.	"_____ is from London.
Ich verstehe **sie** gut."	I understand _____ well."
„Wissen **Sie**, wo **sie** wohnt?"	"Do _____ know where _____ lives?"
2. „Kommen **sie** aus Berlin?"	"Do _____ come from Berlin?"
„Nein, **sie** kommen aus Köln.	"No, _____ come from Cologne.
Ich kenne **sie** gut."	I know _____ well."
„Wissen **Sie**, wo **sie** wohnen?"	"Do _____ know where _____ live?"
3. „**Sie** geht in meine Klasse.	"_____ is in my class.
Ich sehe **sie** jeden Tag."	I see _____ every day."
4. „Ich finde diese Bücher gut.	"I think these books are good.
Sie können **sie** überall kaufen."	_____ can buy _____ everywhere."
5. „Hast du Ken und Tom gesehen?"	"Have you seen Ken and Tom?"
„Ja, Ich habe **sie** im Hof gesehen.	"Yes, I saw _____ in the playground.
Sie spielten Fußball."	_____ were playing football."

Die Reihenfolge der Objektpronomen im Satz

Wie bereits auf S. 138 erläutert, gibt es im Englischen (im Gegensatz zum Deutschen) nur eine Objektform – unabhängig davon, ob es sich um ein direktes oder ein indirektes Objekt handelt.
Bei der Reihenfolge der Objekte im Satz muss dagegen sehr wohl zwischen direktem und indirektem Objekt unterschieden werden.

Folgende Fälle können auftreten:

1. Beide Objekte sind Substantive:

	indirektes Obj.	direktes Obj.
He bought	**his sister**	**an ice-cream**.
Er kaufte	***seiner Schwester***	***ein Eis.***

In diesem Fall steht – wie auch im Deutschen – das indirekte meist vor dem direkten Objekt.

2. Eines der Objekte ist ein Pronomen:

Direktes Objekt als Pronomen:	He bought **it** for his sister.
Indirektes Objekt als Pronomen:	He bought **her** a new CD.

Dann steht das Pronomen immer vor dem anderen Objekt. Dabei ist es egal, ob es sich um das direkte oder um das indirekte Objekt handelt.

3. Beide Objekte sind Pronomen:

	direkt	indirekt
He bought	**it**	**(for) her**.
He gave	**it**	**(to) her**.

In diesem Fall steht meist das direkte Objektpronomen vor dem indirekten. Das indirekte Objektpronomen wird dabei häufig mit einer Präposition angeschlossen – je nach Verb entweder mit *to* oder *for*.

4.

Jetzt sollst du die Objekte in die richtige Reihenfolge bringen! Bilde zehn richtige Sätze aus folgender Schalttafel. Du darfst ruhig „mischen“: also ein Substantiv mit einem Pronomen oder nur zwei Pronomen. Wie wäre es mit je fünf?

		a new CD	
		her brother	to us
My friend Brian		me	a new CD
I	bought	it	it
Her mum	gave	us	them
You	sent	them	to his sister
They	lent	my friend Jack	for his friend Jack
We		some sweets	a postcard from France
		a magazine	for me
		a letter	

5.

In dieser Übung geht es um Objekt- und um Subjektpronomen: Ersetze in folgenden Sätzen die **fett gedruckten** Satzteile:

1. I gave **Paul** the money.
2. **My mother** sent a letter to **her sister**.
3. She bought **her friends** an ice-cream.
4. **Our English teacher** gave **me and the other pupils** a test yesterday.
5. **My friends and I** sent **a postcard** to **our American friends** by airmail.
6. **My brother** gave **the dog the old sausages**.
7. **Our father** bought **those gold earrings** for **our mother** last year.
8, **Our teachers** showed **my friends and me some old photos**.
9. Can **Yvonne** lend **my sister those old jeans**?

Überprüfe deine Lösungen, bevor du weitermachst!

Die *-self/-selves*-Pronomen

Mit den englischen *-self/-selves*-Pronomen kann man:

1. anzeigen, dass die Handlung des Verbs das Subjekt selbst betrifft. In diesem Fall sind sie Objekt im Satz und entsprechen den deutschen Reflexivpronomen (= rückbezügliche Pronomen) „mich/dich/**sich**, uns/euch/**sich**". Vergleiche:

She saw **her** in the mirror.	Sie sah **sie** im Spiegel.
She saw **herself** in the mirror.	Sie sah **sich** im Spiegel.
They helped **them**.	Sie halfen **ihnen**.
They helped **themselves**.	Sie halfen **sich**. ODER: Sie bedienten **sich**.

2. eine Person oder eine Sache besonders stark hervorheben. In dieser Funktion entsprechen sie dem deutschen **„selbst"**. Vergleiche:

I can do it.	Ich kann es machen.
I can do it **myself**. I don't need any help.	Ich kann es **selbst** machen. Ich brauche keine Hilfe.

In beiden Funktionen muss die betroffene Person oder Sache in derselben grammatischen „Person" stehen:

I talked to the President **myself**.	(betont die „ich"-Form: Ich **selbst** ...)
I talked to **the President himself**.	(betont, dass ich mit dem Präsidenten selbst sprach, nicht mit seinem Stellvertreter)

Fassen wir die einzelnen Formen in einigen Beispielsätzen zusammen:

Singular:	**Plural:**
I repaired my bike **myself**. Did **you** see **yourself** on TV?	**We** bought **ourselves** some new jeans. **You** must read the book **yourselves**.
He copied this CD **himself**. Has **she** hurt **herself**? **It** switches **itself** off after an hour.	**They** always do their homework **themselves**.

Beachte:
- Im Plural wird *-f* zu *-ves*: *myself* → *ourselves* etc.
- Es gibt unterschiedliche Formen für *you* in Singular und Plural: *yourself* (Singular) und *yourselves* (Plural).
- Die Redewendung ***by** myself, **by** himself* etc. heißt „allein“ oder „ohne Hilfe“:

I was at the party **myself.**	Ich **selbst** war auf der Party.
I went to the party **by myself**.	Ich ging **allein** auf die Party. (= ohne Begleitung)
I made this model **all by myself.**	Ich habe dieses Modell ganz ohne Hilfe gebastelt.

6.

Setze das richtige Pronomen in folgende Sätze ein. Aber Vorsicht! Es handelt sich nicht immer um eines der *-self/-selves*-Pronomen.

1. “I always do my homework __________. Nobody helps __________.”
   “What about your sister? Does __________ do her homework __________?”
   “Well, she’s younger than me. Sometimes my father helps __________.”
2. Some of the girls in my class make their clothes __________. I’ve tried making my own clothes, but when I put them on and look at __________ in a mirror, I hope that other people won’t laugh at __________ when they see __________!
3. “I’m thirsty,” he asked me. “Can I get __________ a glass of orange juice?” “Of course!” I said. “Help __________!” So he poured __________ a glass of orange juice. “Shall I pour a glass for __________?” he asked me and my brother. “No, thanks,” I said. “We can pour __________ a glass when we’re thirsty.”
4. We have a big garden, so we grow a lot of our own food __________. Our neighbours have tried growing their food __________, but they only have a small garden.
5. My cat is very clever. When it’s hungry, it goes into the kitchen and gets __________ something to eat. The box of cat food is on the floor. The cat knocks __________ over. Some bits of food fall out of it, and the cat eats __________.

7.

Was würdest du in folgenden Sätzen besonders betonen wollen? Subjekt oder Objekt?

"I was in London last week." – "We were in London ______________. We didn't see you there." – "Well, London ______________ is a big city, isn't it? I went on a tour of Buckingham Palace. It was a very expensive tour, so we had to pay for our tickets ______________. Prince Charles ______________ was the tour guide! The rooms ______________ were very interesting, but I wanted to see the Queen ______________. There was a door with a sign 'NO ENTRY'. When nobody was looking, I opened the door and walked right into the private rooms of the Royal Family ____________! They ______________ live right in the middle of the Palace ______________. There was nobody about, so I had to find the Queen's living-room ______________. At last I found it – and there was Her Majesty ______________, sitting in an armchair and reading a newspaper." – "I don't believe you! You made that story up ______________!" – "You're right. But both of you almost believed my story ______________, didn't you?"

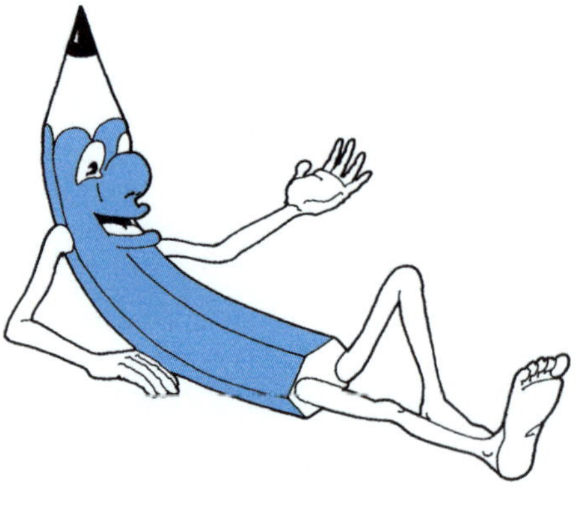

Merke

Im Gegensatz zum Deutschen hat die englische Sprache wenig echte rückbezügliche Verben (Reflexivverben). Die meisten deutschen Reflexivverben (z.B. „**sich** waschen, **sich** anziehen, **sich** treffen, **sich** langweilen“ usw.) brauchen im Englischen also **kein** „mich/dich/sich, uns/euch/sich“.

Vergleiche:

I get up at 7 o'clock. First I wash and get dressed. Then I sit down and have breakfast. After breakfast I set off to school. My friends and I meet at the bus-stop.

Ich stehe um 7 Uhr auf. Zuerst wasche ich **mich** und ziehe **mich** an. Dann setze ich **mich** hin und frühstücke. Nach dem Frühstück mache ich **mich** auf den Weg zur Schule. Meine Freunde und ich treffen **uns** an der Bushaltestelle.

Für Englischsprachige ist es nämlich selbstverständlich, dass man sich selbst wäscht, anzieht usw. und nicht jemand anders. Wäre jemand anders gemeint, würde man die Person als Objekt erwähnen müssen: *I wash* ***my little brother*** *and dress* ***my baby sister***.

Die „reziproken“ Pronomen *each other/one another*

Die reziproken Pronomen *each other* und *one another* drücken aus, dass zwischen Personen eine wechselseitige Beziehung besteht:

Paul and Anna started fighting and hurt **each other/one another**.
(= Paul hurt Anna and Anna hurt Paul.)
*Paul und Anna fingen an, sich zu raufen und verletzten **sich (gegenseitig)**.*

Die beiden reziproken Pronomen *each other* und *one another* sind gleichbedeutend und können beliebig eingesetzt werden.

Achtung:
Verwechsle nicht die reziproken (= wechselseitigen) Pronomen *each other/one another* mit den reflexiven (= rückbezüglichen) *-self/-selves*-Pronomen:

Paul and Anna fell off their skateboards and hurt **themselves**.
(= Paul hurt **him**self and Anna hurt **her**self.)
*Paul und Anna fielen von ihren Skateboards und verletzten **sich**.*

8.
Ergänze folgende Sätze entweder mit *each other/one another* oder mit einem der *-self/-selves*-Pronomen.

1. "Hi, Karen. Have you met my brother Vincent?" – "Oh yes. Vincent and I have known ________________ for years."
2. Some of my friends are not very good at English. So we sometimes meet after school and help ________________ with our homework.
3. A farmer in our village had too many apples last year. He put a lot of apples in a box beside the road with a sign on it: FREE APPLES. HELP ________________. So we helped ________________.
4. She was too big for her old bike, so she bought ________________ a new one.

5. I hadn't seen my cousin for six years. When we met again last week, we hardly recognized ________________.
6. We went to the open-air concert in the afternoon and watched it again on TV in the evening. We saw ________________ in the crowd.
7. "They never think about other people. They are selfish. They only think about ________________." – "I hate selfish people! I think everybody should help ________________."
8. "I painted that picture of the river ________________. Do you like it?" – "The picture ________________ is OK, but I don't like the colours much!"
9. "I grew up in London. Have you ever been to London ________________?" – "No. Only to London Airport, not to London ________________."
10. Nobody can help us. We'll have to do it ________________.
11. "Shall I tell Mum and Dad that I broke your window, Mrs Smith?" – "No, John. I'll tell your parents ________________."
12. "Did I see you and Vera talking to ________________ at the party?" – "That's right. She didn't know many people ________________. In fact she told me she had come to the party by ________________."

Die Possessivpronomen

Neben den Possessivbegleitern *my, your, his, her* usw., die vor einem Substantiv stehen (***my** CD* usw.), gibt es eine komplette Reihe Possessivpronomen, die (ähnlich wie bei den Personalpronomen) ein Wiederholen des Substantivs vermeiden.

Singular:

Personal-pronomen	**Possessivbegleiter**	**Possessivpronomen + Nomen**
I	"This isn't **my English book**."	– "No, it's **mine**." *(meins)*
you	"Can I borrow **your book**?"	– "No. Look for **yours** first!" *(deins)*
he	"I think this is **his CD**."	– "Are you sure it's **his**? It could be **mine**."
she	"Isn't that **her bike**?"	– "No. I don't think it's **hers**. It looks like **Vera's**."
it	The dog is sleeping on **its** bed.	*(keine Entsprechung für* its *!)*

Plural:

Personal-pronomen	**Possessivbegleiter**	**Possessivpronomen + Nomen**
we	"**Our** English teacher is very good."	– "Yes. He's better than **ours**!"
you	"Can we borrow **your bikes**?"	– "What have you done with **yours**?"
they	"Have you seen **their new car**?"	– "No." – "That's **theirs** over there."

Bei Eigennamen oder Nomen im Genitiv wird einfach die Genitivform als Pronomen übernommen:

"Is that **John's skateboard**?" – "No. I think it's **Andy's**."
"I like **your sister's bike**!" – "That's **my mother's**."
"Is that **the Smiths' house**?" – "No. It's **the Browns'**."

Bei mehreren Personennamen ist nur **ein** Genitiv-s erforderlich:

We stayed for a week at **Chris and Geoff's**.

Achtung! Diese Pronomen bzw. Genitivformen werden in der Wendung „ein Freund **von mir**, ein Fehler **von dir**, ein Bekannter **von Kevin**" usw. benutzt: He's a friend **of mine**. (= He's one of my friends – *einer unter mehreren*)

9.

Setze die richtigen Possessivpronomen in folgende Dialoge ein:

1. "Whose bike is that? Is it __________?" – "No, it isn't __________. I didn't bring __________ to school today. Ask Peter – I think it's __________."
2. (After the party) "Where did you put your coats?" – "We put __________ on the bed. I think Barbara and Ken put __________ on the bed, too."
3. "Have you seen my English books, Sheila?" – "No, Helen. These are my books. Where did you leave __________?" – "I left them here, on the table, right next to __________." – "Oh dear! Tania thought those books were __________. She put them in her bag and went home, I think." – "Just a minute, Sheila. There's a bag over there. I think it's __________. She must still be here. I'll find her and ask her about the books."

10.

Ergänze folgende Sätze mit der richtigen Form der in Klammern stehenden Namen oder Substantive. Es sind aber auch einige Lücken **ohne** Vorgaben, die du mit den passenden Pronomen ausfüllen musst:

Beispiel:

"Does this computer belong to you?" – *(my sister)* – "No, it's <u>my sister's</u>."

1. "That must be Mr Jones's car over there." – *(Mr Smith)* "No. I think it's __________."
2. "It wasn't my mistake. *(our headmaster)* It was __________: he ordered the wrong books."
3. "Is that your house?" – *(the Browns)* "No, that's __________. __________ is next door."
4. "Are those your glasses?" – "No, I'm wearing __________. *(Mum)* They must be __________."
5. "Do you know Alice and Paul Smith?" – *(us)* "Of course. They're good friends of __________."

Zusammenfassung

Hier hast du eine Zusammenfassung aller wichtigen Pronomen und der dazugehörigen Possessivbegleiter:

Objekt-pronomen	Subjekt-pronomen	Possessiv-begleiter	Reflexiv-pronomen	Possessiv-pronomen
You know **me**!	**I** bake	**my** cakes	**myself**.	**Mine** always taste best!
I don't believe **you**!	**You** did	**your** homework	**yourself**?	**Yours** got the best mark.
Do you know **him**?	**He** repairs	**his** old car	**himself**.	**His** is that blue car over there.
I don't like **her**.	**She** loves	**her** Jaguar and	**herself**.	**Hers** must be a lonely life!
I've never seen **it**.	**It** sits in	**its** garage all by	**itself.**	*She never drives it.
You really mean **us**?	**We** grow	**our** own food for	**ourselves**.	**Ours** is not for sale!
I don't trust **them**!	**They** help	**their** friends and	**themselves**.	**Theirs** is a selfish attitude.

*Es gibt kein Possessivpronomen zu *it*.

Im Gegensatz zum Deutschen

1. gibt es keine unterschiedlichen Formen für das direkte und das indirekte Objektpronomen: *When she saw* ***me*** *she gave* ***me*** *the money.* – Als sie **mich** sah, gab sie **mir** das Geld.

2. gibt es im Englischen eindeutige Pronomen für das mehrdeutige „sie/Sie"-Pronomen im Deutschen: sie lebt = ***she*** *lives*, Sie leben = ***you*** *live*, sie leben = ***they*** *live*

3. wird im Englischen kein Unterschied zwischen „sich" usw. (Reflexivpronomen) und „selbst" gemacht – in beiden Fällen benutzt man die *-self/-selves-Pronomen*:

She saw **herself** in the mirror.	Sie sah **sich** im Spiegel.
She did it **herself**.	Sie tat es **selbst**.

4. wird im Englischen eindeutig zwischen „sich" usw. als Reflexivpronomen und „sich" usw. als reziprokes Pronomen unterschieden:

   Reflexivpronomen:

They fell off their skateboards and injured **themselves**.	Sie stürzten von ihren Skateboards und verletzten **sich**.

   reziprokes Pronomen:

The skateboarders collided and injured **each other/one another**.	Die Skateboardfahrer stießen zusammen und verletzten **sich**.

Test

Setze die richtigen Pronomen in folgenden Dialog ein. In einem Fall brauchst du auch die Präposition *to* vor dem Pronomen – aber nur in einem!

The twins *(Zwillinge)* Kenneth and Victor are arguing – as usual. Their mother comes in to see what is going on.

1. Mum: Victor? Kenneth? What's all that shouting about? What are _________ doing?

2. Victor: Ken's playing with my game-boy! Give it _________ back!

3. Kenneth: It's not your game-boy, Vic. It's _________!
   Mum: So whose game-boy is this one under the table?

4. Kenneth: Oh! Sorry, Vic. This one belongs ____________. I must have dropped it …
   Mum: Anyway, didn't you two want to go surfing on the Internet this afternoon with Chris and Bonzo?

5. Kenneth: No, they're no friends of _________!
   Mum: Well, I saw their mother at the supermarket this morning. She said you two had invited them to come round here after school to try out your new computer.
   Victor: Are you sure it was Chris and Bonzo's mother? Mrs Brown from Number 193?

6. Mum: Of course I'm sure. I spoke to her _________.

7. Kenneth: We didn't invite them, Mum. They must have invited _________!

8. Mum: What's wrong? Don't you like them? I thought all the boys and girls in your class liked _________.

9. Victor: Most of us do, Mum, and Bonzo _________ is OK. But nobody likes Chris Brown much.

Lösungen

1 Simple present oder present progressive?

1.

Present simple forms:

I live in Carlisle.

My family live in a small house (near the town centre).

My mother works at a supermarket.

I go to the local comprehensive school and my sister goes to the junior school next door.

What kind of sports do you like?

I hate it/my name and everyone calls me Pat.

I don't know your name.

Our teacher says she will send all our letters in one envelope.

I hope that your letter is a bit longer than mine!

Tell me where you live, what you do in your free time (and something about your family).

Auxiliary verbs:

My name is Pat.

Carlisle is a town (on the border between England and Scotland).

It's near the sea.

My father is a bus-driver.

He hasn't got a job.

There is a lot of unemployment ... and it is difficult to find work.

My hobbies are skateboarding, swimming, football and playing computer games.

My full name is Patricia.

This is my first letter to you.

I hope that your letter is a bit longer than mine!

2.

Lösungsvorschläge:

My Uncle Jürgen/Aunt Melanie lives in Bochum.

My Uncle Jürgen and my Aunt Melanie live in Bochum.

I go to school in Neuenstadt.

My brother/sister goes to school in Neuenstadt.

My brothers/sisters/brothers and sisters go to school in Neuenstadt.

My mother/father works at a bank/factory/an office.

My best friend lives in Nürnberg/a small village near me.

Some of my friends go to school in Stuttgart/work at the weekends/live in Berlin.

3.

1. Do you ever go to London? – We often go to London Airport to see the planes.
   And what about you? – We go shopping there every week.
2. We never buy "The Sun". But "The Times" is always very interesting.
3. I rarely have time to read a daily newspaper, but I sometimes buy a weekly paper.
4. Do you go to a disco regularly at the weekend? – I seldom have time – especially at the weekend. At the weekend I often go to the cinema.
5. Does she walk to school every day? – No, I often see her at the bus-stop. She always takes a 49 bus to town.

4.

1. "My Uncle Jeff/He lives in Windsor, too." — 2. "Paul/He goes swimming every Friday, too." — 3. "They like ice-cream, too." — 4. "I/We play football on Saturdays, too." — 5. "She speaks French, too." — 6. "My mother does the cooking." — 7. She/Sheila plays the piano well, too." — 8. "Their mother flies to Spain for her holidays every year, too." — 9. "Patrick/He cleans his bike every week, too." — 10. "The dog often sits beside the fire, too."

5.

a) *Simple form:*
You mean Christian?
He comes from Germany.
In the house where the Jenkins normally live.
I see.
Does Christian speak good English?
He only speaks German at home.
Hardly anyone at our school learns German.
Don't you like French?
Christian says that English is easier (for him than Russian).
Why don't you come to the youth club this evening?

Progressive form:
His father is working over here in England (for a year).
So where is the family living now?
Mr Jenkins is working in Germany (for a year).
He and his family are living in the Meiers' flat/in Dresden.
We're learning German at our school.

b) Die einfache Präsensform wird häufig für Handlungen benutzt, die nicht im Augenblick stattfinden. Die Verlaufsform wird für Handlungen benutzt, die im Augenblick passieren oder (beim Satz *We're learning German at our school*) in einem größeren gegenwärtigen Zeitpunkt ablaufen, der als vorübergehend empfunden wird.

6.

1. The boys are playing football. — 2. The girl is (tele)phoning/ringing (a friend). — 3. The woman is driving to Oxford. — 4. The man is cooking (something/lunch) (in the kitchen). — 5. The/Two/The two girls are playing table-tennis. — 6. The cat is drinking milk. — 7. The book is lying on the table. — 8. The men are (going) shopping/doing the shopping. — 9. The teacher is teaching English/giving an English lesson/standing in front of the blackboard.

7.

1. Now Sylvia is doing her homework. – Sometimes Sylvia does her homework in the garden.
2. We never smoke cigarettes. – We are smoking now.
3. Do you speak English often? – Are you speaking English now?
4. He doesn't sit there every day. – He isn't sitting there now.
5. They are cycling to school this week. – They cycle to school every morning.

8.

1. They aren't/are not German. — 2. Where do you live? — 3. They don't/do not like ice-cream. — 4. His sister Sheila doesn't/does not read comics. — 5. Who is he writing to? — 6. He doesn't/does not (often) write postcards. — 7. Has she got a bike? — 8. We can't/cannot speak Welsh. — 9. Where does your sister work? — 10. How much do those CDs cost? — 11. Which bus are they waiting for? — 12. What's/What is he doing there?

9.

1. is buying — 2. goes — 3. give — 4. like — 5. gets/comes/arrives — 6. phone — 7. go swimming — 8. What time do you usually get/come/arrive back

Test

1. I'm learning English at the moment.
2. She rarely goes swimming.
3. My father owns a big car now.
4. Does John live in Stuttgart?
5. My friend Peter comes to my house every week.
6. He does not know the answer.
7. Where are you going now?
8. I don't like ice-cream.
9. On Mondays I always arrive late at school.
10. Do you like potatoes with your meat?

Simple past oder past progressive? 2

1.

Lösungsvorschläge:

a) I got up at 7 o'clock, had a shower/got washed, got dressed and had breakfast (in the kitchen). I left the house at 7.30 and walked to school. When I arrived at school I talked to my friends. We had English/PE/German and played (football) in the playground (during the break). Then we wrote a test. I went home at 12.30 a.m./1.00 p.m. and I had lunch. Then I did my homework and watched TV/a video/listened to my CDs/music on the radio. I went to bed at 9.45 p.m.

b) While I was having a shower/getting washed, I listened to the news on the radio.
While I was having breakfast (in the kitchen), the doorbell/phone rang.
While I was walking to school, I saw our English teacher on his bike.
While I was talking to my friends in the playground, the bell went for the first lesson.
While we were having English/PE/German, the school caught fire.
While we were playing (football) in the playground (during break), we/I/a boy/girl ...
While I was going home/having lunch/doing my homework/watching TV/a video/listening to my CDs/music on the radio, I heard/saw ...

2.

1. saw, was waiting — 2. was getting, fell — 3. ran, was still lying — 4. was, was examining — 5. was leaving, sat — 6. was baking, went — 7. was looking, came — 8. had to, were waiting — 9. was, was giving — 10. was putting, rang — 11. went, were standing

3.

1. was, arrived — 2. was raining, was blowing — 3. remembered, did not have — 4. went, phoned — 5. was getting, rang — 6. heard, got — 7. took, wrapped — 8. wanted, rang — 9. dropped, walked — 10. was just going, heard — 11. ran, turned — 12. opened, was standing — 13. told, was coming — 14. was, rang — 15. walked, picked — 16. was

4.

While Tania and her Uncle Jonathan were having breakfast, Jethro arrived. Jethro worked on Uncle Jonathan's farm. Jethro sat down at the table and Uncle Jonathan gave him a cup of tea. Aunt Helen came into the kitchen while they were drinking their tea. "Good morning, Jethro," she said. "I saw you in the village yesterday. You were talking to Joe Smith the policeman. What did he want to talk to you about?" "I'm afraid I can't tell you, Mrs Brown," Jethro answered. "It's a secret."

5.

1. During — 2. While — 3. while — 4. during — 5. While — 6. during — 7. During — 8. While

6.

1. During our drive through the forest we saw several bears.
2. While he was walking across the park, he got very wet.
3. I went to Bristol during my stay in England last summer.
4. She phoned her boyfriend while she was having her lunch break.
5. During our performance of "Hamlet" there was a fire in the school hall.
6. While we were flying to New York, the weather got worse.
7. The fans screamed all the time while the Rolling Stones were playing at their concert.
8. We stopped five times while we were driving to Scotland.
9. During his exams he lost about two kilos.

7.

Bei den Lösungen zu diesem Training bieten wir die Sätze in der für Engländer natürlichsten Kombination von Haupt- und Nebensatz an. Normalerweise ist die Reihenfolge dann: *while + was + -ing* am Anfang, *when + past simple* an zweiter Stelle. In den meisten Fällen kann die umgekehrte Reihenfolge auch als richtig gelten.

1. While the boys were playing football, it began to rain.
2. The girl was having a bath when the telephone rang.
3. While the woman was waiting for the bus, she read/was reading the (news)paper.
4. The girl was washing her hair when her friend arrived.
5. While the (two) boys were playing cards, the teacher entered the room.
6. The sun was setting when we arrived at the hotel.
7. While the boy was washing up, the girls were watching/watched TV.
8. When the bus arrived, the girl got on.
9. While the postman was delivering the/our letters, a/our dog attacked/bit him.

Test

Sunday was Aunt Helen's birthday. On Saturday evenings, Aunt Helen and Uncle Jonathan usually visited friends. Tania stayed at home that Saturday evening and watched TV. She was hungry, so she made herself a couple of sandwiches during one of the breaks. While she was watching a film, the doorbell rang. She was alone in the farmhouse, so she looked out of the window before she opened the door. Joe Smith the policeman was standing outside! When she saw that Jethro and five or six other people were with him, she thought that something must be wrong! She opened the door. "Don't worry," said Jethro when he saw her anxious face. "This is our surprise for your Aunt Helen. Your aunt told me that she and your uncle were visiting Mr and Mrs Jenkins down in the village tonight. So we decided to have a little party with a few more friends. After all, they won't be back until nearly midnight – and your aunt's birthday starts then!"

Simple past oder present perfect? 3

1.

1 W	E	2 R	E		3 L			4 S	H	O	O	5 K		
A		A		5 B	I	T		P				N		7 C
8 S	9 A	N	10 G		T		11 F	E	L	L		E		A
	T		O					L			12 S	W	A	M
13 W	E	N	T		14 C			15 T	O	R	E			E
O				16 S	H	O	17 T				N		18 B	
19 R	O	20 S	E		O		H		21 S	A	T		R	
E		A			22 S	T	O	L	E				O	
		23 W	O	24 K	E		U		T		25 S	H	U	T
				E			G				L		G	
	26 S	W	E	P	T		27 H	I	D		E		H	
				T			T				28 P	U	T	
29 F	E	L	T					30 L	O	S	T			

2.

1. got — 2. took — 3. went — 4. ran — 5. were — 6. drove — 7. saw — 8. spoke — 9. knew — 10. stood

3.

a) *Present perfect:*

I haven't seen him for days. — He hasn't been at the pub since last Saturday. — He's been away all week. — He's the only person who has suddenly disappeared. — But I've known Andy for thirty years! — He's never stolen anything! — Have you phoned his sister in London yet? — Maybe he's gone to visit her.

Simple past:

Did you see Andy Wilson (at the pub) last night? — Was he at the pub last night? — What did you want to see him about? — Someone stole three or four sheep (from Farmer Hunt's field one night last week). — What makes you think that Andy stole them? — We found two of the sheep in his barn yesterday. — That doesn't mean he stole them! — I didn't know he had a sister in London. — ... if I were you

b) Andy Wilson has never stolen anything in his life.
Andy Wilson hasn't been to the pub since Saturday.
Andy Wilson wasn't at the pub last night.
Jethro has known Andy for years.
Jethro hasn't seen Andy for some days.
Joe Smith didn't know about Andy's sister.
Joe Smith hasn't phoned Andy's sister yet.
Someone stole some sheep last week.

4.

a) 1. "Have you seen John this morning?" — 2. "No, but I have just arrived. — 3. Perhaps he has already gone to his classroom." — 4. "No. I have already looked in his classroom. There's nobody there."
b) 5. "How's your sister Stella? She hasn't been to the youth club for a few weeks." — 6. "Didn't you know? She has flown to the USA for a year. — 7. She has got a job as an au-pair girl." — 8. "Lucky Stella! Has she written a letter home yet?" — 9. "No, she hasn't had time. She only left yesterday. — 10. But she has promised to phone as soon as she can."
(Kurzformen sind selbstverständlich auch erlaubt.)

5.

1. I just hope you know what you're doing! — 2. He just shouted at me. He wouldn't listen. — 3. She has just gone. If you run, you'll catch her up. — 4. They just didn't listen to their friends' advice. — 5. We just thought you might want to come with us. — 6. I have just seen a ghost. — 7. They have just sold their house. — 8. We have just received a letter from Stella.

6.

1. did you do/were you doing — 2. watched/was watching — 3. was — 4. have seen — 5. Did you watch — 6. didn't/did not have — 7. have been — 8. saw — 9. showed — 10. Have you ever seen — 11. went — 12. have misunderstood — 13. didn't mean; meant — 14. saw — 15. Have you ever seen

7.

1. Have you ever kept sheep in your barn? — 2. Did you see (the) sheep in Farmer Hunt's field last week? — 3. Have you ever been to London? — 4. When was your first visit to London? — 5. Did you stay with your sister? — 6. How long has your sister lived in London? — 7. When did you go back to your farm? — 8. Did you find any sheep in your/the barn? — 9. Did you phone the police? — 10. Why didn't you phone the police?

8.

Johnny Purple was born in 1970.

From 1970 to 1987 he lived in London.

From 1976 to 1986 he went to/attended Croydon Comprehensive School.

From 1986 to 1987 he worked as an assistant in a music shop; he took guitar lessons for 2 years.

From 1988 until/to now he has been a singer in the pop group "Johnny's Purple Hearts".

He/The group has made six singles and one CD so far.

He/The group has been on three tours to Europe and America.

He/They went on a tour to South Africa last year./He/They toured South Africa last year.

He married Sally Johnson in 1994.

He got a divorce/They were divorced one year later.

Test

1. "Have you done your homework yet?"
2. "Yes, Mum. I did it when I got home from school."
3. "That's what you told me yesterday!"
4. "It was true! You just didn't believe me!"
5. "Are you sure you finished everything before you put the TV on?"
6. "Yes, Mum. Has Dad come home from work?"
7. "Yes. He has just arrived. Why?"
8. "Well, a few days ago he said he would test my French vocabulary with me.
9. We haven't had a French vocabulary test for about a month, but we've got one tomorrow."
10. "Didn't your class have a vocabulary test on Monday?"
    "Yes, Mum. But that was for German. French is tomorrow."

4 Simple present perfect oder present perfect progressive?

1.

1. have you been learning — 2. has been living — 3. haven't been standing — 4. has your brother been working — 5. Has Julie been playing — 6. have been listening — 7. has been lying — 8. have you been doing — 9. have been watching — 10. have we been waiting — 11. have been eating — 12. has been drinking

2.

1. "What have you been doing all afternoon?" – "I've been working in the garden."
2. "Have you done your homework yet?" – "Yes, I have just finished it."
3. "Have you written to your uncle?" – "Yes, but I haven't posted the letter yet."
4. "Who has been using my pen? I can't find it." – "I haven't seen it anywhere."
5. "Where have you been? I've been looking for you all morning!"
6. "All the lights have just gone out. What have you been doing?" –
7. "I haven't been doing anything. John and I have been sitting in the kitchen all evening."
8. "You've got chocolate around your mouth. Have you been eating my chocolates again?" – "Me? No – I haven't eaten anything since lunch."
9. "Look at these cigarette ends on the ground under the window! Someone has been standing here for a long time in the dark and has been watching us through the window!"
10. "I have often stood here waiting for a bus." – "Have you ever thought of taking a taxi?"

3.

1. Melanie — 2. Vincent — 3. Jerry — 4. Paul — 5. Claire

4.

"I was born in London 16 years ago but I have lived in Birmingham since my parents moved there in 1986. My father worked as a clerk for 15 years but he had to give up his office job five years ago and has been a postman since 2001. My mother has worked in a kindergarten since I started grammar school five years ago. I have one brother aged 18 and a younger sister aged 12. I am looking for a job now. Since May I have written to several firms. I wrote to your firm some weeks ago but ..."

5.

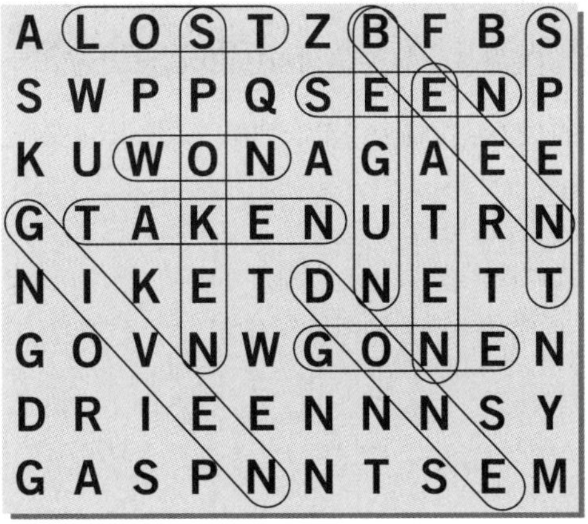

1. lost
2. spoken
3. taken
4. seen
5. eaten
6. gone
7. been
8. begun
9. done
10. won
11. given
12. spent

Test

"Where have you been? I have been waiting for you for half an hour!"
"Sorry I'm late. I waited over twenty minutes for a bus. But in the end I walked here. Let me sit down. I'm so tired! I feel as if I have been walking all afternoon!"
"Never mind. Sit down. If you walked all the way you have deserved a rest!"
"Where's Geoff? Hasn't he arrived yet?"
"He has just sent me an SMS. He's standing outside the wrong disco! He's been there since seven o'clock. I sent him an SMS back. He'll be here in a few minutes."

5 Das past perfect

1.

My boyfriend Geoff had read about it in a computer magazine.
After we had waited for about a quarter of an hour, Peter got out again.
The porter ... told us that the train to Birmingham had left ten minutes ago.
Geoff told the porter that the man at the ticket office had said "Platform 1".
The porter said the man had meant "the front end of Platform 1".
We had got into the last coach.
The train to Birmingham had been the first four coaches ...
They had already gone, and we had been in one of the last four coaches which had been *(= Passiv)* left behind.

2.

1. After they had checked their equipment, they packed their clothes.
2. After they had packed their clothes, they cycled to the Lake District.
3. After they had cycled to/arrived in the Lake District, they found a camping site.
4. After they had found a camping site, they went shopping (in the village).
5. After they had gone/been shopping (in the village), they made and ate supper.
6. After they had made and eaten supper, they went to bed.

3.

1. After/Because we had bought tickets, we went to the pop concert.
2.a) After they had sold their house, they bought a bungalow.
2.b) They sold their house after/because they had bought a bungalow.
3. I phoned the police after/because my car had been stolen.
4.a) After she had left school, she found a job.
4.b) She left school because/after she had found a job.
5. Did you go to Brighton after you had visited London?
6. Because I had phoned the number quickly I got the job.
7. The old woman shouted at the girl because she had burned the cakes.
8. After we had found out their address, we wrote them a letter.
9. He phoned his parents after he had arrived in England.
10. After/Because I had passed my driving test, I bought a motor-bike.
11. I went to the lost-property office because/after I had lost my umbrella.
12.a) After they had lost the match, they drank a lot of beer.
12.b) They lost the match after/because they had drunk a lot of beer.

13. We had come to London because we wanted to improve our English.
14.a) She went swimming after/because she had bought a new bikini.
14.b) After she had gone swimming, she bought a new bikini.
15. After the tourists had visited the castle, they went back to their hotel.

4.

1. We looked at the scenery after the train had left the station.
2. After we had passed Rugby Station, the train went into a long tunnel.
3. Suddenly the train stopped before we had reached the end of the tunnel.
4. After the train had stopped, the guard came into our coach.
5. He wanted to know if anyone had pulled the emergency brake.
6. Nobody said anything because nobody had pulled the emergency brake.
7. Some passengers were frightened because the train had stopped in a/the tunnel.
8. After the guard had told the passengers that there was no need to worry, he spoke to the driver on/over the train telephone.
9. Before the guard had finished speaking, we heard the driver's voice over the coach loudspeakers.
10. He told us that there had been a small fault in the train's computer system but that everything was OK now.
11. Five minutes later the train started to move again.

5.

1. "How long had you been living here before you moved to London?" – "Three years." — 2. He started to learn French after he had been studying English for two years. — 3. People had been drinking 'Wonder-Cola' for years before scientists discovered that it was a serious danger to health.— 4. The bus only arrived after the passengers had been waiting in the rain for almost an hour. — 5. She became the boss's assistant before she had been working at the firm for six months. — 6 "You looked very dirty when I saw you yesterday! What had you been doing?" — 7. "I had been digging the garden." — 8. The pop group had not been playing long when the fire started. — 9. "How long had she been smoking cigarettes before her doctor told her to stop?" – "Only about two years."

6.

1. had been writing; had not written — 2. had been collecting; had now collected — 3. had never travelled; had been travelling — 4. had you been driving; had driven

FOOTBALL IN THE PARK:
5. had been playing; had always played — 6. had been working — 7. had ever seen — 8. had been watching — 9. had been talking

Test

1. After I had finished my homework, I watched TV.
2. I had been learning English for two years before I went to Britain for the first time.
3. She had finished her lunch long before I arrived.
4. My father had been driving for half an hour when he realized that he was on the wrong road.
5. He told me that he had borrowed my book.
6. After he had gone home I saw that he had forgotten to take his CDs with him.
7. When he (had) arrived I told him that he was late.
8. I went out to play football with them after I had finished my homework.
9. Before I got up I had already had breakfast – in bed!
10. We (had) walked to the station before the rain began, so we didn't get wet.

Zeitformen zur Wiedergabe der Zukunft 6

1.

Neutrale Zukunft mit *will/won't*:

(I expect) we'll go to the seaside again. — Won't you need a lot of special equipment? — We won't take more than we need this time! — ... 20 kilos will have to be enough. — ... so I'll ask him. — I'll phone you when I've seen him. Will you be at home at about 6? — We'll see each other at the youth club. — I'll see you there at about half past six.

Verlaufsform der Gegenwart mit Zeitangabe:

John and I are going camping in Turkey this year. — Is John coming to the youth club tonight? — I'm seeing him after school. — I'm not going to my jazz gymnastics tonight.

Absicht mit *going to*:

What are you going to do this summer, Claire? — We're going to fly to Istanbul. — I'm going to bring Barbara with me. — Barbara is going to come anyway.

2.

1. People will (be able to) use language translation telephones. We/They won't have to learn (foreign) languages any more.
2. Pupils/Children won't go to school. They will use home computers. We/They will listen to our/their lessons and see them on the computer screen.
3. People won't have to work. Robots will do everything.
4. We will have electric walkways. We won't (need to) take the bus or walk to school. There will be no pollution.
5. Secretaries won't (need to) write letters and faxes by hand any more. They will only (need to) speak into typing machines.

3.

Example: I'm going to walk — 1. I'm going to cycle — 2. I'm going to visit — 3. I'm going to cycle — 4. I'm going to stay — 5. I'm going to climb — 6. I'm going to pay a visit to — 7. I'm not going to spend — 8. are going to take — 9. are going to follow — 10. I'm going to catch

4.

...

S: Oh, hello, Mr Wilson. Just let me look at my calendar. On Monday I'm flying to Berlin. What about Tuesday?

W: Let me see – No, on Tuesday I'm going to the computer exhibition in London, but I'll be free on Wednesday.

S: On Wednesday I'm visiting our factory in Bremen. What about Thursday?

W: Just a minute – I'm not doing anything on Thursday afternoon. ...

W: Sorry. I'm playing golf with a Japanese customer. Can't we make it the afternoon?

S: No. I'm discussing a new project with my staff on Thursday afternoon. What about Friday?

W: Friday? Well I'm driving to Manchester in the morning and I'm meeting Dr Müller in Leeds in the afternoon. What are you doing on Monday next week?

5.

1. The weather tomorrow will be sunny and very hot. — 2. They are cycling/going to cycle to Brighton on Thursday. — 3. The boy is going to invite the girl to his party. — 4. "Will someone answer the phone?" — 5. "I am not going to visit Spain again." — 6. Flight BE 782 will arrive at 12.15.

Test

Die Verbformen in Klammern sind auch richtige Lösungen.

1. "Bye, Paul! I'll see you at the disco tomorrow!"
2. "I won't be at the disco, Jenny.
3. I'm going (to go) to the cinema tomorrow.
4. Will you come with me?"
5. "I'll have to ask my mother.
6. How much will my ticket cost?"
7. "Nothing. I'll buy (I'm going to buy) your ticket. You paid last time."
8. "Fine! I'll ask Mum as soon as I get home.
9. When will you be (When are you going to be) at home this evening?"
10. "I'm going (to go) swimming this evening, but I should be back at about 9. You can ring me then."

Bedingungssätze

1.

Nebensatz mit *if*	Hauptsatz
"If you turn round,	I'll shoot!"
"If you tell me where the (King of Scotland's) diamonds are,	I will let you go."
if I don't tell you where they are?"	„What will you do

Man erkennt an den Zeitformen, dass die Sprecher die Bedingungen als leicht erfüllbar ansehen: Die Zeitform *simple present* wird im *if*-Teil benutzt, die Zukunftsform mit *will* im Hauptsatz.

2.

2. If I save/she saves enough money, I'll/she'll buy a dog.
3. If I work/he works hard at school, I'll/he'll go to university.
4. If I go/she goes to the party, I'll/she'll meet John.
5. If I get/he gets a well-paid job soon, I'll/he'll go to Spain for my/his holidays.
6. If my/her parents allow it, I'll/she'll invite some friends to a party.

Natürlich kann die Reihenfolge der Satzhälften umgekehrt sein.

3.

1. If I learn a lot at grade school, I will/I'll go to high school.
2. If I go to high school, I will/I'll learn a lot more.
3. If I work hard, I will/I'll pass my exams.
4. If I get good marks in my exams, I will/I'll get a place at college.
5. If I go to college, I will/I'll study hard.
6. If I study very hard, I will/I'll do well at college.
7. If I pass my college exams, I will/I'll get a good job.
8. If I get a good job, I will/I'll earn a lot of money.
9. If I save some of my money, I will/I'll soon be rich.
10. If I am rich, I will/I'll be able to enjoy life while I'm still young.

4.

1. when — 2. if — 3. when — 4. When — 5. If — 6. when — 7. if — 8. If — 9. if — 10. when

5.

Typ II – *if + simple past:*

"If I knew where the diamonds/they were, I wouldn't be here. I'd be on the Bahamas ..." — "If I had the (King of Scotland's) diamonds, I'd be a multi-millionaire!" — "If you found the diamonds, you would keep them all for yourself!"

Typ I – *if + simple present:*

"Unless you tell me where they are, I will shoot you!" — "I won't be able to tell you where I have hidden them if you shoot me." — "If you take me to the diamonds, I'll share them with you!"

6.

1. If I had a bicycle, I wouldn't/I'd not have to walk to the station. — 2. If I did not/didn't have to walk to the station, I would/I'd leave home later. — 3. If I left home later in the mornings, I would/I'd have more time for breakfast. — 4. If I had more time for breakfast, I would/I'd think about new inventions. — 5. If I thought hard, I would/I'd get good ideas. — 6. If I got good ideas, I would/I'd invent useful things. — 7. If I invented useful things, I would/I'd soon get rich. — 8. If I got rich, I would/I'd give up my job on the trains. — 9. If I gave up my job, I would/I'd have more time for experiments. — 10. If I had more time for experiments, I would/I'd invent even better things.

7.

Typ III: *if + past perfect*

"If only the King had hired a real killer (instead of saving money and trying to do the job himself), I would probably have taken him to the jewels." — "But he would have killed you if you had done that!" — "If you had been listening *(past perfect progressive)* to me, you would have realized that there was never any danger for me." — "I would never have taken such a risk if you hadn't been waiting *(past perfect progressive)* at the hiding place." — "If you hadn't received my note, how would you have known where to wait?" — "If I had received a note, I would have been there to help you."

Es handelt sich ausschließlich um Bedingungssätze des Typs III.

8.

1. If I had gone to high school, I would have worked hard. — 2. If I had worked hard, I would have passed my exams. — If I had gone to college, I would not have had time to invent things. — 4. If I had done well at college, I would have become a teacher. — 5. If I had become a teacher, I would never have become an inventor. — 6. If I had not become an inventor, I would not have invented all those useful things. — 7. If I had become a teacher, I would not have had to work so hard. — 8. If I had not worked so hard, I would perhaps have been happier. — 9. If I had moved to Europe, I would have been more successful. — 10. If I had died when I was young, I would never have invented the electric light bulb.

9.

1. If you hit me, I will tell Mum!
2. If I knew her address, I would write to her.
3. If he had waited, we would have taken him with us.
4. If she helps me with my homework, I will help her with hers.
5. If you knew her better, you would like her.
6. If they had asked me to help, I would have done my best.
7. If we walk this way, we'll soon be home.
8. If the sun had shone more often, we would have had a nicer holiday.
9. If the boys brought their CDs, the girls would bring theirs.
10. If we had played harder, we wouldn't have lost the match.

10.

1. would tell — 2. had — 3. see — 4. had stolen — 5. will call — 6. would have bought — 7. had not told — 8. would not have left — 9. won't/will not go — 10. ask — 11. want — 12. say — 13. doesn't stop — 14. were — 15. had known

11.

1.a) If you worked hard, you might/could/should pass your exams.
1.b) If you had worked hard, you might/could/should have passed your exams.
2.a) If I talked to Jenny, she might invite me to her party.
2.b) If I had talked to Jenny, she might have invited me to her party.
3.a) If I borrowed £20, I could/might buy those CDs.
3.b) If I had borrowed £20, I could/might have bought those CDs.
4.a) If he phoned his friends in Germany, he could/might get help with his German homework.
4.b) If he had phoned his friends in Germany, he could/might have got help with his German homework.
5.a) If you helped your sister, she might/should help you.
5.b) If you had helped your sister, she might/should have helped you.

Test

1. "When will you see Pat?" – "This afternoon. I'll give her your message when I see her."
2. "Will you lend me £20 if I promise to pay you back on Thursday?" – "I won't lend you any more money unless you pay me back what you already owe me! If I were you, I'd find a weekend job and earn some money instead of borrowing it!"
3. "Would you come to my party if I invited you?" – "Of course. I'd love to come. I love parties! If you hadn't invited me I would have been angry with you!"
4. "I think she's OK. I saw her yesterday. She would have gone to the doctor's if she had felt ill."
5. "We could be in New York tomorrow if we went by plane." – "If I had known you wanted to fly to New York, I would have brought my passport with me and gone with you!"
6. "You must show your German test to your father when he comes home."

8 Aktiv oder Passiv?

1.

Present passive:

Sometimes strange noises are heard at night, so the room is not often used. I hope you are not disturbed. — All our visitors are told the story of the rich woman.

Past passive:

The old village inn (where we spent the night) was haunted. About fifty years ago, a woman was murdered in this room. — She was found dead one morning. — We were not disturbed (during the night). — (Later) the bullet was put in a special glass box and placed on our mantlepiece.

Present perfect passive:

(A woman was murdered) in the room you have been given.

Past perfect passive:

All the other rooms had been booked. — All her money and jewels had been stolen. — The floor had not been swept for a long time. — Had the rich woman been killed by this bullet? — ... the story of the rich woman who had been killed with it.

Hilfsverb + Passivinfinitiv:

No trace of the murderer could be found. — I hoped that we would be woken by a scream (or the sound of a gun). — The heavy bed had to be moved before we could find the ring.

2.

I will be phoned tomorrow morning. / I am/was/will be woken every morning at 6.30.
Many tourists were stranded at airports last week.
Mount Everest was climbed in 1953.
This car is/was made at the new factory.
When the news was announced, everyone was happy.
After the band had been introduced, the concert began.
Many new hotels have been built so far this year.
She is/was/will be woken every morning at 6.30. / She will be phoned tomorrow morning.

3.

1. Rubbish is often dropped in the playground. — 2. Some money was stolen from my jacket pocket. — 3. The new English teacher is not liked. — 4. Our supper was burned. — 5. The grass is cut every week. — 6. Lunch is served at 1 p.m. — 7. Their house was broken into. — 8. The speed limit is often broken. — 9. The song "Greensleeves" was written in the 12th century. — 10. Many new houses are built every year. — 11. The two young men were arrested

at the airport. — 12. These old pictures are not looked at much nowadays. — 13. Is English spoken in this shop? — 14. Was your fun spoilt? — 15. You are not expected to wait. — 16. Rome was not built in a day.

4.

1. He has not been seen since January. — 2. You will be met at London Airport. — 3. These souvenirs can be bought at any seaside town. — 4. After he had been arrested he was taken to the police station. — 5. This part of the country has not been explored before. — 6. Will the beauty queen be chosen on Saturday? — 7. Don't touch that wire! You would be killed if you did! — 8. Has the Yeti ever been seen? — 9. Hasn't the murder been solved yet? — 10. All the tickets for the open-air concert can't have been sold yet! — 11. The magazine can be ordered from England. — 12. The world record has not been broken yet. — 13. The missing boy was seen in Edinburgh yesterday. — 14. After the police had been called, the burglar was arrested. — 15. This work won't/will not be finished in time.

5.

a) 1. Ten years ago a lot of chemicals were used on the farms. Now farming methods have been changed.
   2. Ten years ago (a lot of) rubbish was put in the river. Now the river has been cleared.
   3. Ten years ago many cars were parked in the village. Motor traffic has now been banned.
   4. Ten years ago a lot of coal was burned. Now the houses have been converted to central heating.
   5. Ten years ago a lot of pollution was caused by the factory. The factory has now been closed.
   6. Ten years ago a lot of litter was dropped in streets. Now more litter bins have been provided.
   7. Ten years ago the houses were/had been made dirty by air pollution. Now they/the houses have been cleaned.

b) 1. After the farming methods had been changed the fields were/the river was cleaner/less polluted, etc.
   2. After the river had been cleaned (up), more fish started to live in it.
   3. After motor traffic had been banned from the village, there was less air pollution/noise/people used the local buses more.
   4. After the houses had been converted to central heating, the air was cleaner/heating the houses was easier.
   5. After the factory had been closed, there was less pollution.
   6. After more litter bins had been provided, the streets were cleaner/less litter was dropped in the streets.
   7. After the houses had been cleaned, they looked a lot nicer.

6.

1. A lot of new houses are being built in our town. — 2. Are new trees being planted in the woods? — 3. New cars are not being bought at the moment. — 4. A piano was being played at the back of the house. — 5. A lot of cars are being stolen nowadays. — 6. Was dinner being served when you arrived? — 7. My car was not being repaired. — 8. Is the roof being repaired? — 9. Was the Queen being photographed a lot? — 10. All the nice food I made is not being eaten!

7.

1. is being interviewed — 2. were already being cleared — 3. was still being dug — 4. were being broken into — 5. are they being asked — 6. are being opened — 7. was just being welcomed — 8. are being changed — 9. are being paid for — 10. are being held

8.

1. The English Channel was (first) swum by Captain Webb in 1875.
2. The first car was built by Gottlieb Daimler in 1885.
3. The song "Yesterday" was composed by John Lennon in 1964.
4. The Football Association Cup was won by Manchester United last year.
5. Basketball was first played by YMCA members in America.
6. The novel "1984" was written by George Orwell in 1948.
7. The first steps on the moon were taken by Neil Armstrong in 1969.

9.

1. The purse was found in the school playground last week. — 2. The letter has already been posted. — 3. The old school is being demolished (by demolition experts). — 4. All the apples had been picked before I arrived. — 5. The clock he broke cannot be replaced. — 6. This letter was written by an idiot! — 7. He took a taxi to the station because his car was being repaired. — 8. The accident must be reported to the police. — 9. We have been asked to turn the music down a bit. — 10. This fine song was written by Paul Simon.

Test

1. I have been invited to meet the Queen.
2. Hundreds of criminals are caught every day.
3. The President wasn't told / was not told the truth about the problem.
4. You will be given a new job when the new factory is opened (when the boss opens the new factory).
5. The garden must be tidied up.
6. A Christmas concert is being arranged at our school.
7. Hundreds of things had been stolen from the shops before the police were (!) called (before someone called the police).
8. He must have been warned that we were coming.
9. Survivors from the plane crash were being interviewed when I arrived.
10. Dozens of good songs have been written by Elton John.

Der Infinitiv

9

1.

1. My mother always makes me finish my homework before she lets me watch TV.
2. It started to rain and we were still five kilometres from the youth hostel. So our teacher made us walk faster.
3. We live in the middle of a big town, so my parents have never let me go to school by bike. They make me walk or go by bus.
4. I was ill when we had our last English test. I hope our teacher will let me take it separately. I think I'll get a good mark for it.
5. I don't like spinach much, but my mother always makes me eat it all up. She says it's good for me.
6. Big sister: "Let me borrow your new CD. I want to listen to it!" – Little sister: "I haven't listened to it myself yet! You can't make me lend it to you!"
7. "Last week our English teacher made us learn twenty-five new English words! I hope she doesn't make us learn fifty this week!"
8. "You're coat is very wet, Eric! Have you been standing out in the rain?" – "Yes, Mum. Our teachers didn't let us stay in the classrooms during break. They made us go out into the playground."

2.

Da es sich um Äußerungen über deinen persönlichen Alltag handelt, müssen unsere Musterlösungen nicht unbedingt bei dir zutreffen:

1. When I get up, my mother makes me get dressed before I have breakfast.
2. Then she lets me watch TV while I'm having breakfast.
3. Then I go to school. If it's raining, I must take an umbrella/wear a raincoat/go to school by bus but I needn't take an umbrella/wear a raincoat/go to school by bus.
4. Our English teacher lets us use a dictionary *(Wörterbuch)* when we have a test, but he/she makes us work hard/learn ten new words a day.
5. During the morning break, we can go into the playground/stay in our classrooms. But we mustn't be too noisy/go outside the school gates.
6. When I/we get home from school my mum makes me do my homework/wash my hands, but then she lets me play/watch TV/visit friends.
7. Before going to bed I may play/watch TV/visit friends, but I'm not allowed to go to discos/to stay up until 10.30.

3.

1. We stood outside Buckingham Palace and saw the Queen arrive.
2. I didn't actually see the accident happen. I was looking in the other direction. I only heard the car's tyres scream on the wet road. When I looked round, the car had stopped and the cyclist was already getting up from the ground.
3. The tourist in the crowded market felt someone quickly put his hand into the back pocket of her jeans. He was probably trying to steal her money.
4. I heard someone shout. I looked round and saw my friend Fred.
5. We were watching a motor race on TV. We saw two cars crash.
6. My friend actually saw the bank robbery. He saw three masked men jump out of a car and run into the bank.
7. I was waiting for my bus when I suddenly heard a car bomb explode.

4.

Zuerst einige „vernünftige" Sätze:
My teacher told / ordered us to work harder.
My teacher warned/told/ordered us not to copy from each other.
My teacher likes his/her pupils to work hard.

The soldier told/ordered us to stay where we were / to go away.
The soldier told/ordered us not to come any closer / not to touch anything.

The boss ordered/told them to be quiet / work harder.
The boss requested/told them not to smoke in the building.
The boss likes us/them to work at weekends.
The boss hates us/them to arrive late for work.

The postman likes / prefers / advised me / us to keep my / our dog indoors when he comes.

The ticket inspector requested / ordered me / us / passengers / them to show him / her my/ our/their ticket(s).
The ticket inspector doesn't/didn't want me/us/passengers/them to show him/her my/our/their ticket(s).

Und jetzt ein paar Nonsens-Sätze:
My teacher prefers his/her pupils not to work hard / not to do their homework.
The soldier advised/warned us not to join the army.
The boss ordered me/us/them to go home early.
The postman hates me/us/them to give him tips *(Trinkgelder)*.
The ticket inspector advised us not to travel by train again.

Es sind unzählige andere Nonsens-Sätze möglich. Sie sind auch richtig, wenn sie unseren Mustern entsprechen!

5.

1. The policeman ordered us to stand back.
2. His boss warned him not to be late again.
3. Our music teacher asked us to tell our parents about the school concert.
4. The teacher told the whole class to listen carefully.
5. The stewardess asked us to sit on the other side of the plane.
6. The boss (said that he) expected his workers to work harder.
7. My mum hates me to tell lies.
8. My father wants me to put on a clean T-shirt every day.
9. Our English teacher told us he would like us to learn five new English words a day.
10. The fireman warned the people not to come too close to the fire.

6.

1. "What's the best thing to do in this situation?" — 2. "I know which way to go." — 3. "I can show you the best vegetables to grow in your garden." — 4. There were no houses for people to live in. — 5. "I've got nobody to talk to," said the old man. — 6. John was the only one to lose his way. — 7. Our teacher told us what to learn for the class test. — 8. He asked me how to ring Germany from Britain. — 9. *Notice:* Will the last person to leave the office please turn the lights off. — 10. She asked me when to meet me.

7.

1. The first person to climb Mount Everest was Edmund Hillary.
2. The first German to win the Men's Singles at Wimbledon was Boris Becker.
3. The last person to rule the Soviet Union was Mikhail Gorbachev.
4. The only racing driver to be World Champion five times is Michael Schumacher.
5. The first woman to swim the English Channel was Gertrude Ederle.
6. The first person to walk on the moon was Neil Armstrong.

Test

1."Good morning. I'd like to talk to Dr Everard, please. I must see her at once!" — 2. "Let me see ... — 3. I think I heard her come in a few minutes ago. — 4. Do you have an appointment, Mr ... ?" – "Gifford, Clive Gifford. It's very important. I'm a new patient, but I'm sure Dr Everard will see me. I feel very ill ..." – "Mr Gifford, there are five doctors in the surgery this morning. Why do you want to see one particular doctor?" — 5. "A friend of mine recommended her to me. He said she was the only doctor to understand all about old people's problems! — 6. I need to see her!" — 7. "I must ask you to sit down for a minute. If you're so ill, you mustn't get so excited." — 8. "You can't make me sit down!" — 9. "You needn't shout, Mr Gifford. — 10. If you want Dr Everard to treat you, please sit down and wait a moment. I'm sure she'll see you in a minute."

10 Das gerund

1.

(Das Kursivgedruckte sind die Wörter, die das jeweilige „gerund" ergänzen)

Skateboarding – skateboarding – skiing – skateboarding – windsurfing or snowboarding? – hurting *yourself* – injuring *other people*

learning *to windsurf* – windsurfing – swimming – climbing *out of the water* – standing *on their boards* – mastering *the basic techniques* – staying *on your board* – windsurfing *on the sea* – skateboarding *in the city.*

2.

Swimming in the sea is one of my hobbies.
Walking (in the mountains/hills) is not among my interests.
Reading (books/comics) is one of my interests/hobbies.
Eating in bed/food/sweets is one of my bad habits.
Listening to good music is (not) one of my interests.
Writing letters to friends is not among my hobbies.
Working in the garden is not one of my weekend activities.
Playing in the park is one of my weekend activities.
Washing the car is not one of my weekend activities.
Drei lustige Sätze:
Swimming in bed is one of my hobbies.
Walking in the sea is not among my interests.
Swimming to good music is one of my bad habits.

3.

1. Dancing (at a disco) is fun/fantastic/a waste of time.
2. Swimming (in the sea) is dangerous/a hobby of mine/wonderful.
3. Hang-gliding is fantastic/dangerous/stupid.
4. Playing football is a waste of time/fun/super.
5. Learning English is a hobby of mine/terrible!
6. Cooking is terrible/interesting/one of my hobbies.
7. Making models is not interesting for me/a wonderful hobby.
8. Writing letters to people is boring/easy/a waste of time.
9. Cycling is easy/wonderful/boring.
10. Camping (in the country) is a hobby of mine/fun/horrible.

4.

Lösungsvorschläge:

1. I like swimming. — 2. I don't mind cooking. — 3. I hate working in the garden. — 4. I prefer sailing to swimming. — 5. I'm keen on riding. — 6. I'm not so keen on cycling. — 7. I love reading. — 8. I'm (not) mad about learning English.

5.

a)	b)
1. No smoking.	"No smoking" means you're not allowed to smoke here.
2. No camping.	"No camping" means you can't camp here.
3. No fishing.	"No fishing" means it's forbidden to fish here/in this river/pond.
4. No parking.	"No parking" means you mustn't park (your car) here.
5. No skateboarding.	"No skateboarding" means you're not allowed to skateboard here.
6. No overtaking.	"No overtaking" means you can't/mustn't overtake other cars here.
7. No cycling.	"No cycling" means it's forbidden to cycle here/on this road.
8. No riding.	"No riding" means you're not allowed to ride (a/your horse) here.

6.

It was June, and John was already looking forward to going on holiday. His parents wanted to spend three weeks at the seaside again, but John was not keen on lying on the beach in the sun. He preferred skateboarding to swimming in the sea. He was not very good at swimming. There was no chance of staying at home while his parents were on holiday, so John asked his father if he could take his skateboard with him.

At first his father was against allowing John to take such a big thing in the car with them, but finally John succeeded in persuading his mother to talk to his father. At last John's dad agreed to let John take his skateboard. ...

Test

1. She prefers roller-skating to skateboarding.
2. Singing is one of my hobbies.
3. I enjoy learning English.
4. She succeeded in passing her exam.
5. We're not used to learning ten new English words a day.
6. It's no use asking him. He doesn't know the answer.
7. Instead of waiting we should leave right away.
8. She's looking forward to getting an e-mail from her pen-friend.
9. "No, I'm not at all interested in meeting you at the disco!"
10. They love eating fish and chips.

11 Die modalen Hilfsverben

1.

1. had to — 2. Must we / Do we have to do; must/do — 3. mustn't — 4. have to; needn't — 5. have to — 6. have to — 7. have to — 8. had to — 9. have to — 10. need not/needn't

2.

1. mustn't — 2. needn't — 3. mustn't — 4. needn't — 5. needn't — 6. mustn't — 7. needn't — 8. mustn't — 9. mustn't — 10. needn't

3.

1. be able to — 2. be able to — 3. could — 4. been able to — 5. couldn't — 6. Are you able to; I won't be able to — 7. would you be able to — 8. was only able to — 9. be able to — 10. can't

4.

1. You: May we stroke the goats, please?
2. Girl: Yes of course. You are allowed to stroke all the animals in this part of the zoo.
3. You: My friend wants to know if it is allowed to feed the monkeys.
4. Girl: Of course you may. But you are only allowed to feed them with food you buy here.
5. You: My friend says that in Hamburg we were allowed to feed them our own peanuts.
6. Girl: I'm afraid you may not feed your own food to the animals here.
7. You: OK, thank you. If the weather is good tomorrow, I might come again with a few friends.

5.

1. Shall — 2. shouldn't; ought — 3. Shall — 4. oughtn't — 5. shall — 6. Shouldn't — 7. ought — 8. Shall — 9. oughtn't — 10. should — 11. oughtn't — 12. should

6.

"What shall we do at the weekend?"
"Let's have a barbecue in the garden. We can invite all our friends: Tania, Paul, Melissa, Jason, Liza."
"Good idea! Shall I phone them or will you?"
"I expect I'll/will see most of them at the youth club tomorrow.
Will Maria be back from Spain by the weekend?"
"I'm not sure. Shall we write her a note?"

"Will you do that? I won't have time. But what shall/will we do if it rains?"
"We'll/will have the barbecue in Farmer Jones's old barn. He won't mind."
"Shall we ask him if we can use the barn even if the weather is fine? It would be even better than a barbecue in the garden."
"Good idea. We'll/will have a wonderful time!"

7.

1.	Mr Sykes:	"Come in, John. Won't you take your coat off?"
2.	John:	"Would you mind if I kept it on, sir? I'm feeling a bit cold."
3.	Mr Sykes:	"No problem. Would you like something to drink? A cup of tea or coffee?
4.		Or would you rather have a glass of water?"
5.	John:	"I wouldn't mind a cup of coffee, sir. If it's no trouble."
6.	Mr Sykes:	"No trouble at all. *(he picks up the phone)* Jenny – will/would you make us two cups of coffee, please?
7.		The coffee won't be long, John.
8.		While we're waiting, I'll/will ask you a few questions."
9.	John:	"I'll/will try to answer them, sir."
10.	Mr Sykes:	"I wouldn't be too nervous if I were you! They won't be too difficult for you!"

8.

When I see this sign ...
At this sign ...

1. ... I should stop and give way at the major road ahead. I may not/mustn't drive straight across – even slowly – because there may be a car coming.
2. ... I should drive carefully and watch out for wild animals. I oughtn't to/shouldn't use my headlights full on/I ought to/should dip my headlights because there might be a deer or a fox on the road, and animals stop when they can't see anything/when they are blinded by headlights.
3. ... I should drive slowly up to the level crossing and look left and right before I cross. There may/might be a train coming. After the first train has passed I must still be careful because there may/might be a second train coming from the other direction.
4. ... I can't/mustn't turn right. I must/may go straight on or turn left, but I needn't slow down.
5. ... I mustn't overtake other vehicles. There may be a dangerous bend ahead, or there might be a narrow bridge. I should drive more slowly and carefully and I shouldn't take extra risks. There is no overtaking on this part of the road.
6. ... I must slow down to 30 mph. I mustn't/shouldn't/oughtn't to drive faster when I see this sign because the maximum speed limit is 30 miles per hour. The road may pass through a town, village or past a school, and there may be more pedestrians and children on the road.

7. ... I should not be surprised if I hear sudden loud aircraft noises. I shouldn't park on the road near the runways because if a plane crashes it might hit my car. I needn't drive slowly.
8. ... there is a river bank, canal or quayside at the end of the road or beside the road. I must drive carefully because there is often mist or fog near water, and I may/might fall into the river or canal. I must not forget to put the handbrake on/I shouldn't park too close to the edge/I shouldn't park here unless I put the handbrake on.

Test

In the street outside the school playground, a pupil is practising skateboarding.
A teacher comes round a corner and nearly falls over the pupil.

1. "Be careful! Why can't you watch where you're going? You nearly knocked me over!
2. Don't you know that you mustn't use a skateboard in the playground?"
3. "I'm sorry. And you needn't shout at me. I'm outside the playground.
4. And this is a play street. You ought to know that. You're a teacher!"
5. "All right. But you should keep your eyes open in future."
6. "Keep my eyes open? You came round a corner! I couldn't see you!"

Sonja has lost her keys. She asks her brother if he has seen them.

7. "I've no idea where they are. They might be anywhere!
8. Shall I help you look for them?"
9. "Thanks. They must be somewhere here in my room."
10. "There they are! On your desk! Right in front of your nose. May I make a suggestion, Sis?" – "What?" – "Get yourself some new glasses." She throws a book at him. "Ouch!"

Die indirekte Rede

12

1.

1. Our teacher had told us to keep our hand baggage with us at all times and not to leave anything on the plane.
2. A voice over the loudspeakers requested us to report any unattended bags or suitcases and not to touch them.
3. The voice over the loudspeakers was ordering us not to panic but to leave the baggage area quietly.
4. The voice also asked us to take all our personal baggage with us.
5. Our teacher told us to leave the baggage hall without it.
6. The voice of the loudspeaker invited us to have a cup of tea and a cake at the airport's expense.
7. Again the loudspeakers warned us not to get too close to the building and to stay away from the windows and glass doors.
8. Finally we were requested to return to the baggage hall and collect our suitcases.

2.

1. Our teacher told us not to wander about. — 2. At the check-in counter the stewardess requested/asked us to put our baggage on the scales. — 3. The passport officer asked/ordered me/us to show him my/our passport(s). — 4. The assistant in the duty-free shop asked me to show him/her my boarding pass. — 5. The stewardess requested/asked passengers in seats 1–40 to board now. — 6. The steward told all passengers to fasten their seat-belts for take-off. — 7. The captain asked us to listen carefully to the safety instructions. — 8. The stewardess warned/told us not to smoke in the toilets.

3.

1. The girl said (that) she went to school in London now, but (that she) had gone to school in Scotland for two years. — 2. My teacher says (that) my pronunciation is good and that I can understand a lot of English. — 3. The young woman said (that) he had phoned her hotel after she had left. — 4. He says (that) he has no idea what I am talking about and that he has never seen me before. — 5. The guests told him (that) they were staying at the hotel for a week and so far had been enjoying their stay. — 6. She tells me (that) she wants to become an airline pilot so she has to do well at school. — 7. The girls said (that) they had seen him yesterday and that he had been standing in the school playground. — 8. Our young African visitor told us (that) his grandmother had never seen the sea. — 9. He said (that) Helena knew the answer but wouldn't tell him. — 10. My French friend Jean says (that) Jim and Vera speak French

very well because they've been living in France since 1990. — 11. She told us (that) she had been having a bath when the phone had rung.

4.

REPORT OF LOST ITEM

The owner said she <u>had lost</u> her rucksack at Victoria Station. She said she <u>had taken</u> it off outside the bank at the station before she <u>had gone</u> into the bank. The owner said that a friend <u>had been looking</u> after the rucksack but that he <u>had been talking</u> to some other people and <u>did not remember</u> if anyone <u>had taken</u> the rucksack by mistake. The two young people from Germany said they <u>were</u> not sure where they <u>were staying</u> but that they <u>would ring</u> us later.

5.

1. My friend said we should take a bus because it would be quicker. — 2. The driver told the girl (that) she could sit in the front of the car and that she did not have to sit in the back. — 3. John said (that) his friends had not been able to help him because they had not had time. — 4. My friend's mother told me (that) I had to go or I would miss my train. — 5. The girl said (that) she would like to talk to my brother if she might. — 6. My friend said she ought to ask her mother if she could come with me. — 7. John told me (that) his sister could not come to my party on Saturday because she was going to London. — 8. The guide said (that) it was going to rain and that we should take our raincoats. — 9. Dad told us (that) it might be too cold for a barbecue in the garden but suggested (that) we could have it on the balcony.

6.

1. She asked me what time it was. — 2. He asked her if she was English. — 3. She asked them if they had been there. — 4. He asked us if we had phoned Phil. — 5. She wondered when the film started. — 6. He asked me how much money we had got. — 7. She asked him if he had seen Penny yesterday/the day before. — 8. He wanted to know if the sun was shining. — 9. She asked me where I had been born. — 10. He wondered whether/if there was anybody there. — 11. He asked his friend how much he earned. — 12. She wanted to know whether/if Paul had phoned. — 13. He asked her if she had ever eaten lamb. — 14. She asked us where we had gone after we had left school. — 15. She asked them what they would like to drink.

7.

1. The inspector wants to know where you were at midnight. — 2. He wants you to tell him what your friend's name is and where she lives. — 3. He says you were seen in Mannheim at 10 pm yesterday and asks how you got to Stuttgart so quickly. — 4. "I took the ICE at a quarter past ten and arrived in Stuttgart at half past eleven." — 5. The inspector is asking how you got to your friend's flat so quickly. — 6. "I took a taxi." — 7. He wants to know how much you paid for the taxi. — 8. "I don't know. I've forgotten." — 9. "Why did/have you come to Stuttgart?" — 10. "I want/wanted to plan another burglary with some friends."

8.

1. The young man suggested going for a ride on his motor-bike.
2. The girl suggested going to the cinema.
3. One driver suggested that the other driver should go back to driving school.
4. Our teacher suggested that we should do exercise 6 again.
5. The tourist suggested going to a museum.
6. The waitress (at the snack-bar) suggested that the boys and girls/young people should have hamburgers and chips.

9.

1. They asked me how long I had been living here. — 2. John wanted to know if my sister was going to the youth club tonight. — 3. Jim and Barbara said they had gone to the disco the previous day/the day before. — 4. They said they were going on holiday next month. — 5. He said he was going to London the following month. — 6. He/She said his/her mother was going to buy a new car that week. — 7. He/she said (that) his/her class test was tomorrow. — 8. He/she said (that) John had told him/her (that) he lived here. — 9. He/she said (that) John had told him/her (that) he lived in that street. — 10. They said (that) they had seen Paul and Jean a few days before/ago.

Test

Die Konjunktion *that* wird in der gesprochenen Sprache meist weggelassen.

1. My mother told me <u>to be polite</u> to my host family.
2. And my father warned me <u>not to go to discos</u> too often.
3. They asked me <u>not to forget to phone them</u> when I arrived.
4. My father said <u>he hoped (that) I would have a good time</u>.
5. My mother told me <u>(that) she had written to my host family / you</u>.
   Did you get her letter? – Yes, we got it last week.
6. She said <u>she hoped (that) you could understand her English</u>.
   – It was quite good, actually.
7. My parents said <u>(that) they would like to visit me in England</u>.
8. My mother wanted to know <u>if/whether it/that would be possible</u>.
9. My father asked <u>if/whether there was an interesting</u> leisure-time programme.
10. And my mother never stops worrying about me! She wondered <u>when we would arrive in London</u> and said <u>(that) she hoped it wouldn't be too</u> late in the evening! Aren't parents the absolute end!

13 Relativsätze

1.

a) 1. A thermometer is a device which tells the temperature. — 2. A bus-driver is a person who drives a bus. — 3. A discjockey is a person who plays CDs and records at a disco. — 4. A plane/An aircraft is a vehicle which has wings. — 5. A teacher is a man or woman who works in a school. — 6. A road sign is a sign that tells drivers what to do. — 7. A pupil is a boy or girl who goes to school. — 8. A lemon is a yellow fruit which is very sour. — 9. An umbrella is a small, portable roof which keeps out the rain.

b) 1. A passport is a document (which/that) you need when you go abroad. — 2. Chewing gum is something (which/that) you can chew. — 3. A bus is a vehicle which/that takes people to work or school. — 4. A cat is an animal which/that can catch mice. — 5. An explorer is a person who/that explores unknown countries or regions. — 6. A walkman is a device which/that plays music while you are walking. — 7. Students are people who/that go to college or university. — 8. A snowboard is something (which/that) you can use in the mountains in winter, like skis. — 9. Rollerskates are things with wheels (which/that) you put on your feet. You can then "roll" along the ground very quickly. — 10. A ghost is something which/that lives in an empty castle or house / something which/that few people believe in.

2.

1. Prince Charles, who is the son of the Queen, has two sons.
2. The blackbird, which lives in trees, has red legs.
3. John Evans, who works in a coal mine, speaks Welsh.
4. The Mini, which is a small two-door car, is still very popular.
5. English, which is spoken everywhere, is a world language.
6. Hamburg, which is a city in Germany, is a large port.
7. Flying doctors, who help sick people, work in Australia.
8. Coal, which is a black mineral, burns very well.
9. John Wayne, who was a film-star, could ride a horse.
10. Bristol, which was once a large port, is west of London.

3.

Bestimmende Relativsätze:

A teenager who stole a car was arrested in Brighton. — The car which he stole was a blue Morris 1100 that belonged to Ms Jane Campbell. — The policemen who followed the stolen car ... are the same men who stopped two joyriders last month.

The police car which they were driving ... — a busy road that is used by thousands of cars. — ... the car that was following him ... — ... the Morris 1100 which Wilkinson had stolen ran out of petrol.

Nicht-bestimmende Relativsätze:
James Wilkinson, who lives at 69, High Street, Thornton Heath, is only 16. — Ms Jane Campbell, who also lives in Thornton Heath. — James broke into the car, which was parked outside Ms Campbell's house, ... — He was unable to steal the radio, which was firmly fixed to the dashboard, ... — PC Alfred Frazer, who lives in Warlingham. — ... the A 23, which is a busy road, ... — The policemen, who could see that the driver was very young, did not wish to frighten the thief, who was driving at about 65 mph, ... — ... the crew of another police car, which had been waiting ..., caught him.

4.

Come to Tenby for a seaside holiday which/that is different!
People who/that enjoy seaside holidays will love Tenby. This small seaside town in South Wales, which has two wonderful sandy beaches, is also famous for the castle which/that stands at the top of the town between the two bays. Tenby is an ideal place for young people who/that want to do more than lie on the beach. There are many interesting paths which/that follow the rocky coastline, and for those of you who/that are not good walkers, there are plenty of places which/that are worth visiting in the town itself. There are boat trips to the small island of Caldy, which has a lighthouse and a Roman Catholic monastery. Jean Smith, who has been coming to Tenby regularly for over 50 years, says: "Tenby is a place which/that attracts all kinds of people, old (like me) and young (like my granddaughter), who is here with me this year."

5.

(Achte auch auf die Kommas!)

1. This is the man who/that lives in the flat above ours.
2. Do you like ice-cream which/that tastes like toffee?
3. John Brown, who lives next door, is a good friend of mine.
   or: John Brown, who is a good friend of mine, lives next door.
4. She is wearing a long skirt which/that is very pretty.
5. The clothes which/that she buys in Paris are expensive.
6. My girlfriend Alison, who is 19, lives in Cleversulz-bach.
   or: My girlfriend Alison, who lives in Cleversulzbach, is 19.
7. This is the bus that/which goes to Euston Station.
8. Here are the shoes that/which cost me £60.
9. When did you see the man that/who stole my car?
10. This coffee, which smells very fresh, comes all the way from Kenya.

6.

The place I went to for my summer holidays last year was a little village which/that is difficult to find on most maps of Scotland but a place you will easily find on a map of Canada: Calgary on the Island of Mull, which is off the west coast of Scotland. The Canadian town which/that is called Calgary was originally a small fort the Canadian Mounted Police founded in 1875 as Fort Brisebois, a French name few of the policemen could pronounce correctly. The fort was renamed Calgary, which means "clear running water" in Gaelic, by Colonel James F. Macleod, who came from the Island of Mull. The year in which the fort was renamed was 1876. The small hotel we stayed at had a fine view of the bay, which, with its blue sea and pure white sand, was ideal for bathing.

7.

1. The school project we did was about London in the 19th century. — 2. The teacher who helped us collect material was Mr Peters. — 3. Some of the material we collected was very interesting. — 4. Anne Harrap, who I was working on the project with, is a good friend of mine. — 5. Our part of the project was something we didn't know much about: the London Underground! — 6. The first part of the London Underground, which is still the biggest underground network in the world, opened in 1863. — 7. Even in those days the streets which connected the suburbs of West London with the banks and offices of the City were overcrowded. — 8. This first underground railway, which many "commuters" used, was called the Metropolitan Railway. — 9. The name it was given was taken over by underground railways all over the world. — 10. The Paris and Moscow "Metros", which are used by millions each day, are both named after it. — 11. The first real "tube" railway (which) electric trains were used on was built in 1890. — 12. At the end of the 19th century there were many miles of underground lines, which most people preferred to the horse buses above ground. — 13. Londoners are proud of their Underground. But the man who did most to start up the system was an American. — 14. Charles Tyson Yerkes, who had made a fortune in the USA, was the man Londoners should be grateful to for their Underground. — 15. It was he who insisted on electric trains instead of steam engines in the early days. — 16. The Glasgow Underground, which was for many years the only other "Metro" in Britain, had a very small, very dirty circular line with steam trains which lasted until the 1930s!

8.

1. The new Arrow sports car, which is made in Coventry, won a rally which/that was organized by the Automobile Club of Scotland. — 2. A boy of 16 who built his own plane flew 500 metres before crashing into a car which/that was parked in the middle of a field. — 3. Melissa Ryman, who lives in London, will swim for England at the European championships, which begin next week in Paris. — 4. The open-air concert which/that was cancelled last week will take place next week at Folly Farm, which is near Oxford. — 5. The first British spacecraft "Britannia I", which will be launched next month, will carry four astronauts who/that were chosen from over 1000 applicants. — 6. The/A computer which/that was developed by an Irish company will be sold by Eurocomp, which has its headquarters in Dublin.

9.

1. James Watt was an inventor whose steam engine revolutionized industry.
2. Watt was born in Scotland, the capital of which is Edinburgh.
3. This is the rare XL 320 sports car, only 200 of which were built.
4. The man whose car had been stolen was very angry.
5. The Rolling Stones, whose songs have been best sellers since the 60s, are still together.
6. The company the collapse of which was forecast months ago is still doing well.
7. Mr Smith (,) whose son won the prize (,) was very happy.
8. The car the door of which was damaged belonged to Mr Granger.
9. The man whose daughter won the prize was very happy.
10. The villages whose streets were flooded were cut off.

Test

Der Gedankenstrich (–) bedeutet, man kann das Relativpronomen auch weglassen, da es Objekt im notwendigen Relativsatz ist.

1. The house in <u>which</u> we live was built in 1906.
2. Mr Aloysius Prang, <u>who</u> built it, was a rather eccentric man.
3. The materials <u>which/that/–</u> he used were very modern at the time: concrete and steel girders.
4. But the brickwork on the front of the house, <u>which looks</u> like most houses built in 1906, is only painted on the concrete!
5. Few people look twice at our house, <u>which</u> my parents bought five years ago.
6. But a year ago an architect <u>who/that</u> had heard about the house visited us.
7. He told us he had heard about a house the front of <u>which</u> was painted to look like brick.
8. He was writing a book about architects <u>whose</u> ideas had been ahead of their time.
9. He said that Aloysius Prang, <u>whose</u> house we were living in, had been one of them.
10. So now our house is famous! There is a long article about our house in the book by the young architect <u>who/whom /–</u> we talked to that day.

14 Die Pronomen

1.

Yesterday we went shopping by bus. The bus was late. When it arrived, we got on. The bus-driver asked us where we wanted to go. I said: "Tooting Station, please" and she said: "Tooting, too." He smiled and said: "Two to Tooting!" The people in the bus heard him. They laughed at his little joke. We thought they were very silly. We didn't look at them. We gave him the money. He took the money and gave us our tickets and our change. He gave me 5p change and gave her 45p. My ticket said: 45p. Mary looked at it, too. Then she looked at me and I looked at her. "Excuse me," I said to the driver. "You've given her the wrong change. She gave you a pound coin and it's only 45p to Tooting Station. You only gave her 45p change instead of 55p." He gave her another 10p. He was not smiling now. All the other people in the bus were looking at him. "He's given one of them the wrong change!" said an old man. We smiled at him. "I'm going to Tooting, too!" he said. This time everybody laughed – except the bus driver, of course!

2.

"I've lost my keys, Dad. Can you help me to find them?"
"Weren't they on the table in the hall this morning?"
"No, those were Mum's keys. I gave them to Mum. My keys were in my jacket pocket, but I can't find my jacket. Have you seen it?"
"Your old jeans jacket? I think Mum gave it away this morning."
"Gave my jacket away? It was my favourite jeans jacket. I wore it almost every day – and it wasn't old. Only a year or two, anyway."
"There were some people at the door this morning. They were collecting old clothes for the Red Cross. I think Mum gave them your jacket – and a few of my old clothes, too."
"But surely Mum looked in the pockets before she gave the things away!"
"I'm not sure, Carol. By the way, have you seen my old black trousers? They were in the bedroom but now I can't find them. There was a £20 note in the back pocket! Where's Mum, anyway. Just wait till I see her! I'll give her a boot in the head if she's given my trousers away!"

3.

1. "She is from London. I understand her well." – "Do you know where she lives?"
2. "Do they come from Berlin?" – "No, they come from Cologne. I know them well." – "Do you know where they live?"
3. "She is in my class. I see her every day."
4. "I think these books are good. You can buy them everywhere."

5. "Have you seen Ken and Tom?" – "Yes, I saw <u>them</u> in the playground. <u>They</u> were playing football."

4.

Am besten prüfst du deine Antworten „von oben nach unten"! Wir haben die wahrscheinlichsten Kombinationen aufgelistet. Deine zehn Sätze müssten dabei sein. Wenn nicht, kannst du im Zweifelsfall deine(n) Lehrer(in) fragen. Er/Sie wird sich sicher über dein zusätzliches Engagement im Englischen freuen!

My friend Brian bought a new CD / some sweets / a magazine for his friend Jack / for me.
My friend Brian bought me / her brother / us / them / my friend Jack a new CD.
My friend Brian gave a new CD / some sweets / it / them / a magazine / a letter to us / to his sister.
My friend Brian gave me / us / them /my friend Jack a new CD.
My friend Brian sent a letter / a magazine to us / to his sister.
My friend Brian sent me / us / them /her brother / my friend Jack a new CD / a postcard from France.
My friend Brian lent a new CD / a magazine / it / them to us / to his sister.
My friend Brian lent her brother / me / us / them / my friend Jack a new CD.

I bought a new CD / some sweets / a magazine for his friend Jack.
I bought her brother / them / my friend Jack a new CD.
I gave a new CD / some sweets / it / them / a magazine to his sister.
I gave her brother / them / my friend Jack a new CD.
I sent a letter / a magazine to us / to his sister.
I sent her brother / them /my friend Jack a new CD / a postcard from France.
I lent a new CD / a magazine / it / them to his sister.
I lent her brother / them / my friend Jack a new CD.

Her mum bought a new CD / it / them / some sweets / a magazine for his friend Jack / for me.
Her mum bought her brother / me / us / them / my friend Jack a new CD.
Her mum gave a new CD / some sweets / a magazine / a letter to us / to his sister.
Her mum gave her brother / me / us / them / my friend Jack a new CD.
Her mum sent a letter / a magazine to us / to his sister.
Her mum sent me / us / them /her brother / my friend Jack a new CD / a postcard from France.
Her mum lent a new CD / a magazine / it / them to us / to his sister.
Her mum lent her brother / me / us / them / my friend Jack a new CD.

You bought a new CD / it / them / some sweets / a magazine for me / for his friend Jack.
You bought her brother / me / us / them / my friend Jack a new CD.
You gave a new CD / some sweets / a magazine / it / them to us / to his sister.
You gave me / her brother / them / my friend Jack a new CD.
You sent a letter / a magazine / some sweets to us / to his sister.

You sent her brother / me / us / them / my friend Jack a new CD / a postcard from France.
You lent a new CD / a magazine / it / them to us / to his sister.
You lent her brother / me / us / / them / my friend Jack a new CD.

We bought a new CD / some sweets / a magazine for his friend Jack.
We bought her brother / them / my friend Jack a new CD.
We gave a new CD / some sweets / it / them / a magazine to his sister.
We gave her brother / them / my friend Jack a new CD.
We sent a letter / a magazine / some sweets to his sister.
We sent her brother / them / my friend Jack a new CD / a postcard from France.
We lent a new CD / a magazine / it / them to his sister.
We lent her brother / them / my friend Jack a new CD.

5.

1. I gave him the money.
2. She sent a letter to her.
3. She bought them an ice-cream.
4. He/She gave us a test yesterday.
5. We sent it to them by airmail.
6. He gave it them.
7. He bought them for her last year.
8. They showed them (to) us/us them.
9. Can she lend them (to) her/her them?

6.

1. "I always do my homework myself. Nobody helps me."
   "What about your sister? Does she do her homework herself?"
   "Well, she's younger than me. Sometimes my father helps her."
2. Some of the girls in my class make their clothes themselves. I've tried making my own clothes, but when I put them on and look at myself in a mirror, I hope that other people won't laugh at me when they see me!"
3. "I'm thirsty," he asked me. "Can I get myself a glass of orange juice?"
   "Of course!" I said. "Help yourself!" So he poured himself a glass of orange juice. "Shall I pour a glass for you?" he asked me and my brother.
   "No, thanks," I said. "We can pour ourselves a glass when we're thirsty."
4. We have a big garden, so we grow a lot of our own food ourselves. Our neighbours have tried growing their food themselves, but they only have a small garden.
5. My cat is very clever. When it's hungry, it goes into the kitchen and gets itself something to eat. The box of cat food is on the floor. The cat knocks it over. Some bits of food fall out of it, and the cat eats them.

7.

Lösungswörter in Klammern gelten als „weniger wahrscheinlich" richtige Lösungen!

"I was in London last week." – "We were in London ourselves. We didn't see you there." – "Well, London itself is a big city, isn't it? I went on a tour of Buckingham Palace. It was a very expensive tour, so we had to pay for our tickets ourselves. Prince Charles himself was the tour guide! The rooms themselves were very interesting, but I wanted to see the Queen herself/(myself). There was a door with a sign 'NO ENTRY'. When nobody was looking, I opened the door and walked right into the private rooms of the Royal Family itself/(themselves)! They themselves live right in the middle of the Palace itself. There was nobody about, so I had to find the Queen's living-room myself. At last I found it – and there was Her Majesty herself, sitting in an armchair and reading a newspaper." – "I don't believe you! You made that story up yourself!" – "You're right. But both of you almost believed my story yourselves, didn't you?"

8.

1. "Hi, Karen. Have you met my brother Vincent?" – "Oh yes. Vincent and I have known one another / each other for years."
2. Some of my friends are not very good at English. So we sometimes meet after school and help each other / one another with our homework.
3. A farmer in our village had too many apples last year. He put a lot of apples in a box beside the road with a sign on it: FREE APPLES. HELP YOURSELVES / (YOURSELF). So we helped ourselves.
4. She was too big for her old bike, so she bought herself a new one.
5. I hadn't seen my cousin for six years. When we met again last week, we hardly recognised each other / one another.
6. We went to the open-air concert in the afternoon and watched it again on TV in the evening. We saw ourselves in the crowd.
7. "They never think about other people. They are selfish. They only think about themselves." – "I hate selfish people! I think everybody should help each other / one another."
8. "I painted that picture of the river myself. Do you like it?" – "The picture itself is OK, but I don't like the colours much!"
9. "I grew up in London. Have you ever been to London yourself?" – "No. Only to London Airport, not to London itself."
10. Nobody can help us. We'll have to do it ourselves.
11. "Shall I tell Mum and Dad that I broke your window, Mrs Smith?" – "No, John. I'll tell your parents myself."
12. "Did I see you and Vera talking to each other / one another at the party?" – "That's right. She didn't know many people herself. In fact she told me she had come to the party by herself."

9.

1. "Whose bike is that? Is it yours?" – "No, it isn't mine. I didn't bring mine to school today. Ask Peter – I think it's his."
2. *(After the party)* "Where did you put your coats?" – "We put ours on the bed. I think Barbara and Ken put theirs on the bed, too."
3. "Have you seen my English books, Sheila?" – "No, Helen. These are my books. Where did you leave yours?" – "I left them here, on the table, right next to yours." – "Oh dear! Tania thought those books were hers. She put them in her bag and went home, I think." – "Just a minute, Sheila. There's a bag over there. I think it's Tania's/hers. She must still be here. I'll find her and ask her about the books."

10.

1. "That must be Mr Jones's car over there." – "No. I think it's Mr Smith's."
2. "It wasn't my mistake. It was our headmaster's: he ordered the wrong books."
3. "Is that your house?" – "No, that's the Browns'. Ours is next door."
4. "Are those your glasses?" – "No, I'm wearing mine. They must be Mum's."
5. "Do you know Alice and Paul Smith?" – "Of course. They're good friends of ours."

Test

1. Mum: Victor? Kenneth? What's all that shouting about? What are you doing?
2. Victor: Ken's playing with my game-boy! Give it me back!
3. Kenneth: It's not your game-boy, Vic. It's mine!
   Mum: So whose game-boy is this one under the table?
4. Kenneth: Oh! Sorry, Vic. This one belongs to me. I must have dropped it ...
   Mum: Anyway, didn't you two want to go surfing on the Internet this afternoon with Chris and Bonzo?
5. Kenneth: No, they're no friends of ours!
   Mum: Well, I saw their mother at the supermarket this morning. She said you two had invited them to come round here after school to try out your new computer.
   Victor: Are you sure it was Chris and Bonzo's mother? Mrs Brown from Number 193?
6. Mum: Of course I'm sure. I spoke to her myself.
7. Kenneth: We didn't invite them, Mum. They must have invited themselves!
8. Mum: What's wrong? Don't you like them? I thought all the boys and girls in your class liked each other.
9. Victor: Most of us do, Mum, and Bonzo himself is OK. But nobody likes Chris Brown much.